THE
STRENGTH
OF GREAT
POSSESSIONS

STERLING W. SILL

OOOOOOOOOOOOOOOOOOOO

THE STRENGTH OF
GREAT POSSESSIONS

OOOOOOOOOOOOOOOOOOOO

STERLING W. SILL

BOOKCRAFT INC.
SALT LAKE CITY, UTAH
1970

2nd Printing, 1972

LITHOGRAPHED IN U.S.A. BY

PUBLISHERS PRESS
SALT LAKE CITY UTAH

Contents

Preface

Charles Dickens once wrote a great book entitled *A Tale of Two Cities*. In it he presents a picture of the lives of some of the people who lived in London and Paris during the time of the French Revolution some two hundred years ago. Mr. Dickens' description of this period reminds us of some of the conditions of our own day. He says:

It was the best of times; it was the worst of times.
It was the age of reason; it was the age of foolishness.
It was the epoch of belief; it was the epoch of incredulity.
It was the season of light; it was the season of darkness.
It was the spring of hope; it was the winter of despair.
We had everything before us; we had nothing before us.
We were all going direct to heaven; we were all going direct the
other way.

As we live in our world of contrasts, the hazards seem to become greater as the possible benefits are increased. And probably that is exactly as it should be. If we are going to enjoy the greater advantages, it is only logical that we should overcome the greater problems that go with them. The poet has said:

Good timber does not grow in ease,
The stronger wind, the stronger trees,
The farther sky, the greater length,
The more the storm, the more the strength.

It is challenging to try to understand our own future possibilities. The probability is that the coming twelve months will make up the most important year in the history of our world. Quite logically it may also be the most important period of our individual lives. During this coming twelve months, more babies will be born than ever before in history. We will have more educational facilities. We will make more money than ever before. We will have a greater chance to be loyal to the government and the government will need our loyalty more than ever before. We will have a greater chance to be loyal to God and more people will join the Church than in any previous year. We will have greater personal challenges and more opportunities to build strength in ourselves than in any year since creation.

But this is also the very worst of times. In the coming twelve months, more people will die than ever before. There will probably be more crimes committed. We will have more troubles. We will drink more liquor, inhale more pollution and use more dope. More young people will rebel against their parents. There will be more people let their hair grow. More people will join the hippies and more people will smell worse than ever before. In this next twelve months, there will be more sins committed, more people will betray their country and more will go to hell than in any previous year.

In 1835, a French visitor by the name of Alexis de Tocqueville made a study of the United States. Later he wrote in his book: "America is great because she is good, and if America ever ceases to be good, America will cease to be great." That also applies to us as individuals. Our success must always depend upon our righteousness and upon the kind of decisions we make in our choices between the best and the worst.

For example, when we sing "God Bless America," what kind of an America do we have in mind? Certainly not a drunken America, nor an atheistic America, nor a criminal America, nor an irresponsible America, nor a weak America, nor an America filled with those who rebel against God. Every person in the world who loves freedom, righteousness and human dignity, regardless of nation, creed, color or race, should pray for a strong, godly, enduring United States of America; for if any communist combination of nations should reach their goals for enslaving the world, then none of our other problems would ever again seem very important. As Emerson has said:

> Of what avail is plow or sail
> Or land of life if freedom fail?

God offered to save Sodom and Gomorrah if fifty righteous people could be found therein. And God will prosper every nation upon this earth as well as every individual in the world if, because of our choices as his children, we are able to present ourselves before him as strong, clean, industrious, law-abiding, faithful and happy people.

One of the conditions marking our age as the very best of times is the fact that there are more things that need to be

done now than ever before. And we now have our greatest
opportunity to be good soldiers. That does not mean to merely
be dressed in a military uniform, but to possess those sure and
steady qualities of always being faithful, of always going forward, of always being loyal and dependable. Every good soldier
should constantly be waging war — not a war against anyone,
but a war for everyone. We should be waging a war for God
and for our country and for righteousness and for our families
and for ourselves. We should be fighting for health and strength,
law and order, industry and courage, truth and righteousness.
Someone has written:

> To every man upon this earth
> Death cometh soon or late,
> But every man may give his life
> For something good and great.
>
> And how can man die better
> Than in facing fearful odds,
> For the ashes of his fathers
> And the temples of his gods?

The most important responsibility that God has ever laid
upon our human shoulders is that of making the best and the
most of our own lives. To promote the best of times we need
to understand both the positive and the negative factors involved.
One of the most important of all success secrets is the ability
to make some strong decisions about those wrong things that
we must not do. The third month after the children of Israel
were released from their Egyptian bondage, they encamped at
the foot of Mount Sinai. The Lord came down onto the Mount
and initiated their national beginnings by giving them the Ten
Commandments. These are ten great laws wherein certain evil
things are placed out of bounds.

When we have definitely made up our minds about those
things that we must not do, we are free to spend all of our
energy in doing those things that must be done. We should first
get out of our way those things that may hold us back, then
we can go toward our goals at a greater speed. A banker can
build up his net worth as readily by subtracting liabilities as
by adding assets. And the best way to plan for the success of
our lives is by this process of making the most of the good and
the least of the bad. By eliminating the incredulity, darkness

and despair mentioned by Mr. Dickens, we may then turn our
own age of foolishness into an age of reason. Our winter of
despair can then be our spring of hope. Then we can have everything before us, and nothing to hinder our progress toward our
divine destiny. If we make the worst of times the best of times,
we will be going directly toward heaven, whereas if we make
the best of times the worst of times, we will be going directly
the other way.

Emerson once said: "On the brink of an ocean of life and
truth we are miserably dying. Sometimes we are furthest away
when we are closest by. We stand on the brink of an ocean of
power, but each must take the steps that would bring him there."
So frequently we are furthest away when we are closest by.
Think how near they were who lived contemporaneously with
Jesus. They were aware of his miracles, they knew of his doctrines, they saw his example; and yet they were so far away
that they said, "His blood be upon us and upon our children."
And so it has been and so it may be with us. We are so near.
We live in the very best of times and yet we may be so far away.
Success and happiness are not in distant places, or even in our
conditions — they are in us. Everyone carries within himself the
very things that he seeks. If we need more faith and greater
courage, we need only develop that which we already have.
God has already implanted in our own hearts the seeds of faith
and courage, waiting only for us to make them grow, but we
ourselves must take the steps that will bring us there. And day
by day we may increase the strength and value of those great
possessions that God has already implanted in our lives.

It has been said that when anyone reads a book, he should
always get much more out of it than there is in it. A reader may
get everything that the book itself contains, but in addition, as
his mind strikes certain ideas, his thoughts will ricochet out into
space. And if the reader will follow his mind, he may get
acquainted with a whole family of new ideas. After this quest
has exhausted itself he may again take up the book where he
left off. Many of our best ideas are those that something else
made us think about, and it is a pretty good idea to ensnare these
new possessions by writing them down before they are able to
get away.

The Strength of Great Possessions is made up of fifty-two
chapters, one for each week of the year. It is hoped that each

will have some negotiable values for each interested reader. It is suggested that one chapter might be studied each week and that any action it indicates be put into practice. Each chapter is a separate segment and may be studied independently of the others, but it is hoped that, in addition to making its own contributions, each chapter will so trigger your own experience as to offer you the best possible course of action in relation to the point considered. The prayer is offered that this coming year will be the greatest you have ever had up to this point and that your total life for here and hereafter will be made up of the very best of times.

The Strength of Great Possessions

SINCE TIME BEGAN, people have been asking each other, "What is the supreme good? Where are the greatest values? What is the noblest objective? Which are the finest virtues? What are the best thoughts? What activities produce the most happiness? What conditions bring about the most worthwhile satisfactions? How does one reach the highest degree of excellence? Which labor is the most motivating, and what are the most worthwhile possessions?"

Many years ago, while trying to answer some of these important questions, Henry Drummond wrote his great literary classic describing love as the greatest thing in the world. His argument is based upon Paul's famous Thirteenth Chapter of First Corinthians, which is an all-time masterpiece in our literature. Certainly, Mr. Drummond gives us an inspiring answer.

Someone once asked a famous teacher which religious commandment came next to love in importance. The teacher replied that he didn't know there was one. However excellent the answers given by Mr. Drummond and Paul were, they may not fully satisfy everyone. Some may feel that peace, contentment, or happiness is the greatest thing in the world. Some may hunger for greater personal virtues. Some may select industry or courage to be the leaders for their lives. There are so many kinds and varieties of successes. Life itself comes in such an overflowing abundance that one may feel limited in accepting any single answer.

Jesus announced his own mission to our world by saying: "I am come that they might have life, and that they might have it more abundantly." (John 10:10) We might contemplate what it would be like to live the kind of life that Jesus had in mind. The scriptures speak of certain people who had "great possessions." If we were going to audit the lives of a group of great people, we might discover that many of their most inspiring experiences came from their possessions.

Almost unbelievable satisfactions can come from a good family owning a fine home that has been beautifully landscaped, artistically decorated, comfortably furnished, and fully paid for. There is great pride, great joy, and great strength in ownership. Much of the worthwhileness of life itself originates with our possessions. Attitudes and motivations are given strength by holdings in real estate or stocks and bonds. Great possessions are not only important in their own right, but they also give us power when translated into their equivalents in education, security, comfort, peace, influence, the joy of accomplishment, or the ability to help others. Sometimes there is even greater happiness born from the great possessions of faith, character, sound personality traits, and solid reserves of mental power. Ambition, ideals, noble deeds, and great expectations of future accomplishments always increase our strength.

We might try to understand what was contemplated in the statement made by the Master about the ownership of eternal things. In the greatest sermon that was ever preached, the greatest man who ever lived gave some of the wisest counsel that has ever been given when he spoke about laying up for ourselves treasures in heaven. The thing that we spend more time doing than almost any other thing is laying up for ourselves treasures upon the earth. By learning to labor effectively, we increase our abundance in so many ways. As Leonardo da Vinci once said: "Thou, oh God, doth sell us all good things at the price of labor."

Labor is the way we build up that wealth which serves as our medium of exchange. We can also make our labor negotiable by converting it into wealth. Wealth is stored-up accomplishment; it is preserved industry; it is one way to measure our effort. But wealth is much more than all of these put together. Our wealth is actually a part of us. It might serve as a kind of sinking fund whereby we can set up a reserve to replace us as our lives diminish. During our lives or after our deaths our great possessions can be converted into hospitals, universities, temples, places of worship, and self-increasing endowment funds.

About the treasures that we store up on the earth, someone has said: "You can't take them with you." Then a pessimistic friend pointed out that with taxes like they are, you can't even keep them while you are here.

Someone who was even a little more negative said that even if you could take them with you, they would only melt. Actually many of our greatest possessions really can be taken with us.

There are two primary reasons why we don't do better than we do in laying up treasures upon the earth. One is that we sometimes get into the wrong business. There are many businesses that don't lend themselves very well to any substantial accomplishment. There are other people who do have a good business, but they never learn to conduct it very well. In the light of eternal values, what would we rather have our lives identified with than that great enterprise, which Jesus referred to as "my father's business"? That is the business of building integrity, character, ability, righteousness, and godliness into human lives. This business always yields good return, both here and hereafter.

This is the business in which God himself is engaged. He has said: ". . . this is my work and my glory — to bring to pass the immortality and eternal life of man." (Moses 1:39) Now he has invited us to serve in this family firm in which he spends his entire time. Demosthenes once said that "No man can have a high and noble character while engaged in petty or mean employment, for whatever the pursuits of men are, their characters will be similar." Our own internal values always reflect our outside activities.

In the very first commandment given after the expulsion from Eden, God said to our first parents: "In the sweat of thy face shalt thou eat bread. . . ." (Gen. 3:19) That is not a command of punishment; it is a command of opportunity. Work is not just the way we get our bread; it is also the way we solve our problems, overcome our difficulties, build our homes, educate our children, develop our characters, and do almost every other worthwhile thing in the world. We must take our works with us; otherwise they wouldn't be able to stand up for us on Judgment Day.

Recently a friend showed me a Bible that he had bought ten years ago, intending to transfer its contents into the minds, the hearts, and the "works" of his family. While the Bible is one of his very valuable possessions, it has never been used for the purpose intended. During these ten years it had served primarily as an ornament for his living room. When I saw it, it was employed to hold up a vase of flowers. While this great religious possession has been misused, it contains 921 printed pages with enough religion, philosophy, poetry, and culture to educate several Abraham Lincolns, as well as to save their souls.

There are some fantastic possessions in the Bible if they are properly translated into human emotions, divine inspiration, and active faith. The Bible contains many treasures that can be developed and taken with us through eternity. The dictionary says that a possession is something that we may obtain mastery of. If we can get a mastery of these great treasures of faith, honesty, devotion, understanding, and righteousness, we can convert them into both earthly and heavenly treasures.

Recently I listened to a recital of some distressing disadvantages of being poor. My informer was a 65-year-old man who had just lost his job. He completely convinced me that he had lived a very hard life. His boyhood had been spent in a miserable kind of poverty. His father's drinking and sloth had made employment impossible. Their family residence had no central heating, no inside plumbing, and no wall plaster. They also had an assortment of social and spiritual problems to match. This man recalled how sorry he felt that his mother lacked the means to properly feed and clothe her family. He had often wished that his mother could have had just one nice dress or just a little happiness. This man himself has not done much better. He has practically no equities in his faith, or in pleasant memories, or in good deeds performed. In other words he has no great possessions. To see wretched physical, mental, or social poverty is depressing, but the scriptures speak of some who were also poor toward God.

On many occasions the Lord has indicated that he is not pleased with any of the conditions that bring about depressing poverty. On one occasion the Lord scolded the Laodiceans because of this problem. He said: ". . . thou sayest, I am rich, and increased with goods, and have need of nothing; and knowest not that thou art wretched and miserable, and poor, and blind, and naked." Then, trying to help them to do better, he said: "I counsel thee to buy of me gold tried in the fire, that thou mayest be rich; and [wear] white raiment, that thou mayest be clothed, and that the shame of thy nakedness do not appear. . . ." (Rev. 3: 17, 18)

In describing the transfiguration of Jesus upon the high mountain, the scripture says: "And his face did shine as the sun, and his raiment was white as the light." (Matt. 17:2) The angel that attended Jesus at his resurrection is described by saying: "His countenance was like lightning, and his raiment white as snow." (Matt. 28:3) Certainly those who live with God will all have beautiful countenances, wear shining apparel, and have a wonderful variety of wealth.

We describe God as being omnipotent and omniscient, but he also has great possessions. It would be very difficult to think of God living in any kind of poverty. He has said: "Worlds without number have I created," but he has also created a great abundance of gold, real estate, beauty, and happiness. He has created the greatest intelligence, the most worthwhile morality, and the finest virtues. The scripture says that God is love, but God is also light and success and ability. God not only wants his children to be rich, but he also wants them to be able to produce their own wealth in the greatest abundance. God has given us a fine start by creating us in his own image, and he has ordained that, according to the universal laws of heredity, the offspring of God may hope to eventually become like their eternal parents.

God has also given us these wonderful, beautiful, physical bodies and has endowed us with these potentially miraculous minds, these godly spirits, and personalities with fantastic possibilities. Jesus indicated the limitlessness of our potential possessions when he said: "For he that receiveth my servants receiveth me; And he that receiveth me receiveth my Father; And he that receiveth my Father receiveth my Father's kingdom; therefore all that my Father hath shall be given unto him. And this is according to the oath and covenant which belongeth to the priesthood." (D&C 84:36-39) Everyone likes to inherit from a wealthy parent. Try to think of something more exciting than to inherit from God, to get everything that God has. Why should faithful children of God be deprived of those important things so necessary to their happiness? The Lord indicated how he feels about this material abundance when he said, ". . . the fulness of the earth is yours, the beasts of the field and the fowls of the air, and that which climbeth upon the trees and walketh upon the earth; Yea, and the herb, and the good things which come of the earth, whether for food or for raiment, or for houses, or for barns, or for orchards, or for gardens, or for vineyards; Yea, all things which come of the earth, in the season thereof, are made for the benefit and the use of man, both to please the eye and to gladden the heart; Yea, for food and for raiment, for taste and for smell, to strengthen the body and to enliven the soul. And it pleaseth God that he hath given all these things unto man; for unto this end were they made to be used, with judgment, not to excess, neither by extortion. And in nothing doth man offend God, or against none is his wrath kindled, save those who confess not his hand in all things, and obey not his commandments." (D&C 59:16-21)

One of the most important characteristics of our earth is its abundance. A single potato carried to England by Sir Walter Raleigh in the sixteenth century multiplied itself into food for millions. Ten forests come out of one acorn. One tomato seed can multiply itself a million times in a single year. Jesus spoke of mansions in heaven and the possibilities of a fulness of the glory of God. (See D&C 88:29) We might try to understand what that would be like. God put the great treasures of diamonds, gold, oil, and uranium in the earth, but he put his greatest wealth into his own children, and he expects us to manifest his abundance in every part of our lives.

Many years ago, Ray Stannard Baker won the Pulitzer prize for his eight-volume work, *The Life and Letters of Woodrow Wilson*. With the pen name of David Grayson, he wrote nine volumes under the title *Adventures in Contentment*. In one of his articles he talks about great possessions. He moved his place of residence from the city out onto the farm in the country and took his philosophy and literary talents with him. From the top of the hill he liked to look across the fields where the white daisies, the purple fleabane, and the yellow buttercups made a tangle of beauty. He enjoyed watching the breezes as they moved across the billowing fields. Bobolinks and meadow larks delighted his heart with their symphony. The old fences had wild hedgerows of chokecherries, young elms, and black raspberry bushes. He felt a strange thrill of strength in the glory of his possession of fields and crops. David loved these scenes, and their magic utility and beauty all belonged to him.

He often talked with Horace, his more humdrum neighbor. David felt that Horace never really had any spiritual ownership of the land to which he had a legal title. David claimed that he owned more of Horace's farm than Horace did. Horace harvested the crops and put the money in his pocket, but David harvested the beauty, the miracles, and the wonder that were produced on these same acres, and the returns went into his heart and soul. David once wrote a magazine article about one of Horace's fields, and the royalties amounted to more than Horace received from the crops.

God will give us a title to as much of life as we can understand and appreciate. Someone once said: "I own the landscape." We can also own the glory of the sunrise and the great possessions of the beauty and wealth of all of his other creations.

When God first looked out upon the work of his hands, he pronounced them very good. What a great thrill it would be for us to own the mountains, the warmth and vitality of the sunshine, as well as the beauty of our neighbor's flowers! One rancher in California recently told of a summer rain in which 10,000 tons of water had fallen on his land. He had estimated that this rain had a value to his crops of five dollars per ton. All of God's greatest gifts have a thrill value, an inspiration value, a beauty value, and a utility value. Every farmer who cultivates his land should also spiritually possess it and harvest at least four crops instead of one.

When we have title to our lives, we ought to live them. We should have mastery of our great literary and spiritual possessions. Certainly we should not lose our strength by letting our great possessions go to waste, because we may be like the Laodiceans who were wretched and miserable and poor and blind and naked. Great possessions do not consist merely in those things that we have. More accurately they are what we *are*. We don't work merely to acquire; we work to become. Success in life isn't just what we can get out of it; it is what we can become by it. The gospel isn't just something to think about; it is something to believe in and work at and live by. As we prepare to effectively lay up treasures in heaven, we must develop the great possessions that God has already hidden in us. Before we can be great souls in heaven, we must be great souls here. May we so conduct ourselves that our lives will be rich toward God with the strength of our great possessions.

The Big Three of Success

RECENTLY A SUCCESSFUL sales manager was trying to help a group of less experienced men improve their sales abilities. During a long and successful experience this sales manager had discovered that salesmen seldom fail because they lack sales ability; they fail because they lack manhood and the ability for self-discipline. It is much easier to make a salesman out of a man than it is to make a man out of a salesman.

Aristotle touched one of the important secrets of accomplishment when he said that "we never know a thing until we know it by its causes." In our world of law and order, nothing ever just happens. Every success has a cause. Every failure has a cause. Overweight has a cause. Indigestion has a cause. Righteousness has a cause. Every happiness has a cause and every misery has a cause. If you can find out what causes sales failure, you can eliminate the cause. If you can find out what causes success in life, you can reproduce it.

Recently an Idaho farmer reported that he had produced 500 sacks of potatoes per acre. Interestingly enough the farmer across the fence produced only 150 sacks per acre. Now just suppose that the less successful farmer wanted to increase his yield — how should he go about it? Following the formula of Aristotle he might first try to discover what was causing his poorer yield. His more successful neighbor could probably help him in his research. A soil analysis might disclose some plant food deficiencies. Or it may be that he doesn't know how a good seed bed should be prepared. Or he may have used poor seed, or he may have planted his crop at the wrong time, or the irrigating may have been improperly done, or the plants may have had too much competition from the weeds. Or maybe the poorer farmer should get some better ideas about cultivation.

Thomas J. Watson, the builder of the great I.B.M. Corporation, says that in planning to be successful, one should first set his goals and then work backward to success. Suppose the poorer potato farmer set his next year's goal at 300 sacks per acre.

Then he could work backward to success by figuring out how much more fertilizer he would need to apply, etc.

The laws governing potato yields and sales success are just as definite and as dependable as are the laws of electricity, gravity, light, heat, or growth. If we know what these laws are, we can successfully harness them. And if we can recognize mistakes in advance, we don't need to make them all personally.

A man once said to his friend, "I would give anything to know where I was going to die." His friend said, "What good would that do you?" He replied, "Then I would never go around the place." If we know the causes of failure, we can stay away from them.

The sales manager mentioned above pointed out the three most common causes for failure in selling. These are the three things that every good salesman ought to stay away from. First, is an inadequate decision. Second, is allowing too many distractions. And third, is an unwillingness to pay the price demanded by success. Of course, these are the same reasons that destroy success in every other field, including business, marriage, religion, and life itself. Suppose that we examine these three, one at a time.

First, we must make an adequate decision about those things that are important to us. So frequently we just never really make up our minds on a permanent 100 percent basis. We allow too much mental wavering and half decisions. When one has a 60 percent decision to be a salesman, with a strong 40 percent mental reservation pulling in the other direction, his net effort will be far too weak for any real accomplishment. Without a full and an enthusiastic unanimous vote we might later expect a lot of heckling, with some serious conflicts between our majority and our minority interests. When we go through life with only a bare majority on our side, our net power is low, our faith is limited, our enthusiasm is lukewarm, and the internal conflicts dissipate our strength. Without a firm, enthusiastic decision we will likely be on dead center most of the time. Then we say, "On the one hand this, but on the other hand that."

A psychiatrist once asked a mental patient if he ever had any trouble in making up his mind. The patient said, "Well, yes and no." It is difficult to muster enough strength for a life-sized success while half of our attention is centered in the greener grass on the other side of the fence.

From the top of Mount Sinai, God said: "Thou shalt not covet thy neighbor's wife — or anything that is thy neighbor's." That might be another way of saying, "Why don't you make up your mind once and for all?" In this the Lord was not speaking merely as a moralist; he was also speaking as a success expert. Coveting is not only sinful but it divides our interest and it also weakens every other ability.

One should be very careful in selecting a life's work or a wife or a religion. But after he has once made up his mind and taken action, he should treat them so well that there will never be any rivals, either in his mind or in his affections; otherwise he will be continually drawn off his course. When we have a great love in our hearts centered in our main purpose, our energies and our devotions can be so channeled that we can hardly avoid being successful and happy. The time when most people have doubts about their businesses or their wives or their religions is when they are neglecting them.

A tired businessman is one whose business is not successful. No one ever quits while he is ahead. You never get discouraged while you are winning. If you don't want to waste your energy coveting your neighbor's wife, just keep your own wife so happy that the neighbor's wife will never have a chance in your mind. There is a wasteful ebb and flow that frequently operates in our affairs when our minds are not fully made up. Then our love and our focus and our industry waxes and wanes, depending upon which attitude is dominant at the moment. Then we take turns in becoming encouraged and discouraged, and our convictions and our enthusiasms are always going up and down like a Yo-Yo on a string.

Second, we must avoid distractions. The shortest way to success is a straight line. A straight line permits no detours or explorations down blind alleys or losses of time because of dead-end streets. To be profitably employed or happily married or successful in our spiritual affairs, we cannot afford too many conflicting loyalties or too many dissenting opinions. Neither can we afford too many stoppings where we have to start over again at the bottom. Success in marriage or business or life does not consist in merely finding the right person or the right business. It also depends upon our being the right person. And the fullest measure of success is never possible for one who is always succumbing to distractions. A little piece of magnetized iron ore placed close to the ship's compass can cause the ship to miss its destination by half of a world. It is also true that some little distractions placed near the straight and narrow way leading to life and success can cause us to miss our total destiny.

Many years ago out on the farm the work horses all had blinders on their bridles to help them to resist the distractions. These little pieces of leather were placed on both sides of the horse's head to cut off his view and to enable him to center his attention right down the row. Without side blinders the horse often developed a kind of swivel neck, enabling him to do a little sightseeing as he went along. But when the horse was taking in too much scenery, he was also stepping on too many plants. It seems that this analogy furnishes us with a very constructive comparison for life. Certainly one of the greatest aids to any success, in business or in morality or in marriage or in life, is to have a good set of side blinders so we can keep our minds on what we are doing.

One of the greatest hazards in either husbands or workers or those seeking the most out of religion is that of being distracted by too much sightseeing. Some professional men have their effectiveness reduced because they are distracted by the lure of big profits made in real estate or on the stock market or in some other area outside of their own field. But usually we make our money in our own business and lose it in someone else's business because of this disturbing natural color-blindness that usually makes the grass look greener on the other side of the fence.

Succumbing to distractions usually doesn't solve any problems, as frequently the tenth job is no more permanent than the ninth. Likewise the fourth marriage may not last any longer than the third. A good set of eye blinders intensifies the power that we are able to generate, and it can be an important success factor.

Jesus was speaking on this subject of limiting our primary interests when he said, "No man can serve two masters." You can't ride two horses in the same race. I heard of someone who tried that once, and just as he thought he had everything going well the horses ran on opposite sides of a tree. And one of the great ideas in holy scripture is given in the dissertation of Jesus about the importance of the straight and narrow way leading to religious success. But the path leading to every success is straight and narrow. We like to think of ourselves as broad-minded, but sometimes when our minds get very broad they also get very shallow. A broad river that is a mile wide and an inch deep never generates very much power. It is the torrent that is narrow and deep that tears down the mountain.

Life has decreed that we may have almost anything that we desire if we seek it over that straight and narrow way which allows no distractions and no stoppings and startings. Life has allotted us enough time to reach for any reasonable success if we are traveling along the straight and narrow way with one thing in our focus. But we probably won't make it if we seek too many things at the same time or if we are required to go on too many detours.

Someone has said:

> He who seeks one thing, and but one,
> May hope to achieve it before life is done.
> But he who seeks all things wherever he goes
> Must reap around him in whatever he sows
> A harvest of barren regret.

The scripture says that a double-minded man is unstable in all his ways. (James 1:8) But if we allow ourselves to be triple-minded, or half-minded, or wrong-minded, or swivel-necked our power will sink to a fraction and our strength will be wasted by conflicts and by the distractions of outside interests.

The third member of the big three of success comes with our willingness to pay the price that is always demanded by success. There are very few things in life that come free, whereas God gives all things to industry. There is an old proverb that says, "What thou would'st have, quoth God, pay for it and take it." Actually there are many people who are not entitled to succeed because they won't pay the required price. But there is a natural eternal law that says that we can have any blessing if we are willing to obey the law upon which that blessing is predicated. (D&C 130:21)

So far as I know, there is only one way for a person to develop big muscles on his arms, and that is to give them a hard job to do. If one wants to get a great brain, he should try using it intelligently over a long period. If one wants to know that the gospel is true, he should live those principles that he wants to believe in. Anyone is kicking against the pricks when he wants to be happy but refuses to take a bath or comb his hair. If one insists on spending his time in idleness, dope addiction, and immorality, he can never be really happy because he is violating the laws of happiness. Happiness is never found in wickedness, and success never comes as a result of idleness and irresponsibility. One who remains rebellious, ignorant, idle, and evil is not likely to become a great captain of industry or to develop a great spirituality. There is no excellence without industry, whereas Leonardo da Vinci has said, "Thou, oh God, doth sell us all good things at the price of labor." The god of success has given us a potentially great character with the integrity, courage, and faith with which to pay the price for what we want. But even if we once develop big muscles, the Lord will still repossess them if they are not continually used to the fullest extent.

We must use our talents and obey nature's laws and pay the full price if we would reach any desired fulfillment. To summarize, we first make up our minds as to where we want to go. Second, we put on our side blinders so that no distractions can pull us off the straight and narrow way. And third, we develop a strong, willing determination to pay the price which life always demands for the particular success that we have set our minds on.

The Albatross

In 1798 SAMUEL TAYLOR COLERIDGE wrote his great epic poem entitled "The Rime of the Ancient Mariner," which one prominent critic has said is in all points one of the greatest creations in all of literature. James Russell Lowell has said: "In the 'Rime of the Ancient Mariner' Coleridge has written one of the most poetical poems in the language which is not only unparalleled but unapproached in its kind."

This great literary work tells some of the experiences of this ancient mariner and his crew as they sailed their ship through distant southern seas. One day as they journeyed pleasantly upon their way, a great albatross appeared out of the ocean mists, and with an attitude of the greatest friendliness, hovered about their ship and accompanied them on their way.

The albatross is the largest of the sea birds. It lives in southern zones and is capable of long continued flights so that it is often sighted great distances from land. But to these sailors far from home this great bird was a very pleasant sight, and they considered it as one of the best of good omens.

In that day it was supposed by some that an albatross brought good fortune to the mariners and success to their causes. Among other things it made the breezes blow and it assured the sailors of good rains to provide fresh water to drink. It also favored the attainment of their other needs. Therefore, when the albatross appeared the sailors greeted it as if it had been a "Christian soul," and they "hailed it in God's name." For days it followed their ship and hovered around it. Occasionally it came aboard for food and to engage in a kind of fraternal association and play with the sailors. It frequently perched on the mast and shroud for evening vespers, and it was generally good company.

Following an evil impulse, the ancient mariner drew his great crossbow, shot the harmless, friendly albatross, and thereby destroyed their omen of good fortune. With no friendly bird to follow their ship, their favorable fortunes began a sharp decline. Because the friendly bond of fellowship that had existed between man and beast had been broken, the breezes stopped blowing, the heavens dried up so that no rain fell, and soon their ship and all aboard were marooned on a hot, dead ocean. The ancient mariner had violated that reverence for life that should exist for man and beast and bird, and because a law had been broken and a crime had been committed, a natural vengeance must surely follow. Mr. Coleridge said:

> Down dropt the breeze, the sails dropt down,
> 'Twas sad as sad could be;
> And we did speak only to break
> The silence of the sea!
>
> All in a hot and copper sky,
> The bloody Sun, at noon,
> Right up above the mast did stand,
> No bigger than the Moon.
>
> Day after day, day after day
> We stuck, nor breath nor motion;
> As idle as a painted ship
> Upon a painted ocean.
>
> Water, water, everywhere,
> And all the boards did shrink;
> Water, water, everywhere,
> Nor any drop to drink.
>
> The very deep did rot: O Christ!
> That ever this should be!
> Yea, slimy things did crawl with legs
> Upon the slimy sea.
>
> And every tongue, through utter drought,
> Was wither'd at the root;
> We could not speak, no more than if
> We had been choked with soot.

Because the ancient mariner had caused the sorry plight of his sailors by killing the albatross, they naturally felt very unkindly toward him. Therefore, he said of their attitude:

> And I had done an hellish thing,
> And it would work 'em woe:
> For all averr'd I had kill'd the bird

That made the breeze to blow.
Ah, wretch, said they, the bird to slay,
That made the breeze to blow!

Then in punishment for his crime the dead albatross was hung about the neck of the guilty ancient mariner. He said:

Ah! well a-day! what evil looks
Had I from old and young!
Instead of the cross, the Albatross
About my neck was hung.

But all on board the stranded ship continued to suffer many disagreeable things that his sin brought upon them, and even death itself visited the ship. Again the ancient mariner said:

There passed a weary time. Each throat
Was parch'd, and glazed each eye.
One after one, by the star-dogg'd Moon,
Too quick for groan or sigh,
Each turn'd his face with a ghastly pang,
And cursed me with his eye.

Four times fifty living men
(And I heard nor sight nor groan),
With heavy thump, a lifeless lump,
They dropp'd down one by one.

Their souls did from their bodies fly —
They fled to bliss or woe!
And every soul, it pass'd me by
Like the whizz of my crossbow!

Alone, alone, all, all alone,
Alone on a wide, wide sea!
And never a saint took pity on
My soul in agony.

The many men, so beautiful!
And they all dead did lie:
And a thousand thousand slimy things
Lived on; and so did I.

I look'd upon the rotting sea,
And drew my eyes away;
I look'd upon the rotting deck,
And there the dead men lay.

I look'd to heaven, and tried to pray;
But or ever a prayer had gusht,
A wicked whisper came, and made
My heart as dry as dust.

I closed my lids, and kept them close,
And the balls like pulses beat;
But the sky and the sea, and the sea and the sky,
Lay like a load on my weary eye,
And the dead were at my feet.

The cold sweat melted from their limbs,
Nor rot nor reek did they:
The look with which they look'd on me
Had never pass'd away.

An orphan's curse would drag to hell
A spirit from on high;
But oh! more horrible than that
Is the curse in a dead man's eye!
Seven days, seven nights, I saw that curse,
And yet I could not die.

After days of enduring this awful living death in company with the slimy things that were crawling over the rotting decks marooned on this rotting sea, the ancient mariner got into his heart a new feeling of sympathy for God's other creatures so that he loved even the lowliest among them. His own suffering and this new feeling of godliness purged out his sins and restored that sympathetic relationship, which should always exist between God's creations of man and man, and man and beast. The ancient mariner said:

O happy living things! no tongue
Their beauty might declare:
A string of love gush'd from my heart,
And I bless'd them unaware:
Sure my kind saint took pity on me,
And I bless'd them unaware.

That selfsame moment I could pray;
And from my neck so free
The Albatross fell off, and sank
Like lead into the sea.

Now that the curse had been removed, the rain fell in abundance into their buckets. The dead men came back to life.

Their throats were slaked, their brows were cooled, and a gentle, peaceful sleep was again made possible after the tiresome weariness of this awful suffering. A friendly wind now arose that would carry the ship and its crew back again to their own country.

A reminder of this awful experience always remained with the ancient mariner, and at intervals it would again return to burn in his memory. His only relief was to get someone to listen as he rehearsed his awful tale. He never knew in advance at what hour his suffering might again come upon him, but he must always be ready to tell again the story of his sin. He said:

> Since then, at an uncertain hour,
> That agony returns;
> And till my ghastly tale is told,
> This heart within me burns.

After giving the account to his most recent listener, he said:

> Farewell, farewell! but this I tell
> To thee, thou Wedding-Guest!
> He prayeth well, who loveth well
> Both man and bird and beast.

> He prayeth best, who loveth best
> All things, both great and small;
> For the dear God who loveth us,
> He made and loveth all.

> The Mariner, whose eye is bright,
> Whose beard with age is hoar,
> Is gone: and now the Wedding-Guest
> Turn'd from the bridegroom's door.

> He went like one that hath been stunn'd,
> And is of sense forlorn:
> A sadder and a wiser man
> He rose the morrow morn.

The stimulating ideas that we get from great literature serve an important place in all our lives.

James Russell Lowell has said: "More bits of Coleridge have embedded themselves in my memory than of any other poet who delighted my youth, unless I should except the sonnets of Shakespeare." And Henry Wadsworth has said: "The two cardinal points of poetry are the power of exciting the sympathy of the reader by a faithful adherence to the truths of nature, and the power of giving us the interest of novelty by modifying the colours of our imagination."

Good poetry is often very effective in producing sublime feelings in us in the place of the images given us by the poet. The thoughts from our great literature frequently help us to feel the elemental truths of life as they strike some responsive chords in us. Some of these thoughts should also become embedded in us. This idea that a part of the punishment of the ancient mariner was for the dead albatross to be hung about his neck to represent his sin reminds us of Nemesis, the Greek goddess of divine retribution. It is one of the universal laws of life that an unseen avenger is constantly standing guard in the world to make sure that no sin ever goes unpunished. This idea of burdening the sinner with his own sin also accords with that graphic way which some of the ancients had for punishing wrong. When any crime was committed the criminal was tied to his crime. If one should kill he had to pay for his evil by being chained to the corpse of his victim. Then wherever he went forevermore he must drag with him the putrefying remains of his sin. There was no possible way that he could disentangle himself from the results of his evil act. If at a later date he should decide to kill again, another dead body would be added to his awful burden.

This punishment is terribly severe, and yet life has a plan of retribution that is exactly like that. The facts are that we must always be chained to our sins with no possible escapes permitted. If a person becomes an alcoholic, his punishment is that a ruinous, driving thirst attaches itself to push him farther and farther down the road to despair. If one fails to study, his sentence is to be chained to his ignorance. He cannot lay it off for even an hour. His own albatross is hung about his neck. If one tells lies, his judgment is that he becomes a liar. And so it is with every other sin. The Apostle Paul may have had this awful custom in mind when he said: "Oh dreadful man that I am, who will free me from the body of this death?" And with some of our own albatrosses about our necks we might say, "Who indeed!"

One of the important characteristics of the people of our own day is that we are loading ourselves down with the dead bodies of so many serious sins. It would be a great source of embarrassment if each of us had to go about his daily affairs with this appropriate albatross hanging about his neck. And yet that is exactly our present situation. Disloyalty is an albatross that is presently dragging our great nation down toward its doom. Atheism is an albatross that is destroying our chances for eternal life. Immorality is an albatross which is placing an awful encumbrance upon millions of human beings.

Recently a broken-hearted mother reported that her fifteen-year-old daughter had taken up the life of a hippie. She had previously been very active in her church class. She had been a scholastic and social leader in her school. Then with some peculiarly dressed, uncombed, evil-smelling companions she had become addicted to dope, lust, and irresponsibility. She now is a mental case in the hospital psychiatric ward, suffering from a venereal disease and from several equally serious venereal attitudes. Some doctors and social workers are trying to get her well enough to send her to the reform school. It is easy to understand that wherever she goes forevermore, both she and her mother must drag with them this girl's dead and decaying albatrosses.

Nicotine is an albatross. It not only hangs itself around our necks but it discolors our fingers, gives us a foul breath, puts cancer in our lungs, and contaminates the very atmosphere that others around us breathe.

Rebellion is an albatross. How pathetic when people hang a load of irresponsibility around their own necks and insist on the immoral pleasures of idleness and sin! They want a prestige and recognition which they have not earned, and if someone objects to their evil ways they think they are being persecuted. An individual can live without integrity, industry, or faith in God, but not very well. How terrible is the mistake that some make of thinking that happiness can be found in idleness, begging, immorality, irresponsibility, and sin. The betrayal of Judas Iscariot not only hung an albatross around his neck, but it also caused him to put a rope around his neck and hang himself.

Atheism is an albatross. What a heavy, dead weight we have to carry when we load ourselves with disbelief and disobedience. And what a tremendous advantage is the privilege we have of relieving ourselves through repentance! Like the ancient mariner the albatross of all our sins may, like lead, drop off into the sea and we can again pray and worship God and love all of his creatures. But if we make the chains of our evil too strong, then even hell itself may not be able to burn out our sins or free us from those monstrous things that we sometimes permit to fasten themselves upon us.

Appreciation

M ANY YEARS AGO the great Harvard psychologist William James said: "The deepest hunger in human beings is the desire to be appreciated." More than almost anything else we want to feel that our lives themselves are worthwhile. Everyone has a natural need to love and to be loved. It pleases us when other people manifest a sincere interest in our welfare.

On the other hand one of the biggest problems in our world comes because we allow selfishness and hate to destroy our friendly relations with others. The most harmful characteristics of many nations, racial groups, and individuals is that they *hate* each other and try to reduce each other in importance. Our world has too many jealousies, too many occupational differences, and too many religious dislikes. Some people hate their country. Often we hate life, and we even hate God. Then we are frustrated because we usually get back in kind whatever we give. To develop a real appreciation we should also have a more discriminating concern about what is right and wrong, and we should also do more of those things that foster the best interest of others.

To get effective appreciation we also need to be more mindful of our relations with God, for when we get too much godlessness in our success formula, we make many mistakes that are not good for us. The longer we continue in our sins, the more we load ourselves down with the feelings of guilt and the attitudes of discouragement and inferiority. Then we are thrown into unpleasant moods and destructive depressions. The one thing that our human mechanism cannot endure for very long without losing its mental balance is that devastating feeling of one's own worthlessness.

Probably the best way to solve all of our individual and group problems is to follow that great success formula given nearly two thousand years ago when Jesus said: "Thou shalt love the Lord thy God with all thy heart, and with all thy soul, and with all thy mind. This is the first and great commandment, and the second is like unto it, Thou shalt love thy neighbor as thyself. On these two commandments hang all the law and the prophets." (Matt. 22:37-40)

One of the best ways to get the appreciation that we seek is to be worthy of it. If we effectively foster love and appreciation, we must first root out hate and evil. Practising this great success law of love can work wonders in our lives. There are actually three main subheadings that the Master presented for our consideration.

The first part of the commandment was that we should wholeheartedly love God. That is also the most important. God is all wise and all good and all knowing. In order to love God we must know him and believe in him and agree with him. Then we will want to do as he says, not only because he said it but because it is right and is also profitable. If we adequately loved God, most of our problems would disappear more or less automatically. On the other hand, nothing could be more disastrous to our own best interests than to hate God. When we are antagonistic our course is contrary and failure is the result. Someone has said: "He who forgets his friend is ungrateful to his friend but he who forgets his Savior is unmerciful unto himself." To love God and to keep his commandments is the shortest possible route to success, happiness, and the appreciation of others. It is also the best-known way to every other worthwhile benefit. Someone has said: "The best possible argument in favor of an eternal life is the existence of someone who deserves it."

The second part of this important success formula is to love our neighbor as ourselves. There are many difficulties involved in hating our enemies. By this process we keep live poison in our hearts. If limitlessly followed, this old philosophy of an eye for an eye would eventually make everybody blind. Jesus reminded his listeners that even the worst and the weakest people could love their friends and hate their enemies. However, the very best way to get the best of any antagonist is to be friendly to him. The hottest coals of fire ever heaped upon the head of an enemy are the coals of human kindness. It is pretty hard not to like someone while we are being friendly to him.

One of our most productive potential abilities is to love people, even though we may think they don't deserve it. It has been said that many teen-agers need to be loved most when they are the least lovable. But that is also true of us, and we seriously weaken our own problem-solving ability when we use scorn, hate, bitterness, or our abilities for rejection as the tools of our negotiation.

Some time ago a meeting was attended by a group of psychiatrists, psychologists, and ministers. The matter for consideration was to discover what single success factor was most important in a counselor who was trying to help other people solve their problems. As possible answers, they discussed the qualities of insight, experience, professional training, and counseling techniques. But when the opinions were all in, the one answer that had emerged most frequently indicated that the counselor most likely to get the best results was the one who had mastered the art of paying sympathetic attention to the one he was trying to help. Just to be listened to has a powerful therapy. It gives people the feeling of being appreciated and important. Each of us has had woven into the fabric of his life this need which must be satisfied if we are to remain at our best in mental and emotional health. When we receive inadequate attention a psychic pain is created that few people can endure without unpleasant consequences.

To some extent the tearful child tugging at his mother's skirts, the rebellious teen-ager, the ridiculous hippie, the philandering husband, the nagging wife, and the race rioters in the street are all voicing some version of the same despairing cry, saying, "Pay attention to me!"

A couple took their shaggy-haired, 14-year-old son to the American Foundation of Religion and Psychiatry. He had been one of the 130,000 teen-age runaway fugitives that are reported each year by the F.B.I. Finally the boy came home, but things were no better. "We give him everything," the mother said distractedly. "We don't know what is the matter with him."

When one of the therapists had finally gained his confidence, the boy said: "My parents don't care about me. We never do anything together. My father never looks at me when I try to talk to him. My mother is always nagging me about my hair, but she never listens."

Most parents and most children want to do the right thing but mostly we just don't know how. This boy may have been largely to blame, but these parents were advised that maybe they should work a little harder learning to pay more attention to their child who was having trouble.

I suppose that this phrase "to pay" means that we should part with something that has value. In this case it would probably mean that the parents should part with some time or give up some preoccupation in their affairs and invest more of their interest in their son's welfare, in spite of the fact that the son himself may be unlovable.

We have so many dozens of ways of rejecting people. No matter what its form, rejection always hurts; it always leaves wounds, whereas attention always heals. A mother can actually cure a child's pain by taking him in her arms and kissing away the hurt. Husbands and wives can also heal each other by this same process. Even a doctor can make a sick patient feel better by lavishing a little attention upon him.

Every sick person who has suffered the apprehension of being in the hospital knows the feelings of inner security and soul satisfaction that come when the doctor shows a genuine and expert interest. Everyone likes to be reassured occasionally that he is getting along all right. In addition to his medicines a doctor can also heal by kissing away, so to speak, the pains and fears that make so many patients sick. There are many people who consciously or subconsciously actually make themselves sick, physically, mentally, spiritually, or socially, because of the attention that they will get as a consequence.

The story is told of an escaped convict who risked his freedom by going into the post office to sit and gaze at his reward picture. Under the picture was written: "Wanted $10,000." Someone asked the convict why he took such a chance and he replied: "It just felt so good to be wanted."

Think of the other reasonable and subreasonable things that we do in order to get attention. During the courting period a young man develops the attention-getting techniques of washing his face and combing his hair. And it is very fortunate when this desire for affection is continued throughout one's life. When we take pains to be at our best, then the ship of matrimony and almost every other ship usually runs smoothly. For above most other things everyone likes to be courted. We like to feel that our lives have enough merit to win the favorable attention of others. It pleases us when we are well regarded by the community, the church, and God. If honorable ways of winning attention fail, many people employ less desirable means. Some dropouts from success may feel that they can't compete on the level of merit, and so they may go to the other extreme and even become ridiculous, if necessary. Some stop bathing, let their hair grow, and make themselves look as hideous as possible in order to get attention.

There is also an important hidden factor in this formula. When Jesus said that we should love our neighbors as ourselves, he certainly had in mind that we should love ourselves in the right way. Many people regard themselves with little or no self-respect. Whenever we do the wrong things we usually hate ourselves, and too many errors can cause us to lose confidence in our own judgment. Sin can soon destroy the finest character, and if we are going to love our neighbors as ourselves there is a lot of work to be done in building up our relations with ourselves.

If we sincerely love God and if we have a little good, wholesome, merited self-respect and feel a warm, friendly interest in others, we are well on our way toward satisfying that deepest hunger in our lives.

It is an interesting fact that God made hunger one of the most important parts of our nature. If we didn't have a craving for food, we probably wouldn't eat and we would soon break down our health. But our souls need spiritual food and our personalities need appreciation about as much as our bodies need nourishment. We can only get love and appreciation by giving love and appreciation and by being worthy of its return. It is pretty difficult to get what we seek by trying to dominate others. We can't command respect by the use of power, wealth, force, fear, or bribes.

Many times the scriptures mention our possibility of pleasing God. What a great idea it is that we can actually win the attention of God and by what we do we can give him a feeling of contentment and happiness! One of the greatest of all human satisfactions is to be admired and highly regarded by others. Who can think of anything more exciting than to be highly regarded by God, our eternal Heavenly Father?

The scripture says that "God is love," but under the right circumstances that might also be said of us. We can also rest assured that if we love God, he will be paying attention to us. The Psalmist said: "The eyes of the Lord are upon the righteous, and his ears are open unto their cry." (Psa. 34:15) One of our most profitable possible projects is to be the kind of person that God can love, bless, and pay favorable attention to. It doesn't make much sense to think that God will be very happy with us when we are dirty, smelly, irresponsible, sinful, dope-addicted, atheistic, and undependable.

He has specifically said that he hates profanity, all kinds of dishonesty, and immorality. He doesn't like drunkenness, trouble-making, unfairness, or disobedience to any of his holy laws. God is the God of righteousness, and he cannot look upon sin with the least degree of allowance. He is also the best friend of all those who faithfully serve him. They will sometime hear him say: "Well done, thou good and faithful servant. Thou hast been faithful over a few things. I will make thee ruler over many things. Enter thou into the joy of thy Lord." May we satisfy these deep hungers in our own lives in such a way that we will also please God most.

The Articles of Faith

MANY OF OUR GREATEST ideas are received by us in sections. There is an important word in our language called article. It describes a part or a division. Magazine publishers fill their paper with articles. The first written agreement between American colonies was known as the Articles of Confederation. We have articles of association and articles of agreement. The government has a set of rules called the Articles of War. A very important part of the standard works of the Church is that great set of beliefs called the Articles of Faith. It is a great help to have clearly in mind exactly what we believe in and what we should do about each belief.

On March 1, 1842, John Wentworth, publisher of the *Chicago Democrat*, went to Nauvoo, Illinois, for an interview with the Prophet Joseph Smith. He wanted to know firsthand about the doctrines that were taught by this newly organized Church of Jesus Christ of Latter-day Saints. As a result of this interview Joseph Smith wrote out thirteen Articles of Faith, giving a brief authoritative expression to many of the Church's religious doctrines. These articles begin where most other good things begin, and that is with God. Of course, the basic principles of all religion and the basic principles of all other kinds of success must always have a strong central belief in God. God is the Creator of the universe, the chief governor of our world, the giver of life, and the source of all good things. Without God, there is nothing.

The first Article of Faith says: "We believe in God, the Eternal Father, and in His Son, Jesus Christ, and in the Holy Ghost." That is a very important statement, and it does not just mean that we only believe that the members of this great trinity exist, but it also means that we understand the kind of beings that they are. One great modern-day scripture states: "The Father has a body of flesh and bones as tangible as man's, the Son also; but the Holy Ghost has not a body of flesh and bones, but is a personage of Spirit. Were it not so, the Holy Ghost could not dwell in us." (D&C 130:22)

This Article of Faith also means that we believe that they know their business, that we trust them, and that the wisest possible course in life is to faithfully, fully, and vigorously follow their direction. These three individuals make up the Godhead. They are the rulers of the universe. They are the first presidency of heaven. Faith in God was also the subject of the first of those governing principles thundered from the top of Mount Sinai thirty-four centuries ago, when out of fires of that holy mountain God said: "Thou shalt have no other gods before me."

What a tremendous benefit our world would receive if each of its inhabitants had a full, intelligent, unwavering belief in, an adherence to, and an acceptance of God! On numerous occasions God had revealed himself to the prophets. Enoch walked with God. God revealed himself to Adam and to many others. Moses was with God for 40 days in the Mount. God also personally revealed himself to Joseph Smith. That is, in our own day, mortal man has again known God as Moses did, face to face, and we should make the most of that experience.

The second Article of Faith has to do with that thrilling idea of standing on our own feet. The power of faith in God must go hand in hand with a matching power of responsibility in man. The second Article of Faith says: "We believe that men will be punished for their own sins, and not for Adam's transgression." Many people have falsely assumed that they would be condemned for something that they had no part in bringing about. But Adam's transgression was fully paid for by the atonement of Christ. On the other hand we must not disclaim any of our own responsibility or the necessity we have for shouldering the full liability for our own sins. The acceptance by man of our full personal responsibility is one of the foundation principles of religion. It underlies the idea of being judged according to our works. It is also one of the cardinal principles governing our every other success. We ourselves must be strong enough to hold ourselves accountable for everything that we say and think and do and become.

The third Article of Faith also contains a great success principle. It says: "We believe that through the Atonement of Christ, all mankind may be saved, by obedience to the laws and ordinances of the Gospel." We need to fully understand these great laws of salvation that govern our eternal success, and one of the greatest of these is the atonement Christ made for us on the condition of our repentance. By the process of vitalizing our belief in God with a genuine repentance and a full forgiveness, all of our transgressions may be wiped out, forgiven, and forgotten. And certainly it was a great day for us when in that divine decree the Lord said: ". . . though your sins be as scarlet, they shall be as white as snow; though they be red like crimson, they shall be as wool." (Isa. 1:18)

Under the operation of this great law *we* get the benefits and *he* pays the bills.

The fourth Article says: "We believe that the first principles and ordinances of the Gospel are: first, Faith in the Lord Jesus Christ; second, Repentance; third, Baptism by immersion for the remission of sins; fourth, Laying on of hands for the gift of the Holy Ghost."

If fully lived, these four principles alone can almost completely guarantee our success, both here and hereafter. Faith is the foundation of all success. The first step in any accomplishment is to believe in it. We also need to believe in ourselves and to believe in our work and to believe in righteousness and to believe in the Lord Jesus Christ.

Most of our troubles come because we don't believe soon enough or hard enough or long enough. We don't always believe in the right things. There are many people who invest their belief in such evil things as liquor, adultery, force, crime, delinquency, and dishonesty; whereas if we have enough faith in God most of our other problems would be eliminated almost automatically.

Of course, real faith does not consist in following divine instructions just when it suits our convenience to do so. We must adjust our lives to every principle of the gospel under all conditions, and we must wholeheartedly accept this exciting concept of repentance. Ordinarily we don't like to hear or think about repentance, inasmuch as it gives us a painful and unpleasant feeling of guilt. But some day we might discover that repentance is the most thrilling, exciting, interesting idea that there is in the world, providing, of course, that it will not be too late for us to use it for our own relief and comfort.

Closely following repentance comes baptism by immersion for the remission of our sins. Water is the universal element. It is the symbol of life. It is also a symbol of cleanliness. It is the symbol of Christ's burial and resurrection. Baptism is the gateway into the Church. It is by the ordinance of baptism and confirmation that we take upon ourselves the name of Christ and become officially identified with his program for the salvation of the race. Every child of God is given this opportunity to stand up and be counted with those believing in and belonging to and fostering that great Church organization that Jesus himself thought was so tremendously important.

Then comes the bestowal of the gift of the Holy Ghost. The Holy Ghost is the third member of the Godhead. He is a personage of spirit with great intelligence and tremendous power. The blessings of the Holy Ghost enable all worthy people to have a special divine guidance and a special personal direction following the laying on of hands by those having the divine authority so to do.

About the mission of the Holy Ghost, Jesus said: "But the Comforter, which is the Holy Ghost, whom the Father will send in my name, he shall teach you all things, and bring all things to your remembrance, whatsoever I have said unto you." (John 14:26)

Paul said: ". . . know ye not that your body is the temple of the Holy Ghost which is in you, which ye have of God, and ye are not your own?" (I Cor. 6:19)

The possible gifts of the Holy Ghost are among the most important possessions of life. The Holy Ghost will help us to keep ourselves free from sin, and we should be careful to merit this most important relationship under the best conditions. Paul said to the Ephesians: ". . . grieve not the holy Spirit of God, whereby ye are sealed unto the day of redemption." (Eph. 4:30)

The fifth Article of Faith says: "We believe that a man must be called of God, by prophecy, and by the laying on of hands, by those who are in authority to preach the Gospel and administer in the ordinances thereof." In spite of the fact that God is a God of order, for some reason many people believe that anyone can take upon himself the name of Christ and proceed in his name to teach any kind of doctrines that may suit his own fancy. This is a very serious sin, and frequently God has manifested his great displeasure toward those who have presumed to act in his name.

Article number six says: "We believe in the same organization that existed in the Primitive Church, viz., apostles, prophets, pastors, teachers, evangelists, etc." If God did not want this particular organization to endure, why did he organize it in the first place? The scripture is perfectly clear that Christ did not want either his organization or his doctrines to be changed by men. The world has gone far afield, not only in transgressing the laws and changing the doctrines but also in destroying the organization. The divine Church was organized upon a foundation of apostles and prophets with Jesus Christ himself being the chief cornerstone, and that is the way the true Church must always be. The promise was also given that the same signs that existed in the primitive Church would always follow the believer.

Article number seven says: "We believe in the gift of tongues, prophecy, revelation, visions, healing, interpretation of tongues, etc."

Article number eight says: "We believe the Bible to be the word of God as far as it is translated correctly; we also believe the Book of Mormon to be the word of God." When Christ came to the earth in the Meridian of Time, he organized his Church and taught its principles on both the eastern and the western continents, and in each case a scriptural record was kept, which Ezekiel says would become one in God's hand in teaching and in judging his people. (See Ezek. 37:16-17) The compilation of eastern scriptures is called the Bible, and those scriptures compiled on the western continent are called the Book of Mormon. Some people say: "I don't believe." That is unfortunate as they are *both* the word of the Lord. They supplement and support each other and are the books out of which we will all be judged.

Nine: "We believe all that God has revealed, all that He does now reveal, and we believe that He will yet reveal many great and important things pertaining to the Kingdom of God." Those who believe that God has lost interest in his work or that he has retired from business are very seriously mistaken and are missing many great blessings as a consequence. Many of our greatest revelations are yet in the future.

The tenth Article of Faith says: "We believe in the literal gathering of Israel and in the restoration of the Ten Tribes; that

Zion will be built upon this [the American] continent; that Christ will reign personally upon the earth; and, that the earth will be renewed and receive its paradisiacal glory." Our earth has a wonderful history and it has a magnificent future that has already been described for it.

Article number eleven says: "We claim the privilege of worshiping Almighty God according to the dictates of our own conscience, and allow all men the same privilege, let them worship how, where, or what they may." In one of the fundamental laws of the universe God said: "Thou mayest choose for thyself."

Article twelve says: "We believe in being subject to kings, presidents, rulers, and magistrates, in obeying, honoring, and sustaining the law." How badly we presently need obedience to this important article calling for us to obey, honor, and sustain the law! God's house is a house of order and if we obeyed all the laws of the land we would be in a better position to obey the laws of God.

Article thirteen says: "We believe in being honest, true, chaste, benevolent, virtuous, and in doing good to all men; indeed, we may say that we follow the admonition of Paul — We believe all things, we hope all things, we have endured many things, and hope to be able to endure all things. If there is anything virtuous, lovely, or of good report or praiseworthy, we seek after these things." One of the greatest ideas of our world is that God lives and that Jesus is divine. The gospel is true, and we should be constantly reaffirming these great articles in our lives.

The Atheist

THE FIRST AND GREATEST of all the commandments has to do with our relationship with God. When the young lawyer came to Jesus saying, "Master, which is the great commandment in the law?" Jesus said, "Thou shalt love the Lord thy God with all thy heart, and with all thy soul, and with all thy mind. This is the first and great commandment. And the second is like unto it, Thou shalt love thy neighbor as thyself. On these two commandments hang all the law and the prophets." (Matt. 22:36-40)

A similar command was given when God came down onto the top of Mount Sinai in fire to give the Israelites their start as a new nation. As the lightning and thunder played about the top of that holy mountain, God said: "Thou shalt have no other gods before me." The importance of this great command should be obvious. God is all wise. He has all knowledge and all power. He knows every end from its beginning. He wants us to be successful and happy, and he knows what we must do in order to attain these goals. It is God's work and God's glory to bring to pass our eternal exaltation. He wants us to be successful. He is firmly committed to our free agency, and because it is necessary for us to see good and evil side by side, we live in a world of opposites. Yet it is disastrous for us when we make all the mistakes personally.

The Son of God was born into this world the same as we were. His life was outstandingly successful because he fully adopted God's success program. Jesus said: "I came to do the will of him who sent me." He said to God, "Not my will but thine be done." This is exactly what he did, and it is exactly what he has recommended for us. What miracles we could accomplish if we all followed this program as it has been given! For example, just think what a change could be brought about in our world if all the communists strictly obeyed the law of the Lord. But in addition, suppose that all would-be murderers, adulterers, thieves, liars, profanity-users and Sabbath-breakers would also do as he directed. Then suppose that all of the trouble-makers, race-rioters, those that cause wars, stir up hate, and lead rebellions should learn to love God with all their hearts. Then just suppose that all Christians were really Christians in deed as well as in title. We would also all love our neighbors as ourselves, and this earth would not only be God's paradise but our lives would be filled with every success and happiness.

What a change this would cause from the hell of disease, crime, poverty, ignorance and divorce in which we presently live! If we lived his laws, then our nervous breakdowns, our broken homes, our mental illnesses, and our dependence upon force and intimidation would be done away with. Almost all of our problems come because we fail to maintain the right relationship between God and ourselves. For some peculiar reason it has seemed that from the very beginning we have had an inclination to turn away from God and to actually fight against him.

The flood, the confusion at Babel, the destruction of Sodom and Gomorrah, the crucifixion of Christ, the dark ages, the fall of hundreds of ancient civilizations, and our own present miseries are all the result of our unfavorable attitudes toward God and each other. And all of this in spite of the fact that we know better. We also know that God is our best friend and our greatest benefactor. He created us in the first place. It is his Spirit that enlightens our minds and quickens our understandings. He is ". . . the light of the sun, and the power thereof by which it was made." It is his light that proceeds forth from the presence of God to fill the immensity of space. (See D&C 88:5-12) It is his power that gives us strength and purpose. Emerson says: "We live in the lap of an immense intelligence," and God intended that that intelligence should be channeled into our lives to make us as he is.

Our world itself and all of the people in it are completely dependent upon God. The sun's rays are presently bringing us energy, light, vitamins, and heat across 93 million miles of cold, dead space in order to keep us alive. And these wonderful rays only release their precious cargo when they strike our atmosphere. But every day we are being fed out of God's great central storehouse of the sun. If the sun's rays were turned off for a few hours, all life upon this earth would cease. All of the keys of our personal welfare are provided for by God's powerful laws, and he regulates everything in the universe for our benefit and safety. If the earth were allowed to make the slightest change in its degree of rotation, the North Pole would soon be located exactly on top of us.

Our greatest tragedy would take place if God were to withdraw his presence from us or to leave us to our own devices even for a very short time. With all of our demonstrated inabilities to solve even our smallest problems, many human beings continue in their insistence of ignoring or disobeying God. We deny his power, we change his doctrines, we deprive him of his personality, and we refuse to belong to the Church which he has organized for our benefit. Under the influence of our atheism we claim that God has lost his ability to reveal himself, and when we half-believe that he is dead, the dread disease of atheism takes over our lives. Someone has said, "An atheist is one who has no invisible means of support." The dictionary says that atheists are those who disbelieve in God and deny his power. Our atheism is a manifestation that we are suffering from our own ignorance and stupidity. Someone has written:

The Atheist

The fool hath said: There is no God!
No God! Who lights the morning sun
And sends him on his heavenly road,
A far and brilliant course to run?
Who, when the radiant day is done
Hangs forth the moon's nocturnal lamp
And bids the planets, one by one,
Steal o'er the night vales, dark and damp?

No God! Who gives the evening dew
The fanning breeze, the fostering shower?
Who warns the Spring-morn's budding bough,
And plants the Summer's noon-tide flower?
Who spreads in the autumnal bower
The fruit tree's mellow stores around,
And sends the Winter's icy power
To invigorate the exhausted ground?

No God! Who makes the bird to wing
Its flight-like arrow through the sky,
And gives the deer its power to spring
From rock to rock triumphantly?
Who formed Behemoth, huge and high,
Whose draught the river drains,
And great Leviathan to lie,
Like floating isle, on ocean plains?

No God! Who warms the heart to heave
With a thousand feelings soft and sweet,
And prompts the aspiring soul to leave
The earth we tread beneath our feet
And soar away on pinions fleet
Beyond the scene of mortal strife,
With fair ethereal forms to meet,
That tell us of the after life?

No God! Who fixed that solid round
Of pillars strong, that alter not?
Who spreads the curtained skies around?
Who doth the oceans bounds allot?
Who all things to perfection brought
On earth below, in heaven above?
Go ask the fool of impious thought,
Who dares to say — There is no God!

The greatest opportunity of our lives is to discover God and learn to strictly follow every one of his directions. Jesus said: "And this is life eternal, that they might know thee the only true God, and Jesus Christ, whom thou hast sent." (John 17:3)

It is interesting to think about those great days that give meaning to our lives, and one of our most important is the day we were born. That was when a new life came into being. Life is the greatest of all commodities. Henry Thoreau once said: "We should all thank God every day of our lives for the privilege of having been born." And then he went on to speculate on the very unique supposition of what it might have been like if we had never been born, and he pointed out some of the wonderful experiences that we would have missed as a consequence.

Our birthday is the day when we were "added upon" with these beautiful, wonderful bodies of flesh and bones without which we could never have a fullness of joy, either here or hereafter. Birth is the process by which we get our parents and our ancestors. Another important date is the one when we are married. That is when we get our life's companions for time and eternity. That is when a new family is formed. There is another important day and that is when we select our life's occupation. That is when we accept our share of the work of the world.

There is another important event in our lives, and that is when we establish a proper relationship with God. When we are at our best, to know God means to believe in him, to obey him, to love him, to trust him, to follow him, and to serve him.

Because our greatest need is for God, the greatest commandments have to do with establishing the proper relationship with him. And the greatest sins are those that tend to destroy that relationship. An atheist disbelieves in God, and it is pretty difficult to love and obey someone that you don't even believe exists. The greatest of all sins is to become a son of perdition by turning away from God in the face of great knowledge. An agnostic is one who claims that God is unknown and unknowable. He doesn't believe and he doesn't disbelieve. He just hasn't made up his mind. He bases all of his activities on his claims of ignorance. We have the word of the Lord that no one can be saved in ignorance. Therefore, it is natural for the agnostic to form a part of that great company that walks on the broad road that leads to death.

One of the most terrifying sensations for a child is to get lost from its mother. We might try to imagine what it would be like to be lost from God, the source of all intelligence, beauty, and power; or what it would be like to be lost from righteousness, peace, comfort, and the companionship of good people.

An airplane pilot may place many human lives in jeopardy when he loses contact with the airport or the radar beam that is directing him to his destination. How terrible it would be in our quest for eternal life to have our success shot down by our atheism or our ignorance so that we would forever lose our blessings!

Men and women are supposed to live together and love and serve each other and to serve the larger family of God. The man who mixes with his fellows on the proper basis feels a sense of well-being and happiness. He is ever on a voyage of discovery, finding new sources of power within himself, which might have remained forever hidden but for this stimulating association. Everyone that he meets has something to teach him that he never knew before. Everyone has something that enables him to enrich his life and help him on his way. No man ever makes the most and the best of his life by himself. He needs other people to be his discoverers and developers.

We all feel a sense of dependence upon our fellow beings, but in a much bigger way we are all dependent upon God. The soul should always be seeking God, and no one will ever be free from fear, insecurity, and sin until he has found him. As an electric light needs to be connected up with the powerhouse, so man needs to be connected up with God. We can never do our best without the stimulation that comes from the greatest of all our sources of intelligence and power.

Occasionally we might remind ourselves that the most devastating of all human emotions is this sense of being alone, of being unworthy, of being irresponsible, of being unclean, of being unbelieving, or of being lost. God has created us in his image; he has endowed us with a set of his attributes; he has made his Holy Spirit available to ennoble us. God has given us the great scriptures as our guide. He has established his Church upon the earth and has given us a happy sense of profitable association in living together and a constructive companionship to inspire and uplift us.

Each of us should so live that he may have a good opinion of himself, but primarily each of us should thoughtfully obey the greatest of all the commandments and maintain a close contact with the source of all our blessings. It is our greatest opportunity to believe in him, to love him, to obey him, and finally to be able to live with him in eternal happiness and glory.

The Buck Stops Here

FOR MANY YEARS President Truman kept a sign on his desk which said: "The Buck Stops Here." This phrase gets its meaning from what someone has said are the three American traditions — one is the passing of the Indian, another is the passing of the buffalo, and the third is the passing of the buck.

There is a disabling human weakness that sometimes causes people to try to sidestep their problems and shift the responsibility to someone else. It is so easy just to say, "Let George do it," "That isn't my job," or "Why should I stick my neck out?"

As a solution to their problems many people just pass the buck. That is a process of refusing the effort and denying the responsibility. Then we develop the habit of blaming other people or charging up our failures to conditions. For our failures we blame our family or our education, or we sometimes feel that fate itself is against us. Very frequently people blame their sins and weaknesses onto something that happened in their childhood. One says: "Because my parents made me go to church when I was young, I have never been religious since I have grown up." One man said: "The reason I am not successful is because my father was not a pusher." By many and varied processes we learn this irresponsible art of "passing the buck."

Frequently, when someone gets a little droopy or discouraged or prematurely tired, we try to put a little more life into him by telling him to "buck up." That means to take heart, to brace one's self with a stronger courage reinforced by a greater industry. To "buck up" means to brighten up, to get smart, to dress up, to think in bigger terms, and to attack life's assignments a little more enthusiastically.

If any of us should analyze ourselves, we might possibly discover that much too much of our time is also spent in this sinful pastime of "passing the buck." We could greatly help if we would follow the philosophy of President Truman and firmly say to ourselves: "The Buck Stops Here." I am not aware of all of the things that the president may have had in mind, but certainly when one becomes the President of the United States, he is at the end of the line, and there is no one that he may pass his problems on to. He has been elected by the people and is expected to solve all of those problems for which he carries the responsibility. His official advisors were all appointed by him. In the event of their failure they may be removed from office and someone else appointed in their places, but the president is elected and must answer to the people. While he is in office he is a kind of committee of one. His heavy responsibility cannot be passed on to anyone else. It cannot be delegated. If the president abandons his duty, then the power is lost, for no one else receives authority merely because the president may be idle or unwise or derelict in his duty. Ordinarily, the president is all alone and a very lonely man.

When the atomic bomb became a reality, the United States was at war with Japan. Thousands of American lives were being destroyed by an aggressor nation that had initiated a war by a sneak attack upon our military outposts. President Truman had been elected to be the Commander-in-Chief of our armies and was the only man who could decide whether or not a bomb should be used on our enemies. If it were not used, the war would continue and thousands of additional American lives would be lost. On the other hand, he knew the consequences of using this terrible, destructive power. But the decision *must* be made, and the buck stopped at the desk of Harry S. Truman.

President Truman also had other momentous decisions to make. One of them was to relieve of his command a very popular general by the name of Douglas MacArthur. General MacArthur had proven his ability and loyalty to his country many times. Mr. Truman knew that his contemplated action would bring upon him a great avalanche of criticism from those millions who almost worshipped the famous general. How the president must have wished for someone else to whom he could pass this unpleasant responsibility! As this problem was weighing so heavily upon him, he must have looked pretty hard at that little sign on his desk which said: "The Buck Stops Here."

In spite of the fact that General MacArthur had better training in military procedures and knew far more about winning wars than did President Truman, the president was the only human being in the world who had the authority or the responsibility to decide the question, and he must live forever in his country's history with whatever criticisms may come from his decision. All buck-passing must stop at the desk of the president.

And while most of us will never be president, each of us also has an important job to do and each of us must carry the complete responsibility for his own task. This usually requires about as much courage, initiative, industry, punctuality, and actual ability as we are able to muster.

During the Civil War, an energetic color-bearer carried his company's flag a little too far ahead of the troops. The captain called out to the color-bearer to bring back the colors to the line. The color-bearer shouted back what he thought was a better idea. He suggested that the captain bring the line up to the colors. We must also keep ourselves up with the colors, and there is no one to whom we can pass the buck for that responsibility.

There are many disadvantages to this practice of passing the buck, and it is quite likely that some of us could profitably use a similar card on the desks of our own lives, saying: "The Buck Stops Here." Each of us is his own commander-in-chief. And each of us has the responsibility for keeping our accomplishments up with our colors. Every situation in life carries its own responsibility, and each of us has been elected to be his own man. There is no place in life where we can afford to accept the position and then deny its obligations. When one is born into this world of privilege, he is also obligated to accept his share of its work. When God said to man, "Thou mayest choose for thyself," man was not only made his own commander-in-chief, but he was also saddled with the full responsibility for his choices.

There is an interesting phrase used many times in the scriptures where some people are referred to as "the elect of God." The earth is the Lord's and the fullness thereof, and every person born into it has a calling that amounts to an election that he must answer for to God. The duties of our mortality are not easy to sidestep, and they certainly cannot be ignored. To begin with, God created this earth for our benefit, and he has never given a law without also giving a corresponding set of obligations to go with it. It is interesting to remember that all of God's children were not permitted to come to this earth. Satan and the one-third of the heavenly hosts that followed him were rejected as candidates for mortality. But those who won the election must also assume the obligation, and the "buck stops here."

No one can do our deciding or our growing or our repenting for us. Certainly no one can carry our responsibility for us, and no one can sidestep the consequences of his own deeds. The Lord has indicated that we should take upon us his name. We should also square our shoulders for that load of responsibility for making this earth a proper place to live. The Apostle Paul said that each of us is responsible for working out his own salvation in fear and trembling before God. (Phil. 2:12) In substance, Peter was writing out a card for our desks when he said to all Church members: "Wherefore . . . brethren, give diligence to make your calling and election sure. . . ." He was laying the responsibility directly upon us when he said: "And beside this, giving all diligence, add to your faith virtue; and to virtue knowledge; And to knowledge temperance; and to temperance patience; and to patience godliness; And to godliness brotherly kindness; and to brotherly kindness charity." (2 Peter 1:5-7)

When President Truman took office, he also took an oath in which he said: "I do solemnly swear that I will safely execute the office of President of the United States, and will to the best of my ability preserve, protect, and defend the Constitution of the United States, so help me God."

But God has provided an oath of office for each of us, and he laid the responsibility right on the line when he said: "He that believeth and is baptized shall be saved, but he that believeth not shall be damned." (Mark 16:16) We also have other obligations. Once each week we partake of the emblems of his sacrifice and each week we covenant that we will always remember him and keep the commandments which he has given us. One would be ill-advised if he tried to pass off that responsibility, as the consequences of such a choice will last forever.

For four years President Abraham Lincoln carried the same responsibility that President Truman did, and during the bitter years of the Civil War, President Lincoln said that many times he was driven to his knees because he had no place else to go. If we were looking for a better solution, where would *we* go? God is our judge, our law-giver, our highest court of appeal, our only city of refuge, and our only hope of reward.

In the days of Jesus some of the people created a serious problem for themselves by this process of ignoring their responsibility. Of those who were offended by Christ's doctrine the record says that "From that time many of his disciples went back, and walked no more with him. Then said Jesus unto the twelve, Will ye also go away? Then Simon Peter answered, Lord, to whom shall we go? Thou hast the words of eternal life. And we believe and are sure that thou art that Christ, the Son of the living God." (John 6:66-69)

If we sidestep that responsibility our alternate choices are extremely limited, for to whom can we go? To whom can any of us turn if we lose God? But so far as the affairs of our eternal lives are concerned, the "buck stops here," the decision is ours to make, and there is no one to whom we can pass the buck.

One of the most necessary elements in any bid for eternal success is to learn the art of being responsible to God. That responsibility makes our need for right moral decisions an absolute necessity. To live at his best the man created in God's image must have nobility, righteousness, dependability, and be able to carry his own affairs forward effectively. To be responsible one must be competent, solvent, honest, capable, reliable, and trustworthy, so as to be able to discharge all of his debts to God and his fellowmen. When we put all of this on our own card and then sum it up it says: "The Buck Stops Here."

Real responsibility allows no alibiing, no excusing, no rationalizing, no procrastinating, and no shirking. No one else can be held accountable for our dishonesty, or our indecency, or our negative thinking, or our lack of spirituality, or our failure in actual good works. No one can be asked to be decent for us, or honest for us, or constructive for us.

Franklin D. Roosevelt once tried to explain how Russia got along with other nations, and he said, "Of course Stalin is an awful liar." From the very first, communist philosophy has been built on lies. The brutal communist takeover in Hungary, as well as their ruthless maneuvers in Czechoslovakia and East Germany, were all based on false claims, but they had thousands of tanks and guns to back up their treachery. It might help us to remember that when Stalin died, he left this world unarmed and unsupported. With communist backing, the Egyptians and other Arab nations announced their intention of annihilating the little nation of Israel. With this in mind, they amassed their troops at Israel's front door, ready for the kill, but when Israel fought back and destroyed her enemies' arms, the communists went before the United Nations with all kinds of misrepresentations, which everyone knew were untrue. A young boy with a similar philosophy was once asked who started the fight in which he was involved. He said: "Bill started it when he hit me back." We put ourselves in a similar situation when we blame circumstances and events for our evil instead of ourselves.

The communists are professional liars and professional buck-passers, and they are not responsible for their own word. But *everyone* who tries to deceive is irresponsible. What is our situation when we lie to life and to God and to ourselves? When we become aggressors in evil and life punishes us, we often feel as if we are being unfairly treated. But when anyone breaks any of the Ten Commandments or any other divine law, he must answer to God for his irresponsibility. God has given no one the *right* to do *wrong*. It is our *privilege* to do wrong, but because it is not our *right*, we must always expect to suffer the consequences. In every activity we should take our own oath of office before God with a pledge to do right. Whether our goals lie in social, educational, moral, financial, or spiritual fields, we ought to say to ourselves: "The Buck Stops Here." Under God, each of us is his own commander-in-chief, and we pray that God will help us to be fully honest, fully righteous, and fully responsible.

The Catalog

ONE OF THE MOST unusual delights that I remember as a boy on the farm came in early spring, as I looked through the seed catalog. As the winter was breaking up and we began looking forward to planting our crops, we always received in the mail an impressive-looking catalog from some seed distributors. I used to think that this particular volume was about the most wonderful of all books.

When I was a young boy my father used to give me a little land that I could plant and cultivate as my own, and one of my delights was to go through the seed catalog to make the proper planting selections. This miracle book showed beautiful colored pictures of what, to me, were the most tempting fruits, berries, and vegetables. It showed exactly what one could expect the finished product to be like if he planted the particular seeds shown in the catalog and then took proper care of his plants. Since those early days I have visited many of the great art galleries of the world, but I don't remember any impression that was ever made on my mind comparable to that which came in visualizing the miracles and wonders that could be brought about by effectively doing what was described in the seed catalog.

The dictionary says that empathy means "the imaginative projection of a subjective state into an object so that the object appears to be infused with it." By a projection of my imagination I learned to make carrots, radishes, onions, apples, peaches, watermelons, and blackberries a part of me. I could bring the most wonderful and the most useful products out of the raw ground. In their material form they not only satisfied my stomach and gave my body strength, vision, heat, and energy, but this useful production also stimulated my brain. With the right seeds I could bring about what, to me, is still one of the greatest miracles in the world. With a little topsoil, some fertilizer, some irrigation water, and a little labor, I became a kind of creator and produced an assortment of life's wonders in an appetizing and colorful array. I suppose that a great deal of my motivation came from the fact that I have always seemed to be hungry.

We used to have an early bearing cherry tree out in our front yard, and I used to stand under it all spring, waiting for the cherries to get ripe. When the first touch of red appeared, I would climb up into the tree and pick the cherry. I had no competition with the birds, because my appetite made cherries acceptable to me long before the birds were interested.

My early craving seems to have stamped a love of cherries into my brain, and several years later I joined with a friend in planting twenty acres of cherry trees. The excitement was increased because we selected the stock and budded the trees ourselves. Even now there are still a lot of cherries in my brain and occasionally I dream about the most beautiful cherry orchard where the limbs are all burdened down with an overload of the most beautiful, fully ripened, delicious, juicy black cherries. When I awake in the morning there is always a hunger for cherries that must be satisfied that has been left with me by my dream.

A lot of other things were also stamped into my brain by my seed catalogs. One of my great present-day joys is to go into a well-ordered supermarket and see the tremendous display of colors, tastes, calories, and vitamins that have been produced from seeds.

Many years ago I memorized an interesting poem that says:

> I paid a dime for a package of seeds,
> And the clerk tossed them out with a flip.
> "We have them assorted to every man's needs,"
> He said with a smile on his lip.
> "Asters and poppies and pansies and peas,
> Ten cents a package and pick as you please."
>
> Now, seeds are just dimes to the man in the store,
> And the dimes are the things that he needs;
> And I've been to buy them in seasons before,
> And have thought of them merely as seeds,
> But it flashed through my mind as I took them this time,
> You have purchased a miracle here for a dime!

You've a dime's worth of something no man can create,
You've a dime's worth of life in your hand,
You've a dime's worth of mystery, destiny, fate
That the wisest cannot understand.
In this bright little package, now isn't it odd,
You've a dime's worth of something known only to God.

There is an old philosophy to the effect that the heart of the lover lives in the soul of the beloved, and our hearts live in those places that nourish our various interests and keep our motivations strong. It used to be a great joy to me to see how readily my plants responded to a good seed bed, a generous application of fertilizer, a little cultivation, and a good drink of water at the right time. Of course, we know that plants have life, and there are some who believe that they respond to human love and consideration the same as animals and humans do. Even a tomato plant may produce better tomatoes if it is given a little love and thoughtful care along with the fertilizer.

As I have grown older I have discovered that there are many other kinds of catalogs. Some are filled with books and some are catalogs of music. There are some catalogs of faith, out of which we may feed our minds and hearts. And just as watermelons come from seeds so do love, courage, industry, ambition, enthusiasms, and ideals. If the right kind of seeds are planted in a proper seed bed, and if they are given good care, they will grow into the most substantial accomplishments.

With an emotion that matches my interest in the supermarket, I love to browse around in a good bookstore and read the interesting book and chapter titles. I like to exercise my imagination in regard to the mental vitamins and pleasures they make available to my mind. It can be a lot of fun to buy a book that especially challenges one's interest and then see how many mental cucumbers and blackberries can be made to grow in his life.

In addition, a resourceful reader always gets more out of a book than there is in it. As you read a book you are free to fully absorb all of its contents, but occasionally when your mind strikes one of the book's ideas it will go ricocheting out into space. Don't be too quick to pull it back, but rather let it go where it wants to go and follow it to its lair. An inspired book needs an inspired reader. People get many good ideas from what they read, but some of the best ideas often come from what one's reading makes him think. Interestingly enough, ideas never come singly; they always come formed in chains or clusters or in family groups. An idea that is followed will frequently introduce you to the other members of its family, and from one chance acquaintance we may sometimes get to meet a whole family of the most worthwhile ideas. In this way you get all that there is in the book, plus a lot of additional ideas that the book makes you think about.

A good dictionary is also a kind of catalog. It can make words grow in our minds with every color and shade of meaning. The world's great literature is a kind of catalog made up of life's finest meanings and greatest experiences. Through the world's great literature we may live through every kind of life situation in such a way that we may get the experience without the risk. We may have the profit without the penalty.

Shakespeare wrote 37 plays and staffed them with a thousand characters, each one being a personification of some personality trait. Shakespeare said that his purpose in writing was to hold the mirror up to life, to show virtue her own image and scorn her own likeness. He said: "I your looking glass will be, and will modestly discover to you qualities which you yourself know not of."

It was Shakespeare's mission in life to show us every human experience of good and bad without the need of a dangerous and costly personal experience. From Shakespeare's plays we can make about the same kind of selection made possible from the use of a seed catalog. Reading Shakespeare can be like going into a personality store where we can try on for size and usefulness any and all of those interesting traits that we ourselves would like to possess. Shakespeare said: "Assume a virtue if you have it not."

With a few personality fertilizers and a little effective cultivation, we can soon have the finest human qualities responding at their peak in us. Every human trait comes from some seed, just as onions and radishes do, and they are just as productive. The tomato seed pays us back a million for one in a single year, and that is about what a well-cultivated personality seed can do.

The great scriptures serve as one of our finest catalogs with a wide assortment of ideals, virtues, spirituality traits, and soul qualities to choose from. In the great scriptures a divine agency has brought together beautiful psalms, wise proverbs, instructive parables, gracious beatitudes, stimulating philosophies, and uplifting commandments. They also contain the blueprints on which every worthwhile success is built. The scriptures also include an interesting catalog of biographies, and they show us some of the most colorful personalities of good and bad all the way from Cain, Nimrod, Judas, and Satan up to Abraham, Moses, the Apostle Paul, and the tremendous person known as Jesus of Nazareth. From this colorful display we may pick out the best from each and use them as seeds to produce happiness and success in us.

Some time ago someone who was properly concerned about my surplus weight suggested that he would give me some weight control pills that would kill my rather vigorous appetite. While I do need to hold a tighter rein on my intake, one of the things that I don't want to part with is my appetite. Always being hungry is a bit miserable to cope with at times, yet I would rather have an appetite that had to be restrained than one that had to be coaxed and bribed to do its job. I like to feel the wholesome power of my taste buds. When I run good food over them they light up my entire personality with some of the most exquisite feelings of pleasure and other sensations of fulfillment. But I also appreciate the strength of those other taste buds that have their attention centered in the bookstore. With some good spiritual taste buds the reading of the scriptures can also light us up with zones of substantial spiritual satisfactions so that they make all great ideas taste good. With some healthy, spiritual taste buds we will never have that awful feeling of rebellion against authority or that disabling disbelief in God or that serious affinity for evil that afflicts so many people. A doctor judges health by the appetite, and so can we. When our food doesn't taste good, it is a sign that we are sick, but when our spiritual appetite is in good working order, we want to practice those great doctrines of Christ that will bring about our eternal exaltation.

Jesus said, "Blessed are all they who do hunger and thirst after righteousness, for they shall be filled with the Holy Ghost."

(3 Ne. 12:6) This is one of the greatest of all promises, and we should never take any pills that will tend to kill this kind of an appetite.

We know that the stomach shrinks when it is empty and so does the mind and so does the spirit. There is nothing like a thirst for righteousness to give one a whole-souled sense of fulfillment. We need to have our faith, our dreams, and our ambitions fulfilled by our appetite. It is very satisfying to be well fed physically, but surpassing almost everything else is that satisfaction that comes from great faith and from our righteous dreams and ambitions. When we can feel that our lives themselves are worthwhile we can build up enough strength to overcome anything that can happen to us. When we live by "every word that proceedeth forth from the mouth of God," then we are cultivating the soil in which the seeds of godliness may grow to give us the spirit of contentment and well-being. With a strong enough hunger for righteousness, even God will be pleased with us.

There is an interesting story in Shakespeare's *Merchant of Venice*. Portia of Belmont was an heiress to a princely name, great beauty, and such a colossal fortune that many distinguished suitors came from all parts of the world to court her. But Portia loved only Bassanio and in her affection she placed him far above all others. In pledging the fullness of her love to him she said that she regretted that she was not much more beautiful than she was. She said: ". . . for you I would be trebled twenty times myself; A thousand times more fair, and ten thousand times more rich; That only to stand high in your account, I might in virtues, beauties, livings, friends, exceed account." (Act 3, scene 2)

Our own wishes are granted extra power when we exercise them vigorously enough, and we might take some of the seeds of Portia's wish and plant them in our own hearts. Then we might hunger to be improved a thousand times as a husband, and be a thousand times more worthy as a father, and a thousand times more effective in the uses we make of life.

Above all else we should have an appetite to make our lives a thousand times more pleasing to God, our eternal Heavenly Father. Suppose that we come back to where we began and get out the great catalogs of our lives and plant the seeds of faith, love, and obedience to God — in this way we can develop a hunger and thirst after righteousness that will fill our lives with the Holy Ghost.

The City of Monuments

ONCE HAD OCCASION to spend some time visiting the historic spots in the city of Washington, D. C. I have some little knowledge about other great capital cities, including Rome and Carthage, Tyre and Sidon, Babylon and Nineveh, Athens and Jerusalem, London and Moscow, but Washington surpasses them all. Washington, D. C., is the capital of the greatest nation ever known upon the earth since its creation. The present rulers of most other nations look toward America as the scientific, cultural, military, financial, literary, and religious capital of the world.

While in Washington I was particularly impressed with the reasons that this city has been called the "City of Monuments." There are monuments erected in honor of men; monuments have been built to commemorate causes, ideas, and events. Each monument has its own particular significance and its own identifying spirit. The meanings of these monuments have a particular significance in America, and they also carry a message across the entire earth.

Dominating all other monuments is the one erected in honor of George Washington. Washington was foremost among the founding fathers. He led this nation in its struggle for freedom and then watched over its infancy. Washington loved life and yet he willingly risked it in doing his duty, which was even more dear to him. He wrought out a new nation, became its first president, and guided it on toward greatness. He helped formulate our national ideals, and his grateful countrymen bestowed upon him the everlasting title of the father of his country.

Although Washington fought and suffered, he declined to accept any salary. Even during his lifetime he was almost obscured as a person by the awe-inspiring legends that enveloped him, but behind the legends stands an impressive human being about whom Clinton Rossiter has written: "Washington did the new republic a mighty service by proving that power can ennoble men as well as to corrupt them." And even to this day he remains an Olympian among presidents and other rulers.

The capital city itself was named after him, but the entire nation is animated by his spirit. A few years after Washington's death a divine revelation was given to the Prophet Joseph Smith in which the Lord himself said that God had raised up these wise men to establish the Constitution of this great country. With this nation in mind God had led to these shores many freedom-loving refugees who desired to escape from old world tyranny, and under God's inspiration the new nation was established upon Christian principles. God also prescribed the great American mission of keeping freedom, righteousness, and human dignity alive in the world. (See D&C 101:77-80)

After independence had been won the colonies continued to have many unsolved problems. Some of the states were reluctant to cooperate in the formation of a government of United States. Because some of the states were pulling apart, instead of together, it seemed that even at this date their labors might prove to have been in vain. If ultimate success was to be achieved, there must be a strong central government to hold the states together, and many people felt that the one way to avoid the confusion and escape the storms and divisions that threatened them was to crown Washington as king of this new nation. This was seriously considered by the army, and it was discussed in centers of influence among the states, but when the plan was presented to Washington he was greatly pained that such an idea should have ever been thought of.

He said: "I am at a loss to conceive what part of my conduct could have given any encouragement to such an idea, fraught as it is with the greatest mischief that could befall our country." He further said: "Let me conjure you, if you have any regard for your country, yourselves, or your posterity, or if you have any respect for me, banish these thoughts immediately from your minds."

How grateful we ought to be that God had provided such noble men to stand in the forefront of our civilization and give our country its character and direction! What would be our present state if our early years had been presided over by such power-mad, un-Christian-like men as Stalin, Hitler, Mussolini, Napoleon, and present-day dictators?

Long ago it was revealed to pre-Columbus American prophets that God was sick and tired of dictators. One of them said:

"And he [God] had sworn in his wrath unto the brother of Jared, that whoso should possess this land of promise, from that time henceforth and forever, should serve him, the true and only God, or they should be swept off when the fulness of his wrath should come upon them." (Ether 2:8) It is recorded as an everlasting decree of God that this land shall be free from captivity and from all other nations under heaven, if they will but serve the God of this land who is Jesus Christ.

These are the standards that have been built into the Washington monument to make it the fitting symbol of America. To help us always keep in mind the ideals involved in our national beginnings, there has been erected in our capital city a great white marble obelisk monument as a national memorial to the man who under God gave us our start toward greatness. This impressive shaft is 55 feet square at its base and reaches up over 555 feet into the blue skies of America. It is the loftiest and most imposing monument ever reared by man. It is higher than the pyramids. It reaches far above the cathedral domes of St. Paul or St. Peter. To view this monument not only reminds us of an American hero, but it also reminds us of an American mission and of an American duty.

In addressing a joint session of Congress on the 200th anniversary of Washington's birth, President Herbert Hoover said: "From the room where I conduct my high office, I hourly see the monument. This shaft is a thing of the spirit. There is about it a mantle of pure radiance."

An actual image of Washington could only have displayed one phase of his productive and varied character, but this lofty marble shaft fitly typifies for us the upward reaches of his exalted life, and this unique monument also serves us as an appropriate symbol, reminding us to carry forward with honor our national greatness and destiny. Significantly enough, the Washington monument forms the center for four other meaningful monuments. The national capitol buildings are located on the east with a four-hundred-foot swath of green spanning the considerable distance between the capitol and the monument grounds. The White House is on the north; the Lincoln Memorial is on the west with a 2,000-foot-long reflecting pool as the connecting link; then the memorial to Thomas Jefferson, the author of the Declaration of Independence and the third President of the United States, is on the south.

Engraved inside the marble dome of the Jefferson memorial are some of those inspirational words spoken by the great American patriot who said: "I have sworn upon the altar of God, eternal hostility against every form of tyranny over the mind of man." These words were uttered by Thomas Jefferson, but their spirit speaks for all good Americans. This philosophy is a part of that inspiration that came from God through our founding fathers.

It has been said that one can best judge a people by the kind of men they honor, and we greatly honor ourselves as we identify with those who established our national foundations and who have since successfully carried the mission and tradition of America.

Abraham Lincoln identified with Washington and was one of his greatest admirers. Lincoln was born ten years after Washington's death, but Lincoln's life was greatly influenced by Washington. When he was very young, Lincoln obtained a book entitled *The Life of Washington* by W. R. Weems, and from a very early age Lincoln absorbed both the Bible and Washington.

Lincoln said: "Washington is the mightiest name on earth, long since mightiest in the cause of civil liberty, still mightiest in moral reformation. On that name a eulogy is expected that cannot be. To add brightness to the sun or glory to the name of Washington is alike impossible. Let none attempt it. In solemn awe pronounce the name and in its naked deathless splendor, leave it shining on."

Another of the inspiring monuments in this "City of Monuments" is the memorial erected to the great Civil War President, Abraham Lincoln. Washington became the father of his country, and Lincoln saved it from being destroyed by civil war. The Gettysburg Address and the Second Inaugural are engraved on the inside of this great national shrine which carries the spirit of our famous Civil War president to all Americans. In one of his most significant speeches Lincoln said: "With malice toward none, with charity for all, with firmness in the right as God gives us to see the right, let us strive to finish the work we are in to bind up the nation's wounds: to care for him who shall have borne the battle and for his widow and his orphan — to do all which may achieve and cherish a just and a lasting peace, among ourselves and with all nations."

Then finally, as Lincoln lay dead, Edmund Stanton, his great Secretary of War, looked down upon the lifeless form and said: "Now he belongs to the ages." And so it is and so it will always be. It has now been well over a hundred years since Lincoln's death, but he is still our friend and he is still a living presence in our nation's capital. As his physical likeness sits majestically there in his great chair, his mighty spirit hovers over our nation and permeates the great country that he did so much to save. Every day every real American absorbs something from the spirit of these great God-inspired men. We put them on our calendar and picture them in our minds so that we can think about their good qualities and incorporate these traits of excellence into ourselves. This principle is presently working in favor of America and Americans as we draw greatness from our greatest leaders.

Thomas Carlyle once said that no one could look upon a great man without gaining something from him. And so from day to day we nourish our own souls by absorbing the spirit of our national heroes.

There are many other meaningful monuments in this "City of Monuments." There is one erected to the Unknown Soldier. There is a living flame that burns continuously at the grave of John F. Kennedy. A natural park on the Potomac River recalls the life of the great conservation-minded President Theodore Roosevelt. It was set apart as a bird sanctuary and a memorial site and designed to keep alive a love of freedom and the great out-of-doors. We also have the immense Arlington National Cemetery in which we have many monuments to honor our great host of hero dead. In some cases we have monuments within monuments.

On March 17, 1941, in Washington, D. C., President Franklin D. Roosevelt dedicated the country's first national gallery of art. The building, which required four years to complete, measures 780 feet in length and 305 feet in width. It is constructed of pink marble and cost 16 million dollars to build. It houses a collection made up of 126 paintings by the old masters and 26 pieces of sculpture that in 1941 were valued at approximately 80 million dollars or an average of over $500,000 each.

In planning the building of this national gallery every consideration was given to the importance of distance, light, temperature, and air conditioning. The gallery and the endowment fund to maintain it were presented to the American people as a gift by the late Andrew W. Mellon. At first it might be a little bit difficult to understand how mere painted canvasses or pieces of cast bronze could be worth such great sums. We are challenged by the thought that a few years ago the Italian government exhibited a painting at an American World Fair that was insured for seven million dollars.

Our understanding of this idea might be helped out by remembering that noble ideas and uplifting thoughts are probably our most important national or individual possessions, and if these can be effectively communicated to us by means of painted pictures, then no price could be too great. In several very real ways this "City of Monuments" makes substantial contributions to our own individual welfare, and then in more subtle ways it teaches us to build some statues of our own.

We need some statues erected in our hearts to freedom, righteousness, and human dignity. Certainly we should have some monuments to honesty and fairness shining in our lives. To live in this favored land established under the direction of God should help us to refrain from lying, cheating, or profaning the name of that great being who is the God of this land. Working under his Father, the Son of God was the Creator of our earth. He has also been appointed to be the Savior of our world and the Redeemer of our souls.

His special title of "God of this land" has particular meaning for us. All Americans should help to erect a great spiritual monument that should be built high enough that it could be seen by everyone. Then we ought to live by its spirit. Certainly we ought not to oppress our wives or slight our children or be untrue to our friends. And above all, we should honor God, our Creator. One of the traditions of our Christian heritage centers in the cross on which Christ gave his life for us, and this great symbol of his sacrifice might also become a monument, representing our righteousness and good fortune, as well as our determination to serve him. This should tower above all other earthly things and should remind all people in all lands of the possibility and the spirit of eternal life and eternal happiness in God's presence. We should so conduct ourselves that we may be loyal Americans and worthy of God's many blessings to us.

Thy Dead Men Shall Live

I HAVE ALWAYS been greatly impressed with the life and experiences of the prophet Ezekiel. He was one of 10,000 Israelites who, with their families, were taken into Babylonian captivity in 597 B.C., as a punishment for their sins. But their evil continued and even in their captivity the Lord was ashamed of them. He said of Ezekiel: "Son of man, when the house of Israel dwelt in their own land, they defiled it by their own way and by their doings. . . . And when they entered unto the heathen . . . they profaned my holy name, when they said . . . [We] are the people of the Lord, and are gone forth out of his land. (Ezek. 36:17-20)

It is one of our human traits that we frequently try to bolster up our own shaky reputations by claiming an association with someone in better standing. Like the disreputable Israelites, we say: "We are the people of the Lord," or "We are friends of so-and-so." The Pharisees said: "We are the children of Abraham." But we only shortchange our God-given betterment instincts when we try to rate well without deserving it.

God has always had a kind of holy hunger to be proud of his children, and like the parent of a delinquent child, he tried very hard to get his chosen people to behave themselves. But they had many serious problems with their own conduct. Their sins had already caused them to spend over 200 years in Egyptian slavery. The Lord had released them, on a kind of parole, to give them another chance to make something of themselves, but they couldn't maintain their decency even until they reached their promised land. It was necessary in their own interests for the Lord to punish them again and again.

Even after they had settled in their land of milk and honey after forty years in the desert, they were still unable to live the laws on which their success was predicated. Time after time, they allowed their obedience to lapse, and finally they ended up in Babylon as captives of a heathen nation. The history of the Israelites might serve us a big-scale example of some of our own problems.

Our ambitions to do well are frequently thwarted by our inclinations toward weakness and wrong, and our sins always bring their evil consequences upon us as they did upon the Israelites. One of our most serious errors is that instead of learning from the punishment, we often allow discouragement or rebellion to make our situation even worse.

Some people can learn from both failure and success, but some can learn from neither. Even God can't save us in our sins. How can a child be helped, who not only takes license from forgiveness and love, but also rebels at discipline? This double-edged weakness so feeds upon itself that no matter what happens, the problem is never solved. Someone has said: "Life is like golf; as soon as we get out of one hole, we head for another." If we love God, if we have the right attitude, if we think right, then both punishment and reward operate in our interests. We can dry up life's failures when we learn how to repent of our sins and get pleasure from righteousness. We must not let our God-given success qualities wither and die because of disuse.

There is one success process that might be appropriately compared to God's program of resurrection. For very good reasons, the spirit and body of man were joined together on a temporary basis for the period of mortality. In announcing the separation which takes place at the end of this probationary period, God said: "Then shall the dust return to the earth as it was: and the spirit shall return unto God who gave it." (Ecc. 12:7) This separation called "death" provides the necessary interval for the cleansing, education, and final preparation of both the spirit and the body for the resurrection. After this process has been completed, a permanent association can be made on the most favorable basis.

This wonder of the resurrection was initiated by Jesus. His was the first body on this earth to be inseparably connected with his spirit. However, we know that many others have since been resurrected as the scripture says that immediately following the resurrection of Jesus, ". . . the graves were opened; and many bodies of the saints which slept arose, and came out of the graves after his resurrection, and went into the holy city, and appeared unto many." (Matt. 27:52-53) This important process in our eternal progression was not just discovered nineteen hundred years ago; the people of this earth have been promised a resurrection since the beginning. Both death and the resurrection were decided upon in the pre-mortal council in heaven.

All of God's prophets have taught the people that by their own good works they may obtain a better resurrection for themselves. Several centuries B.C., the prophet Daniel said: "And many of them that sleep in the dust of the earth shall awake, some to everlasting life, and some to shame and everlasting contempt." (Dan. 12:2) Isaiah said: "Thy dead men shall live, together with my dead body shall they arise. Awake and sing, ye that dwell in the dust. . . ." (Isa. 26:19) Through Hosea the Lord said: "I will ransom them from the power of the grave; I will redeem them from death. . . ." (Hos. 13:14)

What more stimulating idea could one have than this promise of a glorious resurrection! It is necessary for our eternal exaltation and a fullness of our joy. Without resurrection, this wonderful mortal body would be lost. Then throughout eternity we would remain spiritual beings just as we were before mortality began.

This word resurrection, like many other great words, also has a symbolic meaning. We sometimes talk about resurrecting someone's faith or bringing his ambition back to life. The Lord may have spoken with a double meaning when he gave Ezekiel his stimulating vision about the resurrection of the Israelites. While they were in Babylon paying the penalty of their sins they became very discouraged, and whatever the reason may be, every discouraged man is a weak man. Though even the beginning of the resurrection was then still some eight hunded years in the future, the Israelites needed some motivation. Therefore, as a means of getting them to revitalize their industry and righteousness, the Lord pointed out this thrilling possibility awaiting them beyond the grave. Their repentance and faith would not only help them to get a better resurrection from the dead, but it would also restore the freedom and blessing of being returned to their homeland. God could resurrect their dead bodies, but to make the most of their mortal situations, they themselves must revitalize their faith. It is a little bit ridiculous to allow a necessary correction to destroy our interest in ourselves with an attitude of not caring. Undoubtedly, the Lord hoped that this double motivation of national restoration and bodily resurrection would overcome their double sin of living unrighteously and then becoming depressed by the correction.

Ezekiel said to the people: "The hand of the Lord was upon me, and carried me out in the spirit of the Lord, and set me down in the midst of the valley which was full of bones, And caused me to pass by them round about: and, behold, there were very many . . . and . . . they were very dry . . . [and] he said unto me, Prophesy upon these bones, and say unto them, O ye dry bones, hear the word of the Lord. Thus saith the Lord God unto these bones: Behold, I will cause breath to enter into you, and ye shall live: And I will lay sinews upon you, and will bring up flesh upon you, and cover you with skin. . . ."

Then Ezekiel said: "So I prophesied as I was commanded: and as I prophesied, there was a noise, and behold a shaking, and the bones came together, bone to his bone. And when I beheld, lo, the sinews and the flesh came up upon them, and the skin covered them. . . ." Then God put the breath of life into them, and they lived and stood upon their feet, an exceeding great army. Then God said to Ezekiel, "Son of man, these bones are the whole house of Israel: behold, they say, Our bones are dried, and our hope is lost: we are cut off from our parts. Therefore prophesy and say unto them. . . . O my people, I will open your graves, and cause you to come up out of your graves, and bring you unto the land of Israel. . . . And shall put my spirit in you, and ye shall live, and I shall place you in your own land: then shall ye know that I the Lord have spoken it, and performed it, saith the Lord." (Ezek. 37:1-14)

A glorious resurrection is such a great benefit that it was highly desirable for even the Son of God, himself. This has some of the elements of a do-it-yourself project, for to obtain the best resurrection, we must revitalize our own faith and animate our drooping, discouraged, sinful spirits. We should get on the job in the right frame of mind; otherwise we might come forth in the resurrection of the damned. With all the great wonders and miracles of our world we should have no doubt about God's ability to resurrect our dead bodies. Our primary problem is to revitalize our sick, sinful spirits.

God has made an atonement for our sins, and he has promised a bodily resurrection to everyone who has ever lived. He has said: "For as in Adam all die, even so in Christ shall all be made alive." (I Cor. 15:22) But the resurrection of the just will be far more glorious than the resurrection of the unjust, and even God cannot make us worthy of celestial bodies without our cooperation. In spite of their many broken promises, the Lord said to the Israelites: ". . . I will make a new covenant with the house of Israel, and with the house of Judah. . . . I will put my law in their inward parts, and write it in their hearts. . . ." (Jer. 31:31-33) This is another of those jobs in which the Lord must have our help.

The Lord's primary project has always been to get his law of success into our inward parts. Jesus said to Nicodemus that we should be born again. This is one of the things that God was trying to bring about in the lives of the captive Israelites. Physical birth can take place only once, but our ambition, our righteousness, and our success can be born a dozen times, and each time they can be born better. We can cause a more enthusiastic repentance to activate our lives. By being born again we can get greater hope, more faith, and a stronger determination in actual operation. In being born again, we can leave out our weaknesses, our ridiculous discouragements, and strengthen our wishy-washy wills.

The Lord said: "Cast away from you all your transgressions, whereby ye have transgressed; and make you a new heart and a new spirit. . . ." If we fail in this, we fail in our lives.

The Lord asked the Israelites a very important question which also applies to us when he said: ". . . for why will ye die, O house of Israel?" (Ezek. 18:31) Some eight hundred years later, Paul echoed this same question when he said, ". . . why stand ye in jeopardy every hour?" (I Cor. 15:30) The answers to both of these great questions are very important to us.

I know a man who makes a lot of money revitalizing sick businesses. He finds a firm whose owner is so negative and discouraged that his business doesn't have a chance to succeed. After a business has been under failing leadership for a while, it can usually be bought pretty cheap. Under new ownership, with a better outlook and a more effective direction, the atmosphere can be changed. Then under the touch of courage, industry, and a determined faith, a dead business can be made to take on new life. It is born again. A practice of the right success principles can get a lot of new customers and make a failing business worth a lot of money.

I know of a man who recently bought an old dilapidated home. The house was unpainted and unsightly, and the yard was rundown. In the evenings he redid the landscaping. He put on a new roof and gave the house a few coats of paint. He rearranged and dressed up the interior until he made this house look like a new place. This is the kind of job the Lord wanted the Israelites to do for themselves. This is also what he wants us to do for ourselves. One man takes over sick businesses and sells healthy ones; another takes over a rundown home and transforms it into a place of beauty and utility.

God wants us to develop this most important revitalizing ability so that we can take over our own sick, discouraged lives and make them into going concerns that are profitable to God and will bring about our own eternal exaltation. This requires that we get a little more of the spirit of faith and intelligent hope into the dry bones of our lethargy and indifference. We need to throw out our evil transgressions and discouragement and install a new heart and a new spirit. We need to develop stronger sinews and greater ambitions, covered with the flesh of industry and the skin of righteousness. Then we will be able to stand up before God, in such strength, that we may make him proud of us and merit his eternal blessings.

The Double Think

A T HIS BEST, a human being is able to do many things impossible to others of God's creatures. For example, a man is able to laugh. In the entire universe there is no other example of this interesting and pleasant response to life. Second, he can pray; third, he worships; fourth, he loves; fifth, he believes; sixth, he plans; seventh, he is able to work with a purpose; eighth, he dreams; ninth, he understands; tenth, he communicates with others; eleventh, he sings; twelfth, he inspires; thirteenth, he remembers; and fourteenth, he thinks. All of these abilities have tremendous significance and a great happiness potential. Outside of God himself all of these great activities belong exclusively to man, and while we frequently use them very ineffectively, in these important areas God is our only fellow in the universe.

To some extent all of these tremendous abilities depend upon what and how we think. Prayer and worship are thoughtful activities. There is one variety of thinking that we call planning. It has been said that planning is the place where man shows himself most like God. Nothing is more Godlike than the planner. He is the one who draws the blueprints for success. He is the organizer, the designer, the originator. He is the one who builds the roadway on which every other accomplishment must travel.

Certainly the human brain is one of the greatest wonders in the universe. It is about the size of my two hands. It is made up of 14 billion cells, and it can contain more information than can be placed in a dozen libraries. A prominent British neurophysicist recently said that no one could construct an electronic computer for three billion dollars that would be the equivalent of a human brain. If God has that kind of an investment in my brain, he is certainly not getting a very good return on his money. It is one of life's tragedies when we fail to use this magnificent human resource as it was intended.

Woodrow Wilson once spoke of this waste when he said: "The greatest ability of the American people is their ability to

resist instruction." Far too many of us have our full share of
that unfortunate talent. Thomas A. Edison said: "There is no
limit to which a man will not go to avoid thinking." Solomon
said: "As [a man] thinketh, so is he." I am not quite certain
just where that leaves us, but if we are what we think and if
we don't think, it is evident that we have a problem.

Sometimes we do our thinking with our stomachs, our sex
impulses, our hates, our fears, and our prejudices, as we determine
what we do by how we feel instead of by what we think. The
brain was created to be the presiding officer of the personality,
and nothing should ever be permitted in our lives until it has
first been passed on and approved by the brain.

The abuse, or the misuse, or the disuse of our minds will
all have the most detrimental consequences for us. When we
fail to use the muscles in our arms, nature takes the muscles
away. The mole didn't use his eyes and so nature took away
his eyesight. If we don't keep the assessments paid on our
talents and skills, nature quickly repossesses them. Our knowledge, our attitudes, our virtues, and our abilities are all like
the manna that was sent from heaven to feed the children of
Israel in the desert — that which wasn't used always spoiled.
We are committing a great sin against ourselves when we allow
our tremendous mental and spiritual resources to deteriorate and
be lost.

The wide differences in men are largely determined by how
and when and what and why we think. The mind is the seat
of reason and the center of logic. It can be trained, balanced,
and given power. The mind also has the ability to inspire others.
Our minds were created for us to think with but we should also
use them a good deal for purposes of re-thinking.

Our judgment can be greatly improved and the number
of our mistakes can be drastically reduced if we know how to
effectively review certain of our decisions. This technique of
re-thinking is related to a valuable ability called hindsight. It
can be used to help one greatly improve his foresight. Many
of our important programs need to be given a second look occasionally. Sometimes someone says: "Let me sleep on it," or
"I'd like to think it over from a new point of view." Sometimes
it is only after the idea or the idea-thinker has cooled off a
little that an idea can be seen in the clear light of day; then
it looks different.

However, a good second think has frequently produced a more solid set of better conclusions. A doctor is doing some second thinking when he performs a post-mortem examination. This is the way he discovers where his diagnosis went wrong, or where the error was hiding which caused him to miss it. A good post-mortem can also tell him what is required for more successful operations in the future. There are many other problems that make a second look profitable, and there are also many questions requiring some double thinking. A "double think" enables us to better reconcile our contradictions and get a more accurate estimate of our margins of error. This is a way by which we can plumb the depths of our power and get a better understanding of the dimensions of our own judgment.

Daniel Webster once used this double-thinking process to bring a lot of fame to himself. A prospective client without money once asked Mr. Webster to help him solve a difficult legal problem. Mr. Webster recognized the importance of the question involved, and because he wanted to know the answer, he decided to take the case without any fee. He worked through the facts as intelligently as he could. Then he wrote out his brief and presented the case in court. The opposing attorney presented many arguments in opposition. In addition the judge poked a few holes in his logic. Finally Mr. Webster won the case by a narrow margin.

However, instead of forgetting it after it had been won, Mr. Webster felt that now was the time that some real case development should be done. With all of this newly acquired experience he was now in a position to give this case an expert and more intelligent second look. He also knew that such an important point of law as was here involved would be very likely to come up again sometime, and he wanted to be ready. He felt that now when he had all of the facts clearly in mind was the best time to get a super mastery of all of the points involved. Therefore, he reworked his ideas in the light of his greater experience and comprehension. Then he rewrote the brief as though he were getting ready for a brand new trial. He also wanted to make this a perfect case in which there would remain not a single flaw. After careful completion he filed away his brief, knowing that he would sometime make good use of it. He didn't have long to wait.

One day on the floor of the Senate some matters were brought up involving this particular point of law. It appeared to many people that the other side had an air-tight case. And in any event with all the complications involved, it seemed that no one could possibly prepare an adequate reply without weeks of preparation. That night Mr. Webster got out his brief that had already been thoughtfully prepared, court tested, rethought, and then still further improved. The next morning when the Senate opened, Mr. Webster took the floor with the attitude and self-confidence of a master. Because of his superior knowledge and better preparation, those on the other side didn't have a chance They seemed like schoolboys by comparison. Mr. Webster not only won the verdict, he also won great prestige among his associates that made his standing among them shoot up like a skyrocket.

This idea of a double think also presents many opportunities for us in many fields. Second thoughts are stronger thoughts. Frequently, we should do a few rewrites of our own on some of our important personal problems. This is one good way to make sure that as many errors as possible have been eliminated. Suppose that we figure up how many important problems we have that would be benefited by a double think. Suppose that we take the various subdivisions of our lives before the court of reason or before the court of the holy scriptures and test them for their righteousness and profitableness. Or suppose that we give God a chance to poke a few holes in our performance. What about our own conduct in the important areas of religion, fairness, and personal behavior?

An almost broken-hearted mother recently talked about her seventeen-year-old son who had gotten in with the wrong kind of friends. He had taken up smoking and, because that had put him in conflict with his Church teachings, he eliminated the Church as an important factor in his life. Such an action should not be taken by anyone without first going over it very carefully. There are many serious consequences involved in rejecting the Church which may not be apparent at the first thought.

The Church is a result of divine revelation, and its doctrines are decreed by the great God of heaven. To reject the Church also frequently destroys the confidence of other people, as well as the members of one's own family. It is no small thing to deny religious principles and refuse the associations coming from Church membership. When one turns his back on the Church he loses a great many things. Other values are lost when one turns off his conscience and blocks the whisperings of the still, small voice. It is interesting to remember that a person who regularly goes to church and faithfully obeys Church regulations will at the end of his life be a different kind of person than the one who rebels against Church authority, or becomes antagonistic toward the uplifting influences of his own home.

We make a great many other errors because we say: "I didn't think or I never gave it a second thought." If we think about our problems more now, we won't need to regret the consequences so much later on. Certainly our own futures are worth thinking about while there is time to do something about them. With a lot of good "double-thinks" and a willingness to act on a well-developed second judgment, we are pretty safe. Snap judgment and an abandoned thinking is still one of the biggest problems of our lives. Usually we don't think straight enough, or far enough, or soon enough, or often enough, or thoroughly enough. We don't have enough good "double-thinks" based on solid facts. Effective double thinking also depends on whether or not we have the courage to carry out our convictions.

The other day two hippies were trying to explain their philosophy of life. They were trying to justify their sex orgies on the basis of their natural need. In their opinion their idleness was also proper because of their natural need to enjoy themselves right now. They even had some reasons for living in ugliness and filth. However, they hadn't thought any of these things through very well. Certainly they hadn't tried to square their philosophies with reason, or with the word of the Lord, or the judgment of good people.

Sometime in the future, after they have spoiled their lives and wasted their opportunities, the novelty of wallowing in immorality and being regarded as an oddity may wear off. Sometimes their venereal diseases and their dope addictions may not give them the permanent peace and satisfaction that they will need in the future. It is also quite likely that their venereal consciences may also turn on them and cause them problems. The period usually devoted to deathbed repentance is sometimes almost the first time that some people ever give their second thoughts a chance to be considered. What a ghastly nightmare it would be to spend one's deathbed period knowing that his own life had not measured up, and that he had made life very unprofitable for all those that he had led astray!

Jesus said: "And if it so be that you should labor all your days in crying repentance unto this people, and bring, save it be one soul unto me, how great shall be your joy with him in the kingdom of my Father!" (D&C 18:15) If our joy shall be great because we have brought one soul unto him, how bitter will be the remorse in remembering those many souls that we have seduced into immorality, enticed into lung cancer, or initiated into the evils of alcoholism and dope addiction. In the end what satisfaction can come from having persuaded others to desert the straight and narrow way, and with the crowd walk down that broad road of dishonesty, atheism, and evil that leads to eternal misery?

If I could choose the conditions of my death hour, I would not like to spend it in a hippie camp, and when that time arrives I would like to have a clean body and a peaceful mind with my hair trimmed and combed. I would then also like to have a happy, satisfied spirit. It would be wonderful to have my family and a few friends on hand to bid me Godspeed on my journey. It would also help out to know that I was worthy of their confidence and that my own life had served some useful purpose. And while there is time to make these preparations we should lift our conduct above the corrosion of sin by giving some good second thoughts in contemplation of the wonders of eternal glory.

The Eleventh Commandment

ONE OF THE MOST important influences in our world has been the Ten Commandments. In ten great declarations the Creator and Ruler of the universe has set down his own unmistakable convictions for our benefit. In strong, uncompromising language he has told us some of those things that we just must not do in order to make our lives successful. This earth and everything in it was created by God. He has granted us our lives. He has made an outstanding success possible for us if we merely follow his direction. One of the first steps toward any accomplishment is to get clearly in mind that some things are out of bounds.

If we fully obeyed the Ten Commandments, every other success in life would be easy. With our minds definitely made up about the Ten Commandments, we could then definitely, irretrievably, and permanently get rid of all those troublesome problems connected with our false gods, our profanities, our Sabbath-day violations, our rebellions, murders, adulteries, dishonesties, and covetousness. With these handicaps eliminated we would then have all of our power to use in a positive way in bringing about whatever success we had chosen.

Of course, we recognize that the Ten Commandments are not all-inclusive. There are some other destructive sins that were not officially mentioned from Sinai. Suppose, therefore, that you were asked to add one more of these holy "Thou shalt nots" to the list. What would it be? All of the Ten Commandments actually have to do with just two subjects: four of the commandments are designed to improve our relations with God, and the other six are intended to increase our ability to get along more successfully with our fellowmen.

If we thought about it, we might feel very sorry for God. For nearly six thousand years, he has suffered a great deal, because he has been right in the middle of our depressing human problems. Anyone who sympathetically listens to the sins of distressed people shares their miseries. The failure of children always brings unhappiness to the parents. God must be even more vulnerable to the suffering of others, as he has officially taken our load of grief upon himself.

The shortest verse in the scriptures says: "Jesus wept." He wept many times and with very good reason. While suffering under the burden of our sins in the Garden of Gethsemane, he sweat great drops of blood at every pore. But our present crime-waves and the deluges of our modern sins are still reaching up to God with no signs of any let-up, and as he sees what we are doing to ourselves, he must still be suffering a lot of pain. He has ordained happiness to be the purpose of life. But how can a gracious, loving Heavenly Father be happy while we continue to heap eternal damnation and eternal misery upon ourselves? Our situation must be even worse in his eyes as our sins are so ridiculous, so unprofitable, and so unnecessary. All that we ourselves are getting from our sins are millions of cases of nervous breakdowns, suicides, and mental illnesses with a lot of pain for ourselves, both here and hereafter.

There is an Article of Faith that says: "We believe that men will be punished for their own sins, and not for Adam's transgression." It is by our own sins too that we are also punishing God and our families and our friends.

Shakespeare said: "Each new morn, new widows howl, new orphans cry, new sorrows strike heaven in the face." "Man's inhumanity to man makes countless millions mourn."

Suppose, therefore, that you were asked to write an eleventh commandment that would be obeyed by everyone, how would it be to say: "Thou shalt not be unkind." In thinking of the benefits of such a law, we might have both God and ourselves in mind as the beneficiaries. Certainly we should be a lot more considerate of our eternal Heavenly Father. We should not follow the pattern of some thoughtless, earthly children who are breaking their parents' hearts. To hurt God is far more serious. For in a way that no earthly parents can, the Redeemer has already agreed to take our sins upon himself. We know that there is an unchanging law in the universe to the effect that every sin must be paid for, but the people of our world are presently taking a cruel and unfair advantage of this situation. With a kind of reckless abandon we sing: "Cast your burdens on the Lord." And certainly we are presently out-doing ourselves in punishing the wrong man.

How would we feel if our children were continually hurting us by willfully heaping unnecessary misery, expense, and shame upon us? And on the other hand, what joy we would feel if they went a little out of their way to reflect honor, credit, and love toward us and demonstrated their willingness to help us carry our burdens? What idea could be more worthwhile than the truth that we can actually bring joy and happiness to our eternal Heavenly Father by our righteousness? With our eternal parents in mind we might enshrine in our own hearts that great command which says, "Honor thy father and thy mother." This is also in harmony with that first great command given by Jesus wherein we are told that we should love God with all our hearts. However, it is pretty hard to love someone very much while we are abusing him. Or we might try to imagine wonderful parents getting joy and happiness out of watching their children destroy themselves with dope, atheism, crime, and immorality. How do we imagine God feels while he is listening to our ridiculous discussions about the new morality, or our boasted right to do wrong? Or how do you think he enjoys our destructive debates about dope, sex perversions, and our other permissive sins?

We frequently conduct Gallup Polls or canvass a group of conditioned young people to get the latest opinion as to good and bad sex practices. It would be interesting to see the results of the Gallup Polls taken in Noah's day about the so-called sex education, or to discover how the people of ancient Babylon voted on the new morality. The fact that many people are presently voting for irresponsibility, idleness, race riots, dishonesty, force, and murder does not make them right. It is our sins and our conflicts of interest that are causing our nervous breakdowns, mental illnesses, and extreme unhappiness. Certainly God is even more unhappy than we are about this sinful indulgence. What a stroke of genius it would indicate in us if we took sufficient interest in how God has voted on the great issues involving every question of right and wrong! And then what a thoughtful kindness we would be showing him by following his all-wise counsel! Therefore, as the first part of our eleventh commandment we might say to ourselves: "Thou shalt not be unkind to God." This idea has a double significance, inasmuch as being kind to God is the very best way to be kind to ourselves. Someone has said: "He who ignores his friend is ungrateful to his friend, but he who ignores his Savior is unmerciful unto himself."

God has had a lot more experience than we have, and he is a lot wiser. He can see the end from the beginning, and he fully understands the relationship between deeds and their consequences. Because his decisions are always based on truth we do not need to worry about him changing his opinion about fundamental truths every time a new wind blows. Fickleness is only a human frailty. Our frequent Gallup Polls about the popularity of the President of the United States show that in our minds he may be a hero today and a byword tomorrow. Actually he may be doing his best job when he is the least popular.

However, history proves that even our majority opinions are almost always wrong. We ought not to forget that the Gallup Polls taken in Jerusalem before and after the crucifixion had the wrong answers. Even the people who knew Jesus best were not very consistent in their attitudes. On the first day of his last week of life, he made his triumphal entry into Jerusalem while great multitudes of people were spreading flowers and palm branches to carpet the pathway before him, and they were shouting, "Hosanna to the Son of David: blessed is he that cometh in the name of the Lord. . . ." (Matt. 21:9) But by the Thursday evening of that same week the people were crying, "Crucify him, crucify him!" (Luke 23:21) Even his most intimate followers ran away when a little pressure was on. And by that Friday morning the Savior of the world was hanging upon the cross.

God is the same yesterday, today, and forever, and he is always right. The best thing that we could possibly do would be to coordinate our lives with his. Then our crime rate would disappear and we would save our souls. Ibsen said: "Without a fixed point outside myself, I cannot exist." We must have someone more dependable than ourselves to depend upon, and when our fixed point is God's righteousness, then we will always be safe. We have built up our feelings of insecurity only because we do those things that make us insecure, and the primary reason that we have so many inferiority and guilt complexes is because we have done so much to deserve them.

What a help it would be if we had a strong second meaning in this proposed eleventh commandment wherein we agreed to be kind to ourselves, our families, our friends, and our enemies. Presently one of the places where we are most resourceful is in thinking up new ways of being unkind to each other. We have the most bitter feelings and say the harshest words. We rob and steal and cheat one another. We tell lies, plan deceits, scatter rumors, and say unkind things in order to more seriously hurt each other.

Listen to what the Lord himself said about us as he looked forward from his own day to ours. "For nation shall rise against nation, and kingdom against kingdom, and there shall be famines, and pestilences, and earthquakes, in divers places. And then shall many be offended, and shall betray one another, and shall hate one another. And many false prophets shall rise, and shall deceive many. And because iniquity shall abound, the love of many shall wax cold." (Matt. 24:7, 10-12)

What a ridiculous way for us to spend the valuable resources of our lives! Even a sacred marriage relationship is frequently a time when we begin a long series of destructive quarrels and unpleasant bickerings. Under the law of Moses, as soon as a man got married he was given a year's exemption from military service. A little cynically, someone figured out that the purpose of spending this first year with his wife was to teach him how to fight. Very frequently those taking part in our most troubled, unhappy marriages don't even know what they are fighting about. Marriage partners sometimes yell, are unfaithful, irresponsible, and undependable without serious concern as to what they are doing.

When married or single people try to adjust their lives according to their own views, problems always develop, but when all of the parties fully accept the laws of God as the standard for their conduct, then it is much easier for everyone to be harmonious. To believe that something is right or wrong because God said so is quite different than to believe that it is right or wrong because of how we ourselves may feel.

When a basically selfish person leaves himself free to indulge in the unprofitable mental processes of rationalizing and wishful thinking, he can make his life very destructive to everyone around him, including himself. By this process of crooked thinking, based on our own opinions, we bypass reason, avoid self-analysis, trust in the wrong motives, disregard right, and ignore the happiness and rights of other people. Without considering God we can make our own acts seem logical and acceptable, no matter how stupid they may actually be.

Far too frequently we actually enjoy being cruel and take delight in causing other people pain and humiliation. The miserable quality of distorted thinking causes detours from truth, or reason can be made to jump hurdles, or bypass the facts, or ignore those areas that are unfavorable to ourselves.

How grateful we ought to be that God is always fair and righteous and that he can always be depended upon! How fortunate that as a city of refuge there is a heaven available where people will not be ruled by willful, selfish, ungodly men or have ungodly marriage companions! We should all try to develop within ourselves now a firm, dependable sense of what is right and wrong, according to the high authority of God. We should not depend on that kind of logic wherein we try to justify our evil by saying that "everybody's doing it." Some people try to justify themselves by saying, "There are people who do worse things than I do." But that still does not make us any less blameable. If there are worse things than cheating in marriage, how does that alleviate God's punishment or make our cheating any more pleasant to live with? The fact that "everyone was doing it" in the days of Noah didn't save them from the flood. It was because everyone was doing it in Sodom and Gomorrah that God poured out fire and brimstone upon them.

The only way to be kind to ourselves is to have our lives deeply based in righteousness. Only when we have some strong fixed points outside of ourselves can we make ourselves, our friends, and God happy.

A friend once told Abraham Lincoln that he thought that God was on Lincoln's side. Lincoln said that he was not so concerned about whether or not God was on Lincoln's side, but what he wanted to make sure of was that Lincoln was on God's side.

The parent who teaches his children what is right because God said so is in a much stronger position than the one who can only teach them what is right or wrong because the parent says so. Our children soon find out that we are frequently in error and that the school, the society, and their friends often do the wrong things. When this happens to the source of their trust, the children themselves are confused and get a feeling of insecurity and confusion that causes their lives to deteriorate. God promised to spare Sodom if ten righteous people could be found therein, and our righteousness may save the lives of many others.

How grateful we ought to be that we can base our lives and philosophies upon God and his principles of eternal truth and righteousness, and to know that his principles will never be out of date. We know that the Ten Commandments given from Mount Sinai thirty-four centuries ago are sound, and they will still be the law thirty-four centuries hence. Then we might also say to ourselves: "Thou shalt not be unkind." And if we work at it, God will help us to obey all eleven commandments.

Expression

THE STORY IS TOLD about a little boy in school who was asked to give a definition of the word "vacuum." After a little mental fumbling he said: "I've got it in my head, but I can't express it." Many of us have a lot in common with this young man, and anyone's inability in his expression usually rings a bell in us.

A very fine lady said: "I just can't express how I feel," and in her utterance you could feel the helplessness that she was complaining about. She felt that she had many wonderful and worthwhile ideas bubbling up in her mind, and she had a lot of very constructive attitudes swimming around in her emotions, but she had never learned to get them organized and put them into words. She was incapable of making her own greatness negotiable in the lives of other people. She could not give her thoughts a maximum of life, even to herself.

It is interesting that most of life's meaning comes by reason of our own expression. Someone was once asked what he thought about a certain subject and he said: "I don't know, I haven't spoken on it yet." More than almost any other thing the lady mentioned above wanted to be able to give a pleasing verbal form to her feelings, but she was almost completely unable to do so. There are a great many people who have this lady's problem. In fact, to be able to convey good thoughts to others, or to transfer useful feelings, and give a helpful expression to a satisfying ambition is one of the biggest accomplishments in either our occupational success or in the bigger business of adequately living life. We remember that effective expression seemed to be the biggest problem that Moses had to contend with. When he was called to be the leader of that vast nation of Egyptian slaves, he said to the Lord: "I cannot speak." "I am of a slow tongue." "The people will not believe my words." "I am not eloquent." The Lord got after Moses about his inferiority complex. He said to Moses: "Who made man's mouth? did not I the Lord?" The Creator tried to get Moses to understand that God had made man's communication equipment and that it was capable of whatever improvement Moses may want to bring about in it. Because Moses couldn't be convinced, the Lord gave him his brother Aaron as a mouthpiece.

However, this is never an ideal solution, as it is pretty hard for someone else to express our enthusiasm effectively. No successful speaker likes to be limited by the need of speaking through an interpreter. In addition to having to use a substitute mouth, it must have been more than ordinarily inconvenient for Moses to have to look up Aaron every time he wanted to convey an idea.

The prophet Jeremiah was also bothered with this problem about expression. Jeremiah answered his own call to divine service by saying, "I cannot speak. I am but a child." The Lord also got after him for his feelings of inferiority.

If we knew all of the story we would find that almost every person in the world has felt that he was poorly equipped in this field of communication. Salesmen and missionaries have trouble getting their ideas over as effectively as they would like to do. Teachers, speakers, and all others also have trouble in this field. Some can't speak loud enough to be heard. Some can't speak clearly enough to be understood. Some public speakers don't know how to organize their material or how to illustrate it, illuminate it, or make it interesting. The biggest problem in maintaining successful marriage relations comes because of ineffective communication.

A wife was contemplating divorce. While discussing her grievances she was asked, "What does your husband think about these things?" She said: "I don't know, I never talk to my husband." Many men say: "My wife doesn't understand me." And most women feel that they are not appreciated. Children say: "I can't get close to my parents." Parents are often afraid of their children.

A wife was discussing some promotion and sales ideas for a new business that she was getting started. Then it occurred to her that some of these same ideas may help her to put a little interest and new life into her own marriage. Even after living with her husband for twenty-five years she seemed not to have the slightest idea as to whether or not he loved her, and she was just as indefinite about her own feelings for him. Both of them had "slow tongues." Neither of them was very eloquent in the language of love, and each needed a marriage counselor to serve them as a mouthpiece to the other. Each of them also needed an analyst to help them make an appraisal of themselves and to assist them in making up their minds about some of the key issues of their lives. They needed help in getting themselves organized for a greater accomplishment.

We remember Demosthenes, who in his early years had a disabling speech defect. But his situation was a little different. In the first place he had a more serious problem. He had such a bad speech impediment that he couldn't be clearly understood. Unlike most people, Demosthenes did something about his situation. He went down to the seashore and filled his mouth with pebbles and practiced shouting to the waves. He developed enough power, clarity of expression, and human interest that he later became the greatest orator in the world. He also had purpose in his speech and was able to motivate others. By way of comparison, it was said that when people heard Cicero, they said "How well Cicero speaks," but when they heard Demosthenes they said: "Let's take up arms and march against Phillip."

If public speakers, husbands and wives, teachers and salesmen would spend as much time working on their expression as did Demosthenes, our effectiveness in communication would be vastly increased. Certainly this is an area that is important enough to deserve our attention. Because we learn to do by doing, we should develop our expression by effectively expressing.

The other day I watched my grandchildren expressing themselves. They had an advantage over many because they did not have so many inhibitions to contend with as some do. They were running, jumping, laughing, squealing, and yelling to their hearts' content, and as they were doing it their faces were radiant with a full glow of childish happiness. Every part of their bodies, minds, and spirits seemed to be active and taking part. Like Demosthenes in shouting to the waves, these children were letting themselves go to the full limit of their capacity.

There is a period of expression common among young females called the giggling stage. At other ages we do different things in order to express ourselves. A football player expresses his feeling by crashing the line, or kicking a goal, or making a touchdown. To win for the school is his means of satisfying those emotional urges that are welling up inside of him. Some of the spectators satisfy themselves by yelling and jumping up and down. Many fans like to shout a lot of fancy phrases at the players of both teams, even though they know they will never be heard. To help fans effectively channel this expenditure of energy, yell masters and cheerleaders are appointed to get everyone organized so that they can pool this community of expression. It seems to be more satisfying for all the people in the stadium to yell, chant, sing, and have a good time together. People distinguish themselves as workers, writers, politicians, and speakers as they develop their ability in expression. One becomes a captain of industry, others make money, some paint pictures, many get married, or play the stock market in order to express themselves.

On each Sabbath day there is a great group of people who go to church for a very helpful kind of spiritual expression. There they sing, preach, listen, pray, and teach. This is the place where people worship God and shake hands and extend a warm Christian greeting to each other. In church we smile and exercise our feelings of reverence as we mingle our faith, our friendship, and our love of God. In addition to being a command of God this custom of greeting and fellowshipping with each other is one of the most stimulating of our human activities.

It has been suggested that our civilization would never have survived for half a century if it had not been for this one day in seven that we call the Sabbath. This is the day when we pay particular attention to the cleansing of our bodies. This is the day when we put on our best clothes, think our best thoughts and read our best books. Then we put a little paint on our cheeks and dress ourselves up in our smiling faces and go to church. We speak a great deal about our right to receive inspiration from God. And what a thrilling idea it is that if we properly direct our lives, we may entitle ourselves to receive guidance and direction from the source of all intelligence and power! But one of the things that we do not always understand is our right to give inspiration to other people. Next to God the most inspiring, uplifting influence in the world is a great human being, and as we express ourselves by setting some good examples, giving service to others, and extending our devotion to God, we can also uplift ourselves and make many other people happy. By an expression of our love, our testimony, our enthusiasm, and our faith, we may exalt and benefit everyone around us.

Some time ago I talked with a young couple that were having marital problems. They had never been very successful in becoming pleasant companions or even very good friends to each other; nor had they learned how to be friendly to anyone else. They didn't have very much to live on, and neither did they have very much to live for. They attended church so irregularly that they never got well enough acquainted to enjoy it. They went to church listlessly and only as a kind of boring duty. They had some guilt feelings which were making them uneasy and a few inferiority complexes were immobilizing their faith and causing them to draw within themselves. Most of their recreation came from drinking coffee and blowing cigarette smoke at each other.

It was suggested to them that they should open the windows of their small living room and let in some fresh air to clear out the tobacco smoke and the smells of stale beer. They should also practice a little mental and spiritual ventilation in themselves by cleaning some of the dark, gloomy, unhappy thoughts out of their minds. It was suggested that maybe she ought to get a new dress and put his best necktie on him and go to church regularly. If they went to the church house a little early and stayed a little late they could give everyone a few good, enthusiastic handshakes and get a few warm, friendly greetings in return. If they learned to love their neighbors, it might soon get a little easier to love themselves and each other. By going to church each Sunday they would soon be looking into the smiling eyes and friendly faces of a lot of good friends.

It has been said that the eyes are the windows of the soul, and when we shake hands and exchange greetings with those created in God's image, we also shake with our eyes, our spirits, and our other personality traits. Through a cordial, firm handshake we may feel the warmth of friendship, see the sparkle in people's faces, and feel the stirring of their spirits. This thrilling interchange of personalities can transport us much nearer toward God.

The other day while walking down the street I met a good friend. I shook his hand and put my arm around him and told him a joke. He also told me an interesting story, and we laughed and engaged in a little friendly small talk. Verbally, physically, and spiritually, we patted each other on the back and fed each other socially. This friendly exercise lasted only for a few minutes, but as I walked on down the street I thought how much better I felt than I had done before I met my friend. What an additional thrill it can be to go to church on the Sabbath day and give an effective expression to our feelings of fellowship and fraternity! As a preparation for church attendance we ought to take a good bath in the soap and water of repentance and let a little fresh air into our souls. We should get rid of that putrefying mass of our old sins and feelings of frustrations. Then we should learn to make the most of our church attendance. It may not always be appropriate to sing as loud as we can, but we ought to get pretty near the limits of our possibilities so far as getting our spirit into it. The song of the heart is a prayer unto God which he greatly appreciates and which he has said will be answered with a blessing upon our heads. We don't express ourselves nearly as enthusiastically as we should, either in song or in thanksgiving or in word. Certainly we ought to greet God with at least as much joy and as much love and enthusiasm as we greet our friends on the street.

Demosthenes learned to express himself by going down to the ocean and shouting to the waves. We should go to church and practice our communications with God in a spiritual equivalent. Expression made Demosthenes the greatest orator in the world, and it will make us a different and better kind of human being. Certainly in our expressions to God is not the time nor the place to have a slow tongue or an unwilling spirit or a slothful heart. Instead we can run the great scriptures through our minds, fill our hearts with reverence, and feel the stimulating emotions of love, faith, ambition, and righteousness influencing our lives. For the most elegant of all expression we should remember that our actions can speak much louder than our words, and they can also help us to get the vacuum out of our hearts and make the finest expression of ourselves to God.

Faith in Your Future

ONE OF THE MOST important ideas in the world is represented by the word "faith." It is the foundation on which every success rests. One of the most inspiring things about it is that we can have faith in the greatest things. We can develop a great faith in our country; we can build up faith in righteousness; we can learn to have faith in God. A productive faith in God not only means that we believe in him but that we understand the kind of person he is, that we trust him, and that we will always follow him. However, one of our most exciting possibilities, so far as I know, is that we can earn the right to have a satisfying, vitalizing faith in ourselves and in our own futures. This is not always easy as faith like most other things must be earned, and to make faith an actual living force in our lives sometimes takes a lot of doing.

As the apostle James once pointed out, "Faith without works is dead." Faith can't live in isolation. There is no such thing as preserved faith. When you take the works away, the faith dies. It always dies. It requires a very special kind of activity on our part to fully believe in God. We must not only believe in him but we must agree with him and understand that he knows what he is doing.

If one desires to believe in the principles of the gospel, he must first live those ideas that he desires to believe in. Jesus said: "If ye shall do my will, ye shall know of the doctrine." It is pretty difficult for one who is dishonest to believe in honesty. It is hard for a booze addict to believe in temperance. Emerson said: "Do the thing and you shall have the power." That is the reverse order of our usual procedures. Ordinarily, we pray for enough power to perform our labor, but there is a better way, and that is to perform the labor in order to get the power.

At one time, I had very large muscles on my arms, but when I gave up the "works" by which I got the muscles, life began a foreclosure procedure and immediately began repossessing my muscles. If I should now decide to be a ditch-digger, I might pray to the Lord to give me my muscles back, but because the Lord always follows the law he would surely say, "Dig the ditch and you shall have the muscles." In my lack of understanding, I might say to the Lord, "That's ridiculous, I need the muscles first so that I can dig the ditch later." That may be a great idea; it may be very logical and a great convenience to me personally, but it is not the law, and the Lord would probably counter by saying, "You don't understand. Muscles are not given out on that basis." He might say, "You must dig the ditch first, and then you can have the muscles later."

If someone wants a strong conviction about the values of morality, honesty, fairness, and righteousness, it can be acquired most easily by first living those laws that he wants to believe in. The Lord himself has decreed that the rewards are deferred until after the trial of our faith. There are certain trials that we must experience in order to win a strong, enduring, deserved faith in ourselves.

In ancient Greece, Pericles once said that no one had any right to fill an important office until he had first filled some small offices well. We can best learn to trust ourselves in big things by proving ourselves in little things. By learning to handle our work and ourselves effectively we may make ourselves stronger than any weakness that can come to us.

We were created in God's own image, and we have already been endowed with a set of all the attributes and potential powers of divinity. We have been granted an unlimited use of free agency, and if we can't trust ourselves, who will we be able to depend upon? A poet has written:

Trust in thine own untried capacity as thou
Would'st trust in God himself.
Thy soul is but an emanation from the whole,
Thou dost not dream what forces lie in thee,
Vast and unfathomed as the grandest sea.
No man can place a limit in thy strength.

Such triumphs as no mortal ever dreamed may yet be thine,
If thou wilt but believe in thy Creator and thyself.
At length some feet shall stand on the heights now attained —
Why not thine own?
Press on! Achieve! Achieve!

However, that kind of faith never comes to one who is continually disappointing himself and always falling down on the job. Real faith only comes after we have invested in it a lot of good works.

A famous athletic coach once said that muscles grow fastest when they are tired and stretched to the limit. It is when the champion runner is the most weary that he begins the sprint. No fighter ever becomes a champion until he has fought victoriously many times. Jesus expressed a similar idea when he said: "He that endureth to the end shall be saved." And no one has earned the right to really believe in his own future until he has been tested in the fire. Only then can he have a strong, sound faith in his own possibilities. The future is where all of the really important values are to be found.

Charles F. Kettering, the great mechanical wizard of General Motors, once said: "My interest is in the future because I am going to spend the rest of my life there." At best the present is only temporary and will soon be completely unimportant. It is the future that we should be concerned about, and the first step toward a brilliant future is to believe in it. The miracles and wonders of our present are important, but the possibilities of our futures are beyond our wildest imagination. The apostle Paul said: ". . . Eye hath not seen, nor ear heard, neither have entered into the heart of man, the things which God hath prepared for them that love him." (I Cor. 2:9)

God has arranged for us the kind of a future that he himself has. Jesus said, "In my father's house are many mansions." We can imagine beauty, comfort, and elegance costing billions of dollars, but we can't even imagine the things that God hath prepared for those who believe in him and follow him.

Someone has said that the best argument for an eternal life is the existence of someone who deserves an eternal life. According to the eternal laws of heredity, the offspring of God may properly hope to become like the eternal parents. God hid his treasures of gold, oil, and diamonds in the earth, but he put his greatest treasures into his children. Everyone has within himself a vein of greatness, and we need only to learn to command the shaft by which we draw out the gold.

God has given us our incomparable minds, our potentially magnificent personalities, and our godlike spirits. Just try to imagine what our futures might be when, with quickened senses, amplified powers of perception, and vastly increased capacities for love, understanding, and happiness, we have achieved our destinies of becoming even as God is. God is such a magnificent being that no one in his natural state can endure his presence. A great scripture says: "For no man has seen God at any time in the flesh, except quickened by the Spirit of God. Neither can any natural man abide the presence of God . . . wherefore, continue in patience until ye are perfected." (D&C 67:11-13)

Jesus said, "Be ye therefore perfect, even as your Father which is in heaven is perfect." (Matt. 5:48) What a great condition that will be! God is perfect in knowledge; he is perfect in righteousness; he is perfect in wisdom; he is perfect in glory. Our greatest experiences are mostly in the future. The apostle Paul said: "If in this life only we have hope in Christ, we are of all men most miserable." (I Cor. 15:18) All life is a preparation for the future, and as we plan and work and pray, we are projecting our own futures.

There is an interesting contrast that often takes place between the objectives that we seek and the procedures by which they are attained. That is, if the objective is pleasant, then the pathway that leads to it may be unpleasant. For example, if one desires to become a great surgeon the objectives of prestige, remuneration, and satisfaction will be very pleasant, but the road leading to it, made up of hard study, mental discipline, and temporary sacrifice, may be unpleasant. On the other hand if we make the road of life easy, the end will be difficult.

For example, some people select the easy roadway of idleness and indulgence; then the end will be hardship and remorse. Along the way some people engage in immoral practices, become hippies, dope addicts, gamblers, and bank robbers. But those who thus try to make the road pleasant will surely arrive at an unpleasant destination. When we do evil tonight we hate ourselves tomorrow, and one of the biggest differences between success and failure is that successful people do the things that unsuccessful people refuse to do. The pathway of sin leads to the destiny of condemnation. Satan has no future because he chose the way of disobedience and rebellion. It is a pretty good rule to remember that if the road is difficult, the end will be easy, whereas if the road is easy, the end may be difficult.

If the pathway is filled with excellence, righteousness, industry, planning, and self-discipline, the future will be filled with comfort, peace of mind, satisfaction, and exaltation.

Jesus gave the finest expression to this law governing success and failure when he said: "Enter ye in at the strait gate: for wide is the gate, and broad is the way, that leadeth to destruction, and many there be which go in thereat: Because strait is the gate, and narrow is the way, which leadeth unto life, and few there be that find it." (Matt. 7:13-14) In this statement, Jesus was not only speaking as a moralist, but he was also speaking as a business expert. The way that leads to life and happiness is so narrow that such things as idleness, immorality, dope, and sin are placed out of bounds. The road that leads to death is so wide that everything can be included. The road to death is a broad, easy, meandering road where anything goes. Because the narrow way is straight, it sometimes leads up hills and over difficult places, but it leads to life. The road to death is wide enough to include glue-sniffing, stealing automobiles, idleness, and the love-ins of the new morality, but it has no future as it leads to the death of our souls. While struggle, self-discipline, study, and righteousness may require more effort, they lead to futures that are far more pleasant and satisfying.

In trying to adjust our own lives, it is helpful to study the case histories of those around us as we try to estimate the straightness of their gate and measure the narrowness of their way. Some time ago I read an account of a twice-married woman. She, herself, was a high-minded person, but her first husband had been a compulsive gambler. He wanted an easier way to make a living than by work, study, industry, righteousness, and service. He not only made gambling his way of life, but he got it into his bloodstream so that he could do nothing else. But gambling has no future. He lost all of his wife's savings as well as her respect. He lost his friends, his job, and finally, still looking for an easy way out, he took his own life. He solved his problem so far as this life is concerned by dying, but what about eternity?

Instead of trying to solve his problems by gambling, the other husband tried to hide them under lies and drown them in alcohol. He tried to stimulate his brain with dope and make his way pleasant by adopting the new morality. He had started his life with the greatest possibilities, but his end was miserable because he tried to make the way easy and more pleasant by violating the laws of God. Anyone who has watched a loved one, as he seriously widens the trail on which he is journeying toward his future, might understand how Isaiah felt when contemplating the fall of Satan. He said: "How art thou fallen from heaven, O Lucifer, son of the morning. . . ." (Isa. 14:12) It is interesting that Satan, the father of evil, was once the light bearer, the brilliant son of the morning, but he was disobedient to God.

Satan started the first rebellion against righteousness that is still so popular in our day. He wanted a quicker and easier way to power than by earning it. His procedures of force and rebellion remind us of the disgruntled students who want to run the universities before they learn the most simple facts of education. Those who want to forcibly take other men's goods also belong to this school of force and evil. The troublemakers who incite discord among others are working against everyone's future. So many of our own day want to conquer and burn and intimidate their way to success. If we judge Satan by his rank before his fall we must conclude that he was one of the most capable, but he fell when he tried to make the way wide enough to include rebellion, violence, and sin. We should remember that in spite of his ability, Satan has no future, and those who are following him in any degree will share his fate in the exact proportion that they participate in his evil.

John the Revelator was given a great revelation of the final judgment. He describes Satan's future in the twentieth chapter of Revelations by saying: "And I saw an angel come down from heaven, having the key of the bottomless pit and a great chain in his hand. And he laid hold on the dragon, that old serpent, which is the Devil, and Satan. . . . And cast him into the bottomless pit, and shut him up, and set a seal upon him. . . ."

The greatest idea that I know of in the world is that those who are the most righteous will have the most glorious futures. And if we follow the Savior we may sometime see our names written where the most glorious futures are, and that is in God's book of life.

Footprints

O N JULY 20, 1969, we reached the conclusion of a 24 - billion - dollar American expedition into space when two United States citizens climbed out of their spaceship and walked upon the moon. Since the expulsion of man from the Garden of Eden we have recorded nearly six thousand years of human history upon this planet, but we have seen more changes in the last fifty years than in all of the other generations put together. Our forefathers lived on a flat, stationary earth and plowed their ground with a wooden stick. Until recently most of the work of the world has been done by the feeble muscle power of men and animals. And yet until our recent knowledge explosion got under way very little real progress had taken place in all of that long period.

Some two thousand years ago Julius Caesar went to his place of government in a chariot drawn by horses. Eighteen hundred years later George Washington went to be inaugurated President of the United States by exactly the same means. In programming the world's temporal existence, God gave it a time allotment of seven thousand years — one thousand years to represent each of the seven days of creation. (See D&C 77:7) The first four thousand years began at the fall of Adam and ended at the birth of Christ. To this has been added the 1970 years that have passed since that time. Therefore, we are now living in the year of the world 5,970, which places us very late in the Saturday evening of the world's history. The seventh one thousand years, which may be about to begin, has been set apart as the earth's Millennium or the world's sabbath. This will be ushered in by the glorious second coming of Christ. He will come to cleanse the earth of its wickedness and to make possible his millennial reign of peace and good will. During this most glorious of the seven one-thousand-year periods Christ will reign personally upon the earth. The mortal affairs of this earth will all be finished up during this period. The children of God will be cleansed, educated, and bound together in families so that the earth can be celestialized.

We are now living in the most momentous times. One of the signs that was to immediately precede the final winding-up scene was this great increase that is now taking place in the world's knowledge. The ancient prophets all foresaw our day. Isaiah almost lived in our time. In his vision of our day he was undoubtedly watching our airplanes out of his window when he said: "Who are these that fly as the clouds and are as doves at the windows?" He said: "They shall mount up on eagles' wings." (Isa. 40:31)

God gave Daniel a vision of the wonders and miracles of our day and told him about many of the things that should immediately precede the second coming of the Savior of the world. Among other things he said: "But thou, O Daniel, shut up the words, and seal the book, even to the time of the end: many shall run to and fro, and knowledge shall be increased." (Dan. 12:4) And what a tremendous increase it has been! Most books of science written just fifteen years ago are now out of date. New discoveries and improvements are going forward at such a rate that even the greatest men have trouble just keeping up. It has been said that of all the scientists who have ever lived in the world 80 percent of them are alive today. All evidence points to the additional fact that an entirely new world is now just on the brink of discovery. Even when I was born, the Wright Brothers had not yet made their famous sixty-second flight at Daredevil Hill in Kittyhawk, North Carolina. Then there were no airplanes, no radios, no television sets, no iceless refrigerators, no wonder drugs, no giant earth-moving machines, and no atomic power. The horseless carriage and the telephone were then just struggling to be born. In these last few years we have learned to fly through space faster than sound. We travel in the depths of the sea and sail under the polar ice cap.

Then came that zenith day on July 20, 1969, when two mortal men roared out across space and landed on the moon. Then they climbed down out of their landing craft, and for the first time the footprints of mortal men appeared upon the surface of the moon.

Some time ago in a government laboratory I saw some large colored pictures of the moon. I was particularly interested in the pictures of the footprints that the astronauts left upon the lunar surface. The moon is a dead body. God gave the moon no topsoil, no atmosphere, no rain fall, no oceans, no streams filled with fish. Because there wasn't enough atmosphere to wave the American flag, artificial supports had to be provided to give it its customary appearance of vitality and animation. Even the breath that was breathed by Mr. Armstrong and Mr. Aldrin had to be taken with them. Because there is no rainfall and no air movements the footprints of the astronauts will probably remain there unchanged for a very long period.

It has been said that no one can pass through a room without leaving some evidence of his having been there. The evidence may consist of only a scent or a fallen hair or a footprint, and yet something will witness that a particular person has been in that particular room. Human footprints may always show that Mr. Armstrong and Mr. Aldrin have walked on the moon.

This important event marks a very special milestone in our history. President Nixon has said that our landing on the moon is the greatest event that has ever taken place since the creation of the earth. And in some ways this may be so. However, Billy Graham has called our attention to some other important events that have taken place upon this earth. It was wonderful for our astronauts to spend two hours and fourteen minutes on the moon, but it was much more important when the Son of God spent some 33 years walking upon our earth. He left some more important footprints that will never be erased, as these were made in the minds and hearts of people.

When Jesus said, "Follow me," he meant that we should follow him in his faith, and in his love, and in his religion, and in his righteousness as we make some of our own footprints. We often see a young child on a snowy day trying to step in the footprints of his parent. It is a pretty good idea to regularly walk in the footprints of the right kind of people. Great highways have been built up as one generation has followed the trails made by those who have gone before, but great characters, productive personalities, and profitable businesses have also been built that way.

Example is the way that we acquire most of our manners, our morals, our convictions, our enthusiasms, as well as our sins. Some people choose to follow the communists, some follow the hippies, some follow dope addicts, and some follow Satan.

The moon has served us long and well in its assigned task of ruling over the night and reflecting light to the earth. Apparently God did not intend it as a place for human habitation. It is interesting to picture what our good earth must have been like in the beginning. The scripture says: "And the earth was without form and void; and darkness was upon the face of the deep. . . ." (Gen. 1:2)

We might try to imagine what it must have been when that brooding, unbroken darkness covered the earth. And then picture the change that took place when God's spirit moved upon the face of the waters. And then in that great march of progress God first said: "Let there be light." God set the sun to rule the day and the moon to rule the night. He gave our earth its great laws, its seasons, its utilities, its beauty, its wonderful natural resources. He gave us our refreshing streams and beautiful oceans, our fertile topsoil, our life-giving atmosphere, and our wonderful food supply in all of its variety. What a thrill even God must have felt when he looked out upon our earth and called it very good!

God granted Job a kind of flash-back into his own ante-mortal life when the foundations of the earth were being laid and "when the morning stars sang together and all the sons of God shouted for joy." (See Job 38:1-7) What a tremendous prospect it must have been to us then to be able to look forward to living upon this wonderful new earth! It was created by the Son of God under the direction of his Father. What a great compliment it was to us when he himself chose to spend his mortality upon our earth!

He was the Creator of the earth, but he also came here in his official capacity of Savior of the world and the Redeemer of men. As he walked the dusty roads of this earth, he was also subject to its laws. His footprints showed us the way to righteousness. He organized his Church here with the important intention that we should all belong to it and be faithful in it. He announced the great natural doctrines that should govern our lives as well as his own, but most of the wonders of our lives and the earth itself are in the future. God instituted the universal resurrection and established the principle of eternal progression. He has made known that a thousand-year Millennium of peace and good will is about to begin. This will be the period when the earth and its people will receive their final preparation for celestial glory. In the meantime the most important thing we need to learn is to walk in his steps.

God first gave his life-giving and life-saving commandments to Adam, and he has also instructed all of the prophets since that time. Some 3,460 years ago he came down onto the top of Mount Sinai in a kind of a space suit made of fire. The scripture says: "And it came to pass on the third day in the morning, that there were thunders and lightnings, and a thick cloud upon the mount, and the voice of the trump exceeding loud; so that all the people in the camp trembled. . . . And Mount Sinai was altogether on a smoke, because the Lord descended upon it in fire: and the smoke thereof ascended as the smoke of a furnace, and the whole mount quaked greatly." (Exo. 19:16-18) As one of those evidences that he had been here, he left a set of laws, which if followed would make our earth God's paradise. In the meridian of time the Savior walked upon our earth for thirty-three years. And what a significant compliment it was that he should bless our earth with his example! While he was here he made the necessary atonement for our sins, making our own eternal lives possible on condition of our repentance. Many other heavenly messengers have also come to our earth on different occasions and have enlarged these spiritual paths through our minds by giving us additional instructions and directions.

In one of our greatest known examples of space travel a whole multitude of angels came from heaven to Bethlehem on that long-ago Christmas night to celebrate the birth of the Son of God. In carrying out the plan of God many other visitors had come before his birth, and many others have been here since. Moses and Elias visited with Jesus upon a high mountain in the presence of Peter, James, and John. Heavenly messengers attended Jesus during his suffering and death. After his resurrection and ascension into heaven, he paid a post-mortal visit to the people in ancient America, where he organized his Church among them and gave them comparable instruction to that given to the people upon the eastern continent.

However, following his ministry a great universal apostasy from God took place upon both continents. The people transgressed his laws, changed his ordinances, and broke the everlasting covenant that they had made with him. This transgression was followed by the dark ages. For a long period of years the authority to minister in the name of the Lord was not upon the earth. However, some wonderful events have recently taken place. In the early spring of 1820 in upper New York state one of the greatest of all our earth's experiences occurred when God the Father and his son Jesus Christ reappeared upon this earth to re-establish among men a belief in God — the God of creation, the God of Sinai, the God of Calvary, the God of ancient America, the God of the latter days, and the God of our own future. As of old, missionaries are now going out two by two without pay to warn the people, and many great events are even now trembling on the very edge of fulfillment. And we now look forward to that breath-taking experience when he will come again with his holy angels in flaming fire, tremendous power, and great glory to cleanse the earth, execute judgment, and to establish his everlasting kingdom upon the earth. Then all who are fortunate enough to be here will be those who have walked in the spiritual footprints that the Son of God has made upon our earth.

The Gospel Principles

ONE OF THE MOST important words in our language is a wonderful little word called *principle*. The dictionary says that a principle is a general truth. It is a fundamental law. It represents some comprehensive doctrine that is used to guide human behavior. A principle is related to a character trait, and out of a collection of these one may build the cathedral of his success.

Some of the close relatives of the word principle are some words such as maxim, law, truth, or axiom. A principle is an elementary proposition. It is a fundamental assumption. The dictionary says that "a principle is a constituent part which characterizes a substance or gives it its essential properties." With a set of good principles one may form a code of conduct. The best way to any success is to have for that accomplishment a good set of sound, wise, solid, guiding principles.

It is also by good principles that our own lives should be directed. What our individual principles are will determine what we ourselves will become. We recognize some people as living according to high principles, and then there are other kinds of people who live by low principles. There are some people who are unprincipled. Confusion and failure are the characteristics of those who live by their feelings without any well-defined set of fundamental laws to guide them.

Some salesmen try to develop their success by working on the level of sales *methods*, but the greatest salesmen work on the higher level of *principle*. When one understands and is guided by the basic fundamental, unchangeable laws of industry, truth, fairness, faith, and adequate preparation, then selecting successful methods becomes a far more simple matter. One's principles are always of primary importance. As it is much easier to make a salesman out of a man than it is to make a man out of a salesman, similarly, it is easier to make a good husband out of a man than it is to make a good man out of a husband. In any department of success one starts out with a great advantage when he has a good fundamental basic character and when his life is regulated by these great natural success factors. In explaining his success in developing his people, the Prophet Joseph Smith once said: "I teach them correct principles and they govern themselves."

Dr. Henry C. Link once said that "Nothing puts so much order into human life as to live by a set of sound principles." If one were going to be an electrician, he should understand the laws of electricity. One who expects to be a mathematician should understand the principles of mathematics. And every child of God should understand the principles of manhood and righteousness. We give credit to Sir Isaac Newton for discovering gravity, but actually gravity has not yet been discovered. What Newton discovered was merely some of the laws of gravity. They are those unchanging principles on which gravity works. For example, Newton discovered this interesting phenomenon that any two material bodies, if free to move, will be accelerated toward each other. This action is due to an unseen, unfelt force of attraction between the bodies. Newton's law of gravitation states that this force is proportional to the product of the masses of the two bodies and inversely proportional to the square of the distance between them. This law has a great significance in our world. We have an even more important law of attraction interacting between people and God. There is also a great attraction between some people and Satan. We need to understand these principles that like attracts like and that opposites repel each other. When we understand all of the principles involved, then we ourselves may attract an unlimited amount of success and love and righteousness and the favor of God. We ourselves gravitate toward the conditions represented by those basic fundamental principles that we believe in and live by. The author may be God or Satan.

As we plan our own success we ought to remember that God has prepared a wonderful set of basic principles for our guidance as groups and as individuals. We can use these principles more effectively and more profitably as we increase our understanding of them and our belief in them. It would be very helpful to us if we governed ourselves by that very important set of principles known as the principles of the gospel of Jesus Christ. They are the basic fundamental laws of life on which all of our eternal success depends. They govern every department of our existence and have special application in social and religious areas. The principles of the gospel involve our basic standards of honesty, morality, sobriety, faith, worship, fairness, reason, and integrity. To live in ignorance or defiance of these natural laws means certain failure. For example, the farmer who plants his corn in the chill of the December blizzard may not expect to get the same kind of harvest as if his planting is done in the warmth of the May sunshine. We also need to know about the laws of health and the laws of industry. We should be familiar with the laws governing the mental and spiritual realms.

Some 3,460 years ago God gave us those fundamental laws called the Ten Commandments. In the meridian of time, Jesus enlarged upon these principles as he talked to people about faith, repentance, baptism, and the gift of the Holy Ghost. He also gave us more instruction about honesty, integrity, courage, morality, industry, righteousness, obedience, patience, charity, love, temperance, humility, and diligence. God has decreed a principle called eternal progression which concerns the future everlasting lives of all his children. We sometimes think that our lives will be finished at death, but actually they are then only beginning.

Jesus is our example to go by. He was born here as we were. He lived by every one of those great principles that he taught. He died as we will sometime die, and he was resurrected and glorified as a part of God's great program of eternal, everlasting life. If we break the law and allow ourselves to become the victims of ignorance, disobedience, and sin, or if we violate those principles on which our exaltation depends, we lose the attached blessings. In introducing the Word of Wisdom to the people, the Lord said that it was "given for a principle with a promise." (D&C 89:3)

But all of the Lord's promises are based on how well we obey his principles. He has said: "I, the Lord, am bound when ye do what I say; but when ye do not what I say, ye have no promise." (D&C 82:10) Again he said: "I command and men obey not; I revoke and they receive not the blessing." (D&C 58:32)

The Lord's promises are immutable and unchangeable. He said: ". . . inasmuch as those whom I commanded were faithful they should be blessed with a multiplicity of blessings. But

inasmuch as they were not faithful they were nigh unto cursing."
(D&C 104:2-3) The best way to succeed is to make the principles of the gospel the principles of our lives and then live
by our convictions, as our success and happiness throughout
eternity depend upon our principles. As our obedience to them
brings success and joy to us, so our sins heap upon us the most
serious oppressions. God has instituted a great program of repentance, reformation, restitution, and forgiveness by which we may
be constantly turning our lives upward to more worthwhile
things. By practicing the principles of repentance leading to
forgiveness, we may permanently cleanse ourselves of all evil
and failure and arrive at a condition of "pure" joy and "pure"
success and "pure" good.

It might help to free us from the contamination of evil,
wrong, selfishness, and hate to examine the negative side of this
proposition and think about what a human life might become,
if it went on forever without cleansing itself.

In his youth, King David was called a man after God's
own heart, but during his life he wronged many people, including himself. Two of his sins violated major commandments.
In one of his Psalms, David tells us what his life had become
because he had gone to a point where forgiveness had become
very difficult. He said:

O Lord, rebuke me not in thy wrath:
Neither chasten me in thy hot displeasure.

For thine arrows stick fast in me,
And thy hand presseth me sore.

There is no soundness in my flesh because of thine anger;
Neither is there any rest in my bones because of my sin.
For mine iniquities are gone over mine head:
As an heavy burden they are too heavy for me.

My wounds stink and are corrupt because of my foolishness.

I am troubled; I am bowed down greatly;
I go mourning all the day long.

For my loins are filled with a loathsome disease:
And there is no soundness in my flesh.

I am feeble and sore broken.
I have roared by reason of the disquietness of my heart.

Lord, all my desire is before thee; and my
Groaning is not hid from thee.

My heart panteth, my strength faileth me:
As for the light of mine eyes, it also is gone from me.

My lovers and my friends stand aloof from my sore;
And my kinsmen stand afar off.

They also that seek after my life lay snares for me:
And they that seek my hurt speak mischievous things.
And imagine deceits all the day long.

(Psa. 38:1-12)

From the top of Mount Sinai God gave Ten Commandments. In his sermon on the Mount, Jesus gave nine Beatitudes. Suppose that we make up our own list of gospel principles and give our faith a feeling of completeness by giving specific attention to each one. If we don't have all of the gospel principles available to our minds in one place, we may overlook some very important considerations. That is, much of the benefit of our lives would be lost if we overlooked that tremendously important principle of eternal marriage, wherein it has been decreed that the family is to be the basic unit of society forever. What important possibilities are contained here so far as association, love, education, and happiness are concerned!

There is a gospel principle concerning salvation for the dead by which the members of God's family will be brought together, purified, sanctified, and united forever. No one individual will then be unimportant. We have the principle of continual revelation from God whereby we are kept informed concerning the things that we should do. Then we have that tremendous principle of vicarious help. This centers in the atonement of Christ, where our sins may be blotted out and we can also help others. There are principles of order in God's kingdom involving the proper authority in the Church and how it should be delegated and used. God has also ordained that everyone of his children shall have a literal bodily resurrection from the dead, and we should understand the principles involved therein. As a final reward for his children, God has ordained three great degrees of glory with many intermediate stations to correspond with the various degrees of merit that our lives are entitled to.

To the Corinthians, Paul said: "There are also celestial bodies, and bodies terrestrial: but the glory of the celestial is one, and the glory of the terrestrial is another. There is one glory of the sun, and another glory of the moon, and another glory of the stars: for one star differeth from another star in glory. So also is the resurrection of the dead. . . ." (I Cor. 15:40-42)

There are also principles involving punishment and the purification of spirits. This makes possible that only a very few will eventually be lost. Speaking of those Sons of Perdition who have committed the unpardonable sin, the Lord said:

"These are they who shall go away into the lake of fire and brimstone, with the devil and his angels —

"And the only ones on whom the second death shall have any power;

"Yea, verily, the only ones who shall not be redeemed in the due time of the Lord, after the sufferings of his wrath.

"For all the rest shall be brought forth by the resurrection of the dead, through the triumph and the glory of the Lamb, who was slain, who was in the bosom of the Father before the worlds were made.

"And this is the gospel, the glad tidings, which the voice out of the heavens bore record unto us." (D&C 76:36-40)

A knowledge of these great principles will not only bless us here, but it will continue to bless us forever. As the Lord has said: "Whatever principle of intelligence we attain unto in this life, it will rise with us in the resurrection. And if a person gains more knowledge and intelligence in this life through his diligence and obedience than another, he will have so much the advantage in the world to come." (D&C 130:18-19) And so we return again to this great idea that nothing puts so much order into human life as to live by a set of sound principles.

Great Expectations

THERE IS AN INTERESTING word in our language called *expectation*. It stands for one of our most important attitudes of success. A strong expectation even goes beyond the function of mere belief and gives a more powerful pitch to whatever accomplishment we contemplate. Even as people, we become about what our expectations make us. An ancient American prophet once said that God grants unto every man according to his desires. Our desires are closely entwined with our expectations, and both are parts of our finest constellation of success traits. A great expectation includes an intense hope and a real anticipation that our clearly outlined future objectives may be attained. It involves a love of, and a longing for, the things expected. It is made up of a vital hope that the desire will be realized, and it has a substantial self-belief to help bring it about.

There is an ancient Chinese tradition to the effect that if you went into a Chinese home and admired some particular article, you may find that the Chinese would wrap it up and send it to you as a present. They believed that when you admired it, that made it yours. Life has a program that is exactly like that. Whatever we truly love and admire, we get. If we love honesty we get honesty; if we love industry we get industry; if we admire great faith in God, life wraps it up and sends it to us free of charge.

Charles Dickens made an important contribution to our success many years ago when he wrote his book entitled *Great Expectations*. Across its pages he shows us those human ambitions and motivations that operate in people's lives on various levels of expectation. The story itself is centered in the experience of a little orphan boy by the name of Phillip Perip. As he grew up under the most humble circumstances, he was called "Little Pip." But his little education, his little opportunities, and his little abilities were enlarged by his great expectations. In fact, the size and quality of one's expectations always exert a powerful influence in every field of human interest.

We sometimes speak of the "expectation of life." The average length of life as experienced by others is used as an expectation of our own possibility. Nineteen hundred years ago in Jerusalem the life expectancy at birth was 19 years. By George Washington's day in America it had been increased to 35 years. When I was born it was 48 years, but the baby that was born in an American hospital this morning has a life expectancy of 70 years. We have greatly increased our expectation so far as life's length is concerned. But life comes in four dimensions. There is the length of life, or how long we live; there is the breadth of life, or how interestingly we live; there is the depth of life, or how much we live; and then we have that more or less mysterious fourth dimension (corresponding to the fourth dimension in space), which is the purpose of life, or why we live. The greatest commodity in the universe is life, and we get life's total volume by multiplying its dimensions. That is, we multiply how long, by how interestingly, by how much, by how come, to get our total score. And we can get a more powerful set of expectations for each dimension by watching life as it is actually being lived and learning to understand those forces by which our success may be turned upward or downward.

Someone has told of standing before a lighted house at night when the lights were all ablaze and the shades were all undrawn, so that he could see into every corner of space and observe every reaction to life as it took place on every level of accomplishment. The house's occupants are seen at their dinner, at their prayers, and in their various other duties, taking them from one floor to another.

Now suppose that we draw aside the mental shades of life and shine the lights of our comprehension into every corner of human action and reaction. We may find that some of the characteristics on which our life's successes depend are small and poorly developed. Some of our personality traits may appear to be withered and unpromising, and our expectations are affected accordingly. It is largely our expectations that determine whether we are traveling toward a higher or a lower floor in life. We can get some extra zest into our expectations by studying the great literature. We can watch the most accomplished authors draw aside the shades and make us familiar with those techniques by which "a Little Pip" can climb to greatness and nobility, merely by increasing the effectiveness of his expectations.

The world's finest vision of beauty is to see a great person living at his best. The human form and personality have always been used by artists and sculptors as models for their finest masterpieces. Imagine the human countenance ablaze with joy, radiance, color, purity, faith, vision, and magnificence! It is said that God is such a glorious personage that no mortal unquickened by his Spirit can stand in his presence and live. God has given us a program where our increased dimensions may include resurrection and immortality. To reach our divine destiny means that we may be celestialized, glorified, and made beautiful, successful, and happy beyond all imagination.

Each of us has been created in God's image and endowed with a full set of his potentialities. The apostle Paul says that we now see through a glass darkly, but sometime God will draw those shades of darkness aside that all may see what we have become. When his searchlight shines upon our souls, we will desire to see a full maturity for the grace, love, righteousness, and nobility, the seeds of which he has already implanted in us. What a thrilling satisfaction to look forward to the privilege of living with God and beholding those Godly traits of honor, courage, ambition, and faith operating at the maximum in our souls! The apostle Paul has said that faith is the substance of things hoped for and the evidence of things not seen.

Our great expectations can carry us beyond the limits of faith, and hope, or even love. Many people have faith without works. One may have a hope for wealth with no thought or intention of ever attaining it, or one may love greatness but feel that it is beyond his reach. But in addition to these wonderful traits, when one has some "great expectations," he must be ready to do whatever is necessary to bring about the projected accomplishment.

Several years ago I knew a young man who had some great expectations about becoming a medical doctor like his father. He loved learning, and he had a strong desire for that skill necessary to produce health in sick people. He had a strong appetite to serve and a full confidence in his own potentiality. This was all supported by a great expectation and a complete determination to do whatever was necessary to reach the objective.

He felt bigger than any obstacle that could bar his way, and stronger than any temptation that could draw him from his course. He had an unshakable expectation that he would never get off schedule in becoming a great medical man. The power of his expectation pushed every doubt aside. It overcame every fear and eliminated every weakness. The compass of his expectations always pointed straight toward its star. The beckoning lights that distracted smaller people and won away the affections of those who were less resolute had no power over him. He was constant and true to an unwavering purpose that never varied, either in sunshine or in storm, and he is now one of the most competent of medical men.

The most productive area for great expectations is in the field of the spirit. The purpose of God's original endowment was that we might become "even as he is." This objective will allow for no little plans nor tolerate any weak compromises with failure or wrong. God has placed no limitations upon our success, and we must permit none of the fruits of ignorance, disbelief, indecision, or indifference in our personal religious programs. Rather our souls should be surcharged with those great expectations that will assure our success and will please God.

Among Christians the seventh Sunday after Easter is known as "Expectation Sunday" or "Whitsuntide." This is included in "Expectation Week" and commemorates a part of that ten-day period between Ascension Day and the day of Pentecost. On Ascension Day, Jesus said to his disciples: ". . . ye shall be witnesses unto me both in Jerusalem and in all Judea, and in Samaria, and unto the uppermost part of the earth." (Acts 1: 8) In his final commission to them he said: "Go ye therefore, and teach all nations, baptizing them in the name of the Father, and of the Son, and of the Holy Ghost: Teaching them to observe all things whatsoever I have commanded you: and, lo, I am with you alway, even unto the end of the world." (Matt. 28:19-20) Then he said: ". . . behold, I send the promise of my Father upon you: but tarry ye in . . . Jerusalem, until ye be endued with power from on high." (Luke 24:49) He told them that they should receive this power when the Holy Ghost should come upon them. (Acts 1:8) Then as he lifted up his hands and blessed them, he ascended up into heaven.

His disciples returned to Jerusalem with great joy and spent the next ten days in expectation, anticipation, and preparation. With prayer, exhortation and supplication some 120 of the followers of Jesus waited for the day of Pentecost. This day is sometimes now referred to as Whitsunday or White Sunday, because of the white baptismal robes that are sometimes worn in commemoration of this historic day. Luke describes the experiences of Expectation Sunday by saying, "And when the day of Pentecost was fully come, they were all with one accord in one place. And suddenly there came a sound from heaven as of a rushing mighty wind, and it filled all the house where they were sitting. And there appeared unto them cloven tongues like as of fire, and it sat upon each of them. And they were all filled with the Holy Ghost, and began to speak with other tongues as the Spirit gave them utterance." (Acts 2:2-4)

Some great speeches were made about the resurrected Savior, and the people also discussed their own assignment of carrying on his work. A great group had assembled from many nations, the members of which spoke different tongues. But on Expectation Sunday they all understood the messages in their own language. Then the people were pricked in their hearts and said to the apostles, ". . . Men and brethren what shall we do? Then Peter said to them, Repent, and be baptized every one of you in the name of Jesus Christ for the remission of sins, and ye shall receive the gift of the Holy Ghost. For the promise is unto you, and unto your children, and to all that are afar off, even as many as the Lord our God shall call. Then they that gladly received his word were baptized: and that same day there were added unto them about three thousand souls." (Acts 2:37-41)

Certainly our own eternal exaltation should be our greatest expectation. As children we used to do a lot of thinking about what we were going to be when we grew up, and we should now have an even greater concern for our eternal welfare.

We should keep in mind that the place where most people fail most miserably is in their expectations. There can be no great expectations for those who can't even believe in God or in their own divine destiny. What dismal expectations must belong to those who accept the Devil's doctrine that says: "Expect nothing so that you will never be disappointed." One without expectations never arrives. A discouraged man is always a weak man. Doubters, weaklings, and sinners do not develop great expectations. A person who is ignorant as to God's laws will always be found working against his own interests. Jesus said: "All things are possible to him that believeth," and we ought to try to understand that fact.

With a personal testimony of the truth and a strong determination in righteousness, we can build enough strength into our expectations to destroy all of our doubts and sins. We can also replace our weaknesses with enough strength to make us what we really expect to be.

A Great Time to Be Alive

MANY YEARS AGO Harry Emerson Fosdick wrote an interesting book en-
titled *It's a Great Time to Be Alive*. He pointed out some of the
miracles and wonders that make our age the most exciting
since creation. We enjoy the highest standard of learning and
the highest standard of living ever known in the world. In
a material way, we live better than any king lived just a hundred
years ago. Any one of us would count it an incredible hardship
to have to live as Solomon lived in all his glory.

However, I suppose that *any* time is a great time to be
alive. The early American philosopher Henry Thoreau says
that we should thank God every day of our lives for the privilege
of having been born. Then he went on to speculate on the
rather unique supposition of what it might have been like if
we had *never* been born, and he pointed out many of the blessings
that we would have missed as a consequence. What Mr. Thoreau
may not have known was that one-third of all the children of
God never were born and never can be born, because under the
leadership of Lucifer, they rebelled against God in their pre-
mortal state and forever forfeited their right to any further progress. Therefore, they must continue eternally as Satan and his
angels with all of their opportunities for growth and happiness cut
off. Some of these unembodied evil spirits appeared to Jesus in his
day, preferring the bodies of swine rather than to have no bodies
at all. I am sure that if we understood their eternal importance
we would prefer the most broken, twisted, unsightly bodies to
no bodies at all. We would have preferred to live in the most
benighted, backward times, under the most unfavorable conditions than not to have lived at all. How great our gratitude
should be to live in the most important age in the greatest
nation, under the most favorable conditions ever known in the
long history of human life! We live in a day when we may have
all the education that we desire.

The first thing that Adam and Eve were asked to decide
when they were placed in the Garden of Eden was whether or

not they would eat the fruit of the tree of knowledge of good and evil. After they had eaten, God said: "The man is now become as one of us to know good and evil." And I would just like to point out in passing that the right kind of knowledge still tends to have that effect upon people. It still tends to make men and women become as God. A flaming sword was placed in the Garden of Eden to guard the tree of life, but fortunately for us there is no flaming sword guarding the tree of knowledge, and each of us may eat to his heart's content.

We live in a day when the knowledge of medicine gives us strong bodies and clear minds. Since George Washington's day our life expectancy has been exactly doubled, but the length is not the only dimension of life that has been increased. There has also been an improvement in its breadth and its depth, and yet no one is satisfied.

The only kind of life that is permanently satisfactory is eternal life. God holds out the promise that if we live according to his directions we may someday qualify to eat the fruit from the tree of eternal life. God has said that his greatest gift to us is eternal life and he has made clear how it may be attained.

Jesus announced his own mission by saying, "I came that ye might have life, and have it more abundantly." Life is the greatest commodity in the world, and it is the one thing over which God himself has maintained exclusive control. With all our boasted wisdom and science, no one has ever yet been able to produce even a single life cell. The greatest combination of scientists cannot make even one live kernel of corn. All of the medical men in the world put together are unable to produce one live red corpuscle. But God's ultimate objective for us is that someday we may merit the thrilling blessing of an exalted, eternal life. This is the kind of life that God himself has. God has designed and ordained a natural development process for us called eternal progression. If we follow his plan the offspring of God may eventually become like the parents.

Our life's purpose is not just to live long, but to live interestingly, constructively, and well. Success in life is not just what we can get out of it but what we can become by it. Branch Rickey, the famous baseball manager, was once asked what was his greatest day in baseball. He said: "I don't know, I haven't had it yet." And certainly our greatest days are those that we haven't yet had.

William James said the greatest use of life was to expend it for something that outlasts it. Our present lesser days provide the time to prepare for our greater future days. The best use of mortal life is to exchange its energy and discipline for something more important and more permanent. The tragedy of our world is the unpleasant fact that most people have traded their mortality for some mere fraction of life rather than the eternal abundance mentioned by Jesus. Frequently we actually use our time here to bring misery and unhappiness upon ourselves for both here and hereafter. Jesus himself compared our sinfulness with that of those people who lived in the days of Noah. In the creation of our giant crime waves, our vandalisms, and our moral decadence, we are effectively imitating our antediluvian friends who brought a watery destruction upon themselves. Yet in spite of our very serious delinquencies the scriptures still foretell a very bright future for our earth and those who may qualify to live upon it eternally.

After God had created the beautiful paradise called earth, with its peace and plenty, he called it very good. Then came the fall of man and the accompanying curse upon the earth. Deserts and waste places began to appear; a destructive enmity developed involving both man and the beasts. The status of our sphere was lowered from a terrestrial to a telestial rank. During the some six thousand years since that time, our earth has operated in its fallen state. It has continually brought forth thorns, thistles, and noxious weeds, while sin and wickedness have flourished upon its face. At the end of the six thousand years corresponding to the six days of creation, the earth's Sabbath will begin. It will be initiated by the second coming of Jesus Christ to cleanse the earth of the unhappiness and death that have been its chief characteristics.

At the second coming of Jesus Christ, while the earth is being cleansed by fire, those who are ripened in iniquity will be destroyed. The governments of the earth will be replaced by the perfect rule of Christ, who will reign as King of kings and Lord of lords for a thousand years.

During this millennial period, both mortal and immortal people will live upon the earth. The earth itself will be raised to the status of a terrestrial sphere, and it will again be a beautiful paradise like it was before man's sin placed the curse upon it. What a great time this will be to be alive! Then those who have survived the cleansing will live in peace, and their children and grandchildren will grow up in righteousness. Their bodies will be immune to disease, and their minds will be filled with health and vitality. Ignorance will be done away with and the knowledge of the Lord will cover the earth, even as the waters cover the deep. Sin, which has always caused so much trouble, will be done away with, and we will be free from all its sorrow and unhappiness. Then there will be no wars, no crime waves, no delinquency, and no hate. There will be only love, peace, and righteousness everywhere.

Even now what a wonderful sensation it gives us to be at our best and to always feel good and know that everything is going well. With great happiness and joy, mortals and immortals will work together in the temples to perfect their family relationships and complete the other necessary work pertaining to the salvation of the human family. During this one-thousand-year period, children will be born, grow up, marry, and live to old age. Then they will pass through a change equivalent to death and resurrection in the twinkling of an eye. Crops will be planted, harvested, and eaten; industries will be expanded; great cities will be built; education will be fostered; men will continue to care for their own needs, handle their own affairs, and enjoy the full blessings of their God-given free agency. Through the prophet Zephaniah, the Lord has said that he will return to us a pure language, and we will live in a state of peace, happiness, harmony, and beauty beyond our fondest imaginations. We will have a part in the government and will be priests and kings unto God and will reign with him for a thousand years. What a great time this will be to be alive, and what a challenging thought that we may help to bring this condition about!

About the time following this period, John the Revelator says, "And when the thousand years are expired, Satan shall be loosed out of his prison, and shall go out to deceive the nations which are in the four quarters of the earth, God and Magog, to gather them together to battle: the number of whom is as the sands of the sea." (Rev. 20:7-8)

Then will come the great battle in which Satan shall be cast out forever; then will come the end of our earth as we now know it; then will come God's final judgment upon all men. John said: "And I saw a new heaven and a new earth: for the first heaven and the first earth were passed away; and there was no more sea. And I John saw the holy city, new Jerusalem, coming down from God out of heaven, prepared as a bride adorned for her husband. And I heard a great voice out of heaven saying, Behold, the tabernacle of God is with men, and he shall dwell with them, and they shall be his people, and God himself shall be with them, and be their God. And God shall wipe away all tears from their eyes; and there shall be no more death, neither sorrow, nor crying, neither shall there be any more pain: for the former things are passed away. And he that sat upon the throne said, Behold, I make all things new. . . . He that over-cometh shall inherit all things; and I will be his God, and he shall be my son." (Rev. 21:1-7)

After the earth's millennium the work of our world will have been completed. Satan will be disposed of forever — the final judgments will have been made, and the earth will again be raised in status, this time to a celestial sphere, and it will become the permanent abode of those who are qualified as celestial beings. About this situation the Lord has said in our own day: ". . . he that endureth in faith and doeth my will, the same shall overcome, and shall receive an inheritance upon the earth when the day of transfiguration shall come; when the earth shall be transfigured, even according to the pattern which was shown unto mine apostles upon the mount; of which account the fulness ye have not yet received." (D&C 63:20-21)

The celestial order of life is that order to which God him-self belongs. When Charles W. Penrose was a member of the First Presidency of the Church, he wrote an article about this earth's role as the celestial abode of those worthy to live here. He said: "The earth will die like its products but it will be quick-ened again and resurrected to celestial glory." It had been born of the water and will also be born of the spirit purified by fire, from the corruption that once defiled it, developed into its perfections as one of the family of worlds, fit for the Creator's presence. All its latent light awakened into scintillating action, it will move up into its place among the orbs governed by celes-tial time shining like a sea of glass, mingled with fire, every tint and color of the heavenly bow radiating from its surface. The ransomed of the Lord will dwell upon it. The highest beings of the ancient orbs will visit it. The Garden of God will again adorn it. The heavenly government will prevail in every part. Jesus will reign as its king. The river of life will flow from the regal throne. The tree of life whose leaves were for the healing of the nations will flourish upon the banks of the heavenly stream, and its golden fruit will be free for the white-robed throngs that they may eat and live forever. This perfected earth with its saved inhabitants will then be presented to the Eternal Father as the finished work of Christ.

Orson Pratt said: "Who, in looking upon the earth as it ascends in the scale of the universe, does not desire to keep pace with it? Then when it shall be cleansed and take its place among the dazzling orbs of the blue vault of heaven, shining forth in all of the splendors of celestial glory, he may find himself proportionately advanced in intellectual and moral excellence. O man, remember the future destiny and glory of the earth, and secure thine everlasting inheritance upon it, that when it shall be glorious you may be glorious also." And again we might say, "What a great time to be alive!"

Half-A-Minder

IN 1967 DR. NORMAN VINCENT PEALE wrote a book entitled *Enthusiasm Makes the Difference*. In it he describes some of those important situations, the good of which may be made negotiable in other lives. To clearly understand the successes and failures of others teaches us how we can more effectively adjust and adorn our own lives. Dr. Peale is interested in the fundamental causes of certain human responses, and he has helped a lot of people make their lives more effective by learning from each other. Over the years he has spoken to a large number of conventions of business people. On one of these occasions after he had gone to his room, a woman called him on the telephone. She asked his permission to bring her husband up to his room for a personal interview. Far into the night they all discussed the husband's problems.

It appeared that for a long time this woman had been trying to help her husband to be a little more successful. However, this had not worked very well, and her present attitude indicated that she was about at the end of her rope. Evidently her husband was a fine person, but he had never done very well, either in his business or in their home, and apparently his wife was about ready to give up. As a kind of last resort she had brought him to see Dr. Peale with a hope that he might be able to help him. She said: "I wish you could do something for Charlie." Dr. Peale found Charlie to be a pleasant, easy-going, likeable person, but he had not disciplined himself very well and certainly he was not highly motivated. While he had not done very well in his sales job, his firm had been patient with him, for in spite of his shortcomings, they recognized that he had great potential. Dr. Peale attempted to help by meeting with him at intervals over a few months.

As they got better acquainted, Dr. Peale said: "I noticed that Charlie had one stock phrase that he used continually. It was so repetitive that it gave the impression of a phonograph needle stuck in a groove in the record." As each good suggestion was being made, Charlie would say, "You know, I have half-a-mind to do something about that," or "I have a half-a-mind to investigate that." Dr. Peale said, "Once when I was urging him to think a little more positively, he said, 'You know, I have half-a-mind to try that.' " Finally, Dr. Peale said to him, "Charlie, I know what's the matter with you. You're a half-a-minder. Everything you think of doing, you have only half-a-mind to do it."

One of the first requirements for any success is to understand that the human mind is the greatest invention since creation and is capable of any success. However, just half-a-mind is not very effective. To be at one's best, he needs to have a whole mind and to have it all on the job at the same time. It should also be a sound mind and a balanced mind and a positive mind and an enthusiastic mind. Any real accomplishment requires a mind that has been fully made up, fully disciplined, effectively focused, powerfully motivated, and set on fire with a great purpose and a full enthusiasm. When the mind is divided so that it functions only as a fraction, its power is lost. Even an automobile never functions very well when only half of it is in working order. Likewise, even the greatest mind can be corroded by disuse or weakened by indecision. It may lose its balance by wrong thinking, and mental power is soon dissipated when it is not fully disciplined and fully used.

It is an immutable law that when one refuses to use the abilities that God has given him, the abilities are always repossessed. Because the mole didn't use his eyes, nature took away his eyesight. Most people are given a mind that is ample for their needs, but there is none to spare. We are allowed to keep only those abilities that we make good use of. Our mental powers are like the manna that was given to the Israelites in the desert — that which was not used spoiled. However, a whole, fully-used, well-disciplined mind is not only our most productive possession, but its abilities can be increased to suit almost any need. Paul said to the Romans: ". . . be ye transformed by the renewing of your mind. . . ." (Rom. 12:2)

A regenerated mind with perfected vigor is not only able to transform us, but it can transform everything around us. All that Charlie needed was to get his whole mind on the job and fill it with his chosen purpose. That is about the same problem that faces most of us. However, we run serious risks when we allow any part of our great natural endowments to lie unused or undisciplined.

A famous Canadian athletic coach once said that most people both in and out of athletics were hold-outs. What he meant was that so frequently we fail to fully invest ourselves in what we are doing. We have too many reservations about things. We go into life with our fingers crossed, so to speak. And when we hold out on life, life holds out on us. Charlie was a hold-out on his own success. He was a hold-out on his wife, and he was a hold-out on God. He was discrediting his Creator by not making the best use of his God-given abilities. Our Creator has a right to have great pride in his creations, and we dishonor God when we commit such serious hold-out sins as fractional devotion and minimum performance. He is not pleased when we practice marginal morals, half-mindedness, and half-heartedness in those important things that life has given us to do. As Dr. Peale would say: "It is our enthusiasm that makes the difference."

In order to make the best and the most of our lives, the law of success requires us to invest our whole minds and our whole souls and our whole selves in our own destiny. No obstacle can for long obstruct the path of a whole-souled, enthusiastic, industrious, whole-minded person.

The human brain is by long odds the finest piece of equipment ever known. It can bring about any success. It has been said that if you want to hatch out something, just set your mind on it. A prominent British neurophysicist recently said that you could not construct an electric computer for 3 billion dollars, which would be the equivalent of a human brain. After making that kind of an investment in us, God may get a little bit discouraged at the small return he is getting on his money.

The tragedy of life is that so many of us are only half-minders. Woodrow Wilson once said: "The greatest ability of the American people is their ability to resist instruction." Most of us have our full share of that unfortunate talent. Thomas A. Edison once said: "There is nothing a person will not do to avoid thinking." Real thinking is the most unpleasant, disagreeable thing that most of us ever do and yet Solomon said: "As a man thinketh, so is he." I am not quite sure just where that situation leaves us, but if we are what we think, and if we don't think, we may be sure that we have a problem.

The human brain is also the greatest problem-solver. It is the most wonderful creator. Out of the brain of Thomas A. Edison came a whole string of electric lights, phonographs, washing machines, radios, and all sorts of things that no one had ever heard of before. Mr. Edison gave us his own formula for success as "99 percent perspiration and 1 percent inspiration."

We now say that Mr. Edison was a natural-born success, but he was kicked out of school when he was fourteen, because it was thought he was too dumb to learn. However, Mr. Edison disciplined his mind and kept it fully focused until it learned to do whatever he assigned to it. Because Edison was whole-hearted and whole-minded, his actual accomplishment approached his potential about as near as possible. His secret was that each time he used his mind effectively, its powers increased. Our minds are also capable of producing all the attitudes, skills, habits, abilities, and know-how necessary to make our lives outstanding.

The world's greatest literature, as well as its greatest financial successes and scientific miracles, all came from human brains. Someone has said: "I love to lose myself in other men's minds. I love the minds of men, and I love the men who use their minds." A good mind always has a well-developed set of ambitions, and it has usually been definitely "made-up" on all of the important issues with which it is involved. The mind is that part of us that perceives, wills, thinks, decides, solves, resolves, remembers, dreams, reasons, and motivates. It determines moods, regulates dispositions, forms attitudes, creates enthusiasms, and incites desires. But think of the waste when someone becomes a half-a-minder.

The scripture speaks of a related condition when it says that "a double-minded man is unstable in all his ways." (James 1:8) Actually, a double-minded man is only half-a-minder. When one has two things in his mind there can't be more than half-a-mind for each, but a double-mind also loses its focus and its strength as well as its stability.

A certain prize fighter was once badly defeated in the fight ring. After the bout was over, one of his friends was rubbing him with liniment and trying to encourage him by doing a little commiserating. He said to the fighter: "You really did get a pretty bad licking, didn't you?" The fighter said: "Yes, I did, but I now know where I made my mistake; I should have knocked him out in the first round when he was alone."

When any prize fighter procrastinates his success until knocks on his head fill the ring with several phantom opponents, his job becomes much more complicated. In life we also have trouble with a distorted multiple-vision where we are unable to tell which of our opponents are the real ones. Solomon gave us a good idea for avoiding the confusions of life when, in concluding his book of Ecclesiastes, he said: "Let us hear the conclusion of the whole matter: Fear God, and keep his commandments: for this is the whole duty of man." (Eccl. 12:13)

Jesus gave an excellent expression about the weakness caused by our double exposures when he said: "No man can serve two masters." It is pretty difficult to ride two horses in the same race. We heard of a man who tried that once, and just as he was getting everything going to his liking, the horses ran on opposite sides of a tree.

With a double vision, we get involved in too many conflicts of interest where we are fighting ourselves. When one tries to ride two horses or maintain two loyalties or foster two ideologies, he makes himself a half-a-minder. Jesus pointed out that no one could serve God and mammon. One can't look up and down simultaneously; one can't move forward and backward at the same time.

There is one primary purpose for our lives upon this earth and that is to work out our eternal salvation. If we fail in this main objective, then nothing else will ever be of much consequence. As the scripture says, "Whatsoever thy hand findeth to do, do it with thy might. . . ." (Eccl. 9:10) That means to be whole-minded and whole-hearted.

In one of his greatest success pronouncements, the Master said: "Therefore, O ye that embark in the service of God, see that ye serve him with all your heart, might, mind and strength, that ye may stand blameless before God at the last day." (D&C 4:2) The great secret of success in life is to coordinate all our powers into one cooperative effort involving a joint action of the heart, the mind, the might, and the physical strength.

How do we serve God with our hearts? That requires a whole-souled devotion. We can serve him with a full love and an undivided worship. How do we serve God with our mind? That is done through our ability to study, to think, to reason, and to understand. To serve God with one's mind requires a positive mental attitude and an ability to build up a righteous enthusiasm. How do we serve God with our might? That is our physical activity. We are judged according to our works. Then when we get all of these powers coordinated and harnessed, we get success.

Christianity itself is not just a set of ideas; it is a set of coordinated activities. Even faith dies when the works are taken away. Faith has little value by itself. However, by this process of consolidation and joint action, one may make himself whole. He may concentrate all of the elements of personal power into one determined effort. He thereby achieves a wholehearted centrality in his purpose. His effort becomes concentrated, highly focused, and all in one piece, rather than being merely a jumble of many-directioned impulses held loosely together by circumstances. Sometimes we take too much pride in merely knowing that the gospel is true. Satan knows that the gospel is true, but instead of that knowledge helping him, it actually hurts him; whereas the mark of a true follower of Christ is that he fully lives those principles that he believes in. The proverb says: "Wherever thou art, be wholly there."

Jan Smuts, the great South African prime minister, once said that the greatest of all sins is fragmentation, whereas the greatest virtue is wholeism. The great word "holy" came from the word whole, and it means to be complete. It would be pretty hard for anyone to be whole or holy while he was half-minded or half-hearted or half-righteous.

We speak of God as being holy. That is because he is whole. He is complete. He is all wise. He has all knowledge and all power. He is all good. In him there is no darkness, no sin, no indecision, no ignorance, and no indifference. The objective of our lives is that we may someday be holy also. However, before we can be whole, our spirits and our bodies must be inseparably joined together in the resurrection. We must transform our minds by getting rid of our sins and weaknesses. Then we will no longer have half-a-mind, because to be sinful or to be half-a-minder is also to be weak. Above all other things we need to foster our ambition to be whole, to be complete, and to be as God is.

The Head of the House

WE HAVE AN INTERESTING human trait among us that makes us want to be the boss. Almost everyone has a desire to be the leader and march at the head of the procession. We love to command and this helps us to fulfill this natural instinct to feel important. The results of this tendency may be good or bad, depending upon what is done about it. Jesus referred to some of the unfavorable aspects of this trait when speaking about the Scribes and Pharisees. He said: ". . . they *say* and do not. For they bind heavy burdens and grievous to be borne, and lay them on men's shoulders; but they themselves will not move them with one of their fingers. But all their works they do for to be seen of men: they make broad their phylacteries, and enlarge the borders of their garments, and love the uppermost rooms at feasts, and the chief seats in the synagogues, and greetings in the markets, and to be called of men, Rabbi, Rabbi." (Matt. 23:3-7)

Certainly this trait was originally put into human beings for a good purpose. It is a part of that God-given instinct that incites us to go forward, to become better, and to deserve more. We are all supposed to climb upward. Jesus gave us one good way to satisfy this hunger for recognition when he said: "And whosoever of you will be the chiefest, shall be servant of all." (Mark 10:44) The best way to exercise this instinct is to develop our own character and our ability to help others. We should be careful that these natural tendencies are not perverted or abused. One of the best ways to improve our success is to look at ourselves from both the positive and the negative sides.

Some time ago in receiving counsel about their marital problems a man and wife were each asked to prepare a list of the changes that they thought should take place in themselves. At the top of *his* list, and the only thing on *his* list, the husband insisted that he must be recognized as "the head of the house." He thought that this one request was certainly reasonable and small enough, but actually what does it mean? Some 2,500 years ago, Socrates went around Athens telling people to define their terms. It was clear that the success of this marriage depended upon what this man understood his coveted title to mean.

The wife was a devoted church member and the husband was a non-believer. Both had been married before, and each presently had children living in the new home. Both the husband and the wife had full-time jobs. Before their marriage, the wife had owned a little home of her own. When she had married her present husband, he had suggested that she should turn her home in as partial payment on a larger place. Then as "the head of the house," the husband had taken the new title in his own name. He had also insisted that her paycheck should be given to him to be disbursed. Now that they were all one family, he felt that it was his duty to make and enforce the rules governing the conduct of both sets of children. He also felt it was his duty to criticize the wife for the way she had trained her children in the past.

He was opposed to *her* church attendance, on the grounds that any time she spent in church activity was taking away time that belonged to him. He also put an end to the family prayers, blessings on the food, and the religious discussions that had previously been an important part of the family life of his wife and her children. As a consequence of what his step-children thought was a domineering, unfair attitude toward their mother and themselves, a mutual dislike had grown up between the step-father and his household.

Of course, this idea of what his privileges were had some serious problems in it, as people generally do not like to be the victims of impartiality. Ardent church workers do not like to be arbitrarily restricted in their religious worship or their personal affairs by someone who does not believe as they do. The children resented the idea that their mother had to beg to get back a little of her own money for personal needs. This man was doing nothing about this forward, oppressive trait that was upsetting the tranquility of those around him. At first thought, it seemed to the counselor that these differences could easily be worked out, as both parties wanted the marriage to succeed. Certainly the reason, logic, and love that each felt for the other could be counted upon to dissolve their difficulties, but that assumption proved to be an erroneous one.

This man had a deep-seated lust to dominate. This was his third marriage. His two previous wives had divorced him because they couldn't live in the unpleasant mental and spiritual depression that he inflicted upon them. The Lord has indicated that one human mind should not be unjustly dominated by another. He said: "Therefore, it is not right that any man should be in bondage one to another." (D&C 101:79)

This husband also had trouble in his job of supervising the work of several men. They felt that he was too self-centered, which made most of the things he did seem unreasonable and unfair. His problem was a serious inability to be objective about himself. It was very difficult for him to see situations from the point of view of someone else. More or less he worshipped at the shrine of an imagined ability that he did not actually possess. He exemplified the ancient principle that "when a tyrant rules, the people mourn."

It is a good idea to understand that "that king is the strongest when his kingship itself is not so much in evidence." The iron fist is more effective when sheathed in a velvet glove. To bolster his own ego this man claimed that he had always been successful in everything that he had undertaken, and he seems to have a present compulsion to prove that everything he does is right, whether it is or not.

Actually he has made a great many mistakes over the years, which he has refused to recognize. All three of his marriages have been miserable failures — mostly because of his inability for a peaceful co-existence with other people. In the past he has already suffered two nervous breakdowns. And he is presently building up within himself enough conflicts for at least two more. This man could save his health, be happy, and become a great husband if he would make Christ the head of his house. His wife would honor him completely if he carried out his headship under the direction of righteousness. There is an Article of Faith that says: "We claim the privilege of worshiping Almighty God according to the dictates of our own conscience, and allow all men the same privilege, let them worship how, where, or what they may." But this man is unable to grant this privilege to his own wife, though she has made a far greater spiritual development than he has. This causes conflict and unhappiness. Actually this wife wants her husband to be the head of the house, but she doesn't think that he has a proper definition of what that term means. She thinks that his leadership should be characterized by more of God's honesty, fairness, consideration, love, and pleasantness.

Unfortunately her husband doesn't know how to be or to do these things. Most wives want to love their husbands. They want to keep them on a pedestal of respect and admiration. Too many of us keep falling off the pedestal, and sometimes the weight is too heavy for a wife to keep putting her husband back up in the high place where he belongs. Someone said of a husband that he was a good man in the worst sense of the word.

Most children also want to look up to their parents with honor and trust. They want their parents to give them leadership, love, and guidance. Sometimes parents abdicate their high place and abrogate the laws governing parental success. Both the leader and the follower have a difficult time when force, domination, and oppression get too mixed into the leadership formula. Some people would say that the husband mentioned above was mentally ill, and yet it is a self-induced illness that ravages this one part of his life. However, it leaves him able to hold down a responsible job, and he still appears to be above average in intelligence and personality.

The Scribes and Pharisees mentioned by Jesus, as well as this husband, are not the only ones that are having trouble in their efforts to be the boss or to function effectively as the "head of the house." Frequently we are able to get help from the dictionary. It has a long discussion describing the meaning of the word "head." It says that "the head" is the one who occupies the place of leadership, the place of command, the place of honor. It says that the head should stand in about the same relationship to those he leads as his own head does in relation to his other body members.

The head is the headquarters of the intellect, and it should always govern the other members of the body in their own best interests. The head is the center of thought and the source of understanding. When it is said that someone has a good head, it is meant that he has a good mind. He has a good mental balance and a natural aptitude for fairness, kindness, and those other traits that will enable him to effectively coordinate the whole in the best interests of all.

It has frequently been said that occasionally some people lose their heads. Sometimes we lose our tempers. It might also mean that we have lost our heads when we lose our generosity and our courtesy and our kindness. Frequently we also lose our families and even our eternal salvation. The head of the house should not be too headstrong or fail in his comprehension so that he gets involved in problems over the head of his understanding.

The apostle Paul said: "For the husband is the head of the wife, even as Christ is head of the church. . . ." (Eph. 5:23) Christ should also be the head of the family as well as the head of our lives. This requires that we live accordingly and keep ourselves in a heads-up position. There should also be a lot of cooperation between our various departments, as Jesus taught in the parable: "And the eye cannot say unto the hand, I have no need of thee: nor again the head to the feet, I have no need of you." (I Cor. 12:21) Certainly the head has no right to exercise unrighteous dominion or to be unfair or immoral to other members.

The Lord himself forcefully instructed a group of husbands when through an ancient American prophet he said: "For behold, I, the Lord, have seen the sorrow, and heard the mourning of the daughters of my people . . . because of the wickedness and abominations of their husbands.

"And I will not suffer . . . that the cries of the fair daughters of this people . . . shall come up unto me against the men of my people, saith the Lord of Hosts.

"For they shall not lead away captive the daughters of my people because of their tenderness, save I shall visit them with a sore curse, even unto destruction; for they shall not commit whoredoms, like unto them of old, saith the Lord of Hosts." (Jacob 2:31-33.)

What a great accomplishment if we could develop a nation of fine, honest, Christian, God-fearing, moral men who could fully qualify for this important position as the heads of some fifty-million American Christian homes! Their job would be to strengthen the women and make them happy. They should inspire the children and set them a good example. To help get our needs in our minds we might borrow some words written by J. G. Holland who said:

> God, give us men! A time like this demands
> Strong minds, great hearts, true faith and ready hands;
> Men whom the lust of office does not kill;
> Men whom the spoils of office cannot buy;
> Men who possess opinions and a will;
> Men who have honor; men who will not lie;

Men who can stand before a demagogue
And damn his treacherous flatteries without winking!
Tall men, sun-crowned, who live above the fog
In public duty and in private thinking;
For while the rabble, with their thumb-worn creeds,
Their large professions and their little deeds,
Mingle in selfish strife, lo! Freedom weeps,
Wrong rules the land and waiting Justice sleeps.

Mr. Holland points out that wrong rules the land. But wrong can only rule our homes and our personal lives. Recently a very attractive and intelligent young woman came to discuss some of her problems. Over the years she had had several suitors who had been interested in marriage, but she said that she was afraid of men. She knew so many men, including her father, her uncles, and her brothers, who had their closets full of skeletons. She knew of the heartbreak of a great group of women comparable to those mentioned by the Lord in the Book of Mormon. She knew of so many married men who were willing to cheat on their marriage vows. She also knew of many unmarried men who were willing and anxious to do what they knew was wrong and what God himself had forbidden. She wanted a husband whom it was not always necessary to urge and coax and remind and beg to be a man and to do his duty. She wanted a husband who was stronger than she was, who could give her strength, and who was not always falling down before every trivial temptation, but she was afraid of men. She was afraid of their irresponsibility, their selfishness, their lack of self-discipline, and their lack of basic manhood. She felt that far too large a percentage of men had a tendency to be unfaithful to their wives, and even more important, many more were unfaithful to their God.

To begin with, there aren't enough men to go around, but on top of that the fact remains that there aren't enough *really good* men in whom one can have great confidence in every way. It might be pointed out that women are also weak sometimes, but man was given greater strength. He was designed to be the leader in righteousness, to be the head of the house. Satan was a leader, but even in the Council in Heaven he led his followers to hell. There are many who should be good men, who are following that same procedure. So again we pray, "God give us men, God give us a lot of loving husbands, good fathers, loyal citizens, trusted friends, and faithful sons of God."

Health and Strength

HAVE YOU EVER THOUGHT about what you would choose among all of the blessings of the world if you were granted your heart's desire? Suppose that life would let you select from among its most valuable benefits, which would you choose? Life keeps on hand many treasures merely to be able to bestow them upon those who win her favor. For himself Solomon asked for wisdom, and that is what he was given. Others have prayed for love, wealth, and a long life. Some have wanted freedom, beauty, and faith. Certainly all of these gifts are wonderful and can make great contributions to our happiness and joy of living.

I have listened to a great many people pray; I have searched my own heart for some answers, and it seems to me that those things that we want most are health and strength. Probably above everything else we want to be solid, sound, and well in our own persons. The dictionary says that health is the freedom from disease or ailment. It is that general condition of body, mind, spirit, and personality that denotes soundness, vigor, and an abundance of vitality. Health is much more than a mere lack of disease. One needs joy in his heart, enthusiasm in his personality, strength in his muscles, and life and zest in his bloodstream. As real health flows through us it produces a wonderful feeling of well-being. Strength brings with it such qualities as success, excellence, muscular power, mental health, moral balance, and spiritual vitality.

There is also an exhilarating feeling that comes when one has sound logic, moral power, spiritual righteousness, and religious faith. A well-trained, high-spirited, supple-bodied, football halfback feels an enormous thrill of satisfaction as life flows through his being. Almost effortlessly he seems to be able to move the ball forward through the most difficult opposition. As a symbol of our desired health and strength we might picture a skier flying down the mountainside. With rhythm and grace manifesting themselves in all of his senses, he glides across the landscape with all of his faculties harmoniously taking part.

In the best of health, his blood is surging, his eyes are sparkling, his ego is dancing, his spirit is generating life, and he feels in his soul a tremendous enthusiasm for living.

Of Jesus it was said, "In him was life and the life was the light of men." What excitement would be ours if such a statement could be made about us! Jesus announced his own mission by saying, "I came that ye might have life and have it more abundantly." The purpose of our existence is to help generate in the greatest abundance a full measure of life.

One of the reasons why we live in a world of opposites is because white can best be understood when we see it on a dark background. It might help us understand health and strength to see them in the presence of disease and weakness. Our physical health can best be appreciated when its opposites are seen behind sunken eyes and pallid cheeks, and when we are dragging around aching bodies, sick minds, and diseased, droopy spirits. Sometimes severe pains accompany diseased bodies. In fact, some of the most unpleasant of all words in our language are these distressing little words — sick, ill, weak, sore. In various stages and degrees the miserable little words sometimes describe our minds, or bodies, or our souls. There can be no more distressing problems than when one becomes physically sick, mentally ill, morally unbalanced or perverted in his attitudes, or weak in his ambitions. One's personality may exude the awful stench of immorality, and his mind may be distorted by misery, inferiority, or guilt. Probably the most serious problems confronting our entire present socety come from the many varieties of sicknesses that frequently prey upon us.

Our psychiatric wards and mental hospitals are overflowing, our reform schools and penitentiaries are bulging with inmates who in one way or another are too ill to care for themselves. They are tormented by all kinds of confusions, fears, dissatisfactions, conflicts, failures, and miseries. The Book of Mormon gives an interesting account of one of these sicknesses as follows: ". . . Zeezrom lay sick at Sidom, with a burning fever, which was caused by the great tribulations of his mind on account of his wickedness . . . and his many other sins, did harrow up his mind until it did become exceeding sore, having no deliverance; therefore he began to be scorched with a burning heat." (Alma 15:3) After recovery, such a one said: "I was tormented with the pains of hell." There are a lot of people who are presently suffering from these same bitter "hell-pains." There are many times more sick people out of the hospital than there are in it, and the pains that they endure are often much more severe, causing the sufferers to live their lives in a miserable kind of desperation.

Every violation of the laws of health causes some degree of pain, regardless of whether it is a physical, moral, social, spiritual, or mental health law that has been broken. Dr. Paul Tournier, a celebrated European psychiatrist, said: "Every act of physical, psychological or moral disobedience to God's purposes is an act of wrong living and has its inevitable consequences."

When our joints are filled with arthritis, we have pain. When our lungs are filled with cancer, we have pain. And when our hearts are filled with dishonesties, disloyalties, and immoralities, we have pain. We have serious suffering when our minds are full of sin and disobedience to God. When our personalities are filled with unfairness, suffering is bound to result. Unfortunately, this suffering does not confine itself to the one who is afflicted by the disease — it attacks all of those who are associated with him.

If a child were afflicted with leprosy and forced to live apart from others, the suffering may oppress the other family members with greater severity than the one specifically afflicted. I know a father whose immorality and lust have caused him to leave his wife and children. His desertion not only deprives them of the physical necessities of life, but they must also endure the awful shame, loneliness, and soul anguish that he brings upon them. His irresponsibility confuses the children and tends to make them emotionally unstable. When their own father sets them such a bad example, their confidence in mankind itself is placed in serious jeopardy.

Ernie Pyle, the late war correspondent, once said that "nine-tenths of morale is made up of pride in your outfit and confidence in your leaders." Real health tends to be born in us when we have someone that we can trust and something that we can believe in and work at, fight for and live by.

Marriage counselors, marriage partners, psychiatrists, law enforcement officers, and those engaged in psychosomatic medicine are all trying to help us to avoid making these unhealthy

responses to life. This is not only for our own good, but for
the peace of mind and mental balance of the countless others
who are likely to be co-victims, as there is no way that the results
of unfairness, irresponsibility, and sin can be confined within
the body or mind of the diseased person.

We have tried to classify our problems of mental health in
several categories. There are those who are schizophrenic and
who have to deal with a divided or a splintered personality. We
have many dual or multiple personalities. One may be one type
of person at one time and a different type of a person at another
time. Under one set of circumstances, a person may seem to
be perfectly healthy, but in other situations a kind of mental
disintegration causes him to lose contact with his environment.
There are forms of psychosis with serious mental derangements
where people are unable to properly put their thoughts together.
Mental sickness changes the personality and causes all kinds of
sub-reasonable and unfair responses to situations.

In recent years we have had a gigantic increase in psychosomatic medicine. This is the name given to those bodily disorders that are brought about by some unresolved mental and
emotional problems. It has been said that one doesn't get stomach
ulcers because of what he eats; he gets stomach ulcers because
of what is eating him. Many people have actually killed themselves by their own thoughts. We can also kill other people if
we can get a certain kind of ideas into their minds.

Some kinds of neurosis are accompanied by anxiety, physical
exhaustion, or excessive irritation. Various kinds of hysterias
and compulsions frequently grow out of these mental disorders.
Many who are neurotic become pill-takers. There is one category of mental illness that is called paranoia. With this disorder
some people have delusions of persecution; others have halluci-
nations about their own importance, or they have unreasonable
fears, depressing dreads, or distracting suspicions that often
throw their lives out of balance. The mind, attitudes, will, and
spirit may become as weak and unstable as does a physical body
when it is decimated by disease. In fact the mental and social
diseases may be even more devastating, inasmuch as they also
have such a harmful effect upon others.

In seeking a divorce, a despairing wife said: "We were
brought up so differently." Her husband was very selfish and

had the idea that his title as head of the house carried with it some kind of magic power that made him superior to her in every department. He seemed to think that things were right or wrong according to what he thought about them and that his ideas should be accepted by her at their face value whether they were good or bad.

We get sick physically when we take into our bodies things that are not good for them. Adam and Eve fell when they consumed substances that brought about their mortality. If we breathe in enough nicotine, some of our lung cells may become cancerous. If one drinks enough liquor, he may become an alcoholic. Cancer cells in one's body will make him sick, but so will the cells of immorality in his heart or the cells of evil in his mind. Bad cases of mental and spiritual illnesses are just as disabling as heart disease or leukemia.

The Ten Commandments were given to enable us to maintain our health and strength. When we worship false gods, we take unhealthy ideas into our minds and we get sick. When we allow any kind of dishonesty or immorality or profanity or covetousness to get established in our systems, we also become sick. When we violate the Sabbath day or dishonor our parents or break the Word of Wisdom, we become ill to the exact extent of our violation. We can become as deathly ill with greed, hate, lust, irresponsibility, and atheism as we can with syphilis or emphysema. In fact, to know that evil is wrong doesn't help us, unless we abstain from it.

I know of a great cancer doctor who died of cancer. Many heart specialists have died of heart trouble. I know of a marriage counselor who has marital problems that he cannot solve. Some time ago the wife of a psychiatrist sought a divorce because each week she had to prove her sanity to her witch-hunting, problem-causing psychiatrist husband. If she made any responses that were displeasing to him, her sanity was immediately questioned. On the other hand it was of no concern to him that he had a number of disturbing mental problems.

Now just suppose that we each made an intelligent effort to develop an abundance of all kinds of health and strength in ourselves. This could be effectively done if we obeyed those important health principles known as the principles of the gospel of Jesus Christ.

Many years ago Dr. Henry C. Link wrote an interesting book entitled *The Return to Religion*. Dr. Link grew up in a religious home, but as he climbed the educational ladder he abandoned his religion with the idea of making a more intellectual approach to life. Then with his Phi Beta Kappa key on his chest and his name in *Who's Who in America,* he became the head of the psychological service center of New York City where it was his responsibility to help other people solve their difficulties. He discovered that every problem could best be solved by practicing the principles of the religion of Christ. That is, we would have no unsolved problems if we practiced the honesties, the loyalties, the moralities, and the righteousness recommended in the principles of revealed religion. Then the highly intellectual Dr. Link recommended a full scale and complete return to religion as the best means of solving our problems. Such a return would also enable us to "have life and have it more abundantly." We would also have a full measure of spiritual, emotional, and mental health and strength. A return to religion would also eliminate all of our conflicts, spiritual worries, social fears, and moral dreads.

Speaking of the time when this earth shall be cleansed of its sins and God's righteousness shall be established upon it, John the Revelator said: "And there shall be no more death, neither sorrow, nor crying, neither shall there be any more pain." Certainly when we are all obeying the law there will be no more of the pains of lung cancer or atheism or immorality or disloyalty. We will no longer be subject to the pains of heartbreak or disappointment or shame for ourselves or for others. We will have no more guilt complexes or feelings of inferiority. Then we will feel great pride in the goodness of each other and great joy in the pure spirit of life that will be coursing through our veins. What a great idea that each of us may have an abundance of health and strength and live life to our heart's content!

The High Cost of Living

THOSE OF THE OLDER generation will remember that during and after the first World War there was a great deal of talk about the high cost of living. There were many scarcities, and prices were rising very rapidly. Understandably there were a great many people who were highly concerned about it. This seemed to be particularly so in my own family where even with low prices we had a good many serious financial problems.

History is now repeating itself and our inflationary tendencies are presently causing serious concern in every part of our world. It takes a great deal of money to feed, clothe, and house our exploding population. It is also very expensive to provide everyone with automobiles and recreation. Taxes are going up by leaps and bounds. It requires billions to fight in Vietnam and to finance the cold wars in the numerous communist trouble spots around the world.

But we are put to an even greater expense in financing our own crime waves, our devastating labor shutdowns, our various national scandals, our dope addiction, our alcoholism, our appetite for nicotine, and our insatiable lusts for various types of immorality. Through our gigantic government give-away programs, we are supporting many people at home and abroad in idleness. Our national economy is based largely on a program of deficit spending, and the huge interest charges on our public, private, and corporate debts are sending our high costs of living still higher. However, the most disturbing thing about our situation is not the high cost of living but its low return. It seems that as the costs of living have been going up the returns from it have been coming down. We could live on less if only we had more to live for. Our economy has sometimes been referred to as "the profit system," but a much more adequate description would be "the profit and loss system."

In many fields our losses far outnumber our profits. Just think how much we are currently spending on police forces and courts! And yet in spite of our increased expenditures our actual law observance has decreased. Our hoped-for reformation is not taking place and our mental health is getting less in spite of our greater expenditures. Huge sums have been spent to help dissatisfied racial groups, but the more help they get, the more they burn, threaten, steal, and cause trouble.

We have expended vast sums, hoping for better education but never before have teachers or students been so disagreeable, rebellious, and hard to live with as now. We lose vast sums of money on our wars, our sins, and our charities. It costs us huge additional amounts to protect ourselves against ourselves. We hire a large army of attorneys, policemen, lawmakers, courts, and government men to try to force good behavior upon each other. Then think of those costs that are being added by our ignorance, our atheism, and our sloth. Even with our higher standards of spending, our standards of conduct are less now than when our Founding Fathers were laying the ground work for a free Christian America.

The greatest commodity in the universe is life and our success should be judged not only by what it costs to live but what we get from living. If we were properly thoughtful there would be no life losses. God desires that every part of his creation should show a profit.

On one occasion when Jesus and his disciples were walking from Bethany to Jerusalem, Jesus became hungry and searched a nearby fig tree for food. When he found that it had produced nothing but leaves he said: "Let no fruit grow on thee henceforward for ever. And presently the fig tree withered away." (Matt. 21:19) Jesus used this idea as a basis for one of his most important success parables relating to our human activities. He said: "A certain man had a fig tree planted in his vineyard; and he came and sought fruit thereon, and found none. Then said he unto the dresser of his vineyard, Behold, these three years have I come seeking fruit on this fig tree, and find none: cut it down; why cumbereth it the ground?" (Luke 13:6-7)

It was a custom in ancient Palestine to require people to pay a tax on every tree that grew on the land, whether it was fruitful or not. Because it was very unprofitable to pay taxes on trees that did not produce, owners of orchards usually cut down those trees that did not bear a justifiable volume of good fruit. Then in one of his most meaningful parables he said of us: ". . . therefore every tree which bringeth not forth good fruit is hewn down, and cast into the fire." (Matt. 3:10)

No one either in horticulture or in life ever gets ahead very fast by paying taxes on any kind of dead wood. Certainly the Lord is highly displeased with high costs and low returns. The unprofitable servant said to Jesus, "And I was afraid, and went and hid my talent in the earth. . . ." Then Jesus said: "Thou wicked and slothful servant. . . ." And he said to those that were with him: "Take therefore the talent from him, and give it to him which hath ten talents. . . . And cast ye the unprofitable servant into outer darkness: there shall be weeping and gnashing of teeth." (Matt. 25:25-30) Our society takes similar action when it erects scaffolds and gas chambers. When society organizes a firing squad it is attempting to cleanse itself of those members who insist on operating with too many losses and too few profits. We also have penitentiaries, reform schools, and hospitals where we try to help people operate their lives in the black more of the time.

God also runs some reform schools. Hell itself is a divine institution, established for the purpose of purifying the lives of those who have not been able to get rid of their own sins. Because the people in Noah's day were piling up such huge deficits of unrighteousness, God sent the flood to cleanse the world and to enable a new generation to start over on a new page with a new opportunity. Those in Noah's day whose deficit spending was ended by the flood still had to pay their accumulated balances. The apostle Peter tells us that they were sent to one of God's reformatories to make some payments on their sins as spirits in prison. (I Pet. 3:18-20)

The scriptures tell us of another death sentence that is presently hanging over our world. On the last Tuesday of the Lord's life he looked down to our day and made a rather uncomplimentary comparison by saying, "As the days of Noah were, so also shall the coming of the Son of man be." Our present-day activities are not only financially unprofitable, but our debts may involve us in some huge moral and spiritual deficits that may be difficult to settle. A lot of thought needs to be given to what should be done about the high costs and low returns arising from our race riots, our alcoholism, our dope addiction, and our negative thinking. How ridiculously unprofitable it is to seduce each other with our immorality, our dishonesty, and our atheism!

Jesus has always been particularly displeased with those who teach false religious doctrines, and leading his children away from him causes his eternal enterprises to show some losses. In speaking of what he had written in his scriptures he said: ". . . If any man shall add unto these things, God shall add unto him the plagues that are written in this book: And if any man shall take away from the words of the book of this prophecy, God shall take away his part out of the book of life, and out of the holy city, and from the things which are written in this book." (Rev. 22:18-19)

When a man selects an occupation he may choose to labor in any field, but we don't choose ourselves in the work of the Lord. Jesus said: "Ye have not chosen me, but I have chosen you, and ordained you, that ye should go and bring forth fruit. . . ." (John 15:16) It is against the laws of God for Christian ministers to choose themselves and then preach their own doctrines. This has caused hundreds of conflicting sects, many of whom are leading people away from God with their man-made doctrines. The Lord himself has said of them: "This people draweth nigh unto me with their mouth and honoureth me with their lips; but their heart is far from me. But in vain they do worship me, teaching for doctrines the commandments of men." (Matt. 15:8-9) Either nineteen hundred years ago or now this is serious business. It is also pretty unprofitable to trifle with God by disobeying his commandments in our individual lives. We also cause him a loss when we set an evil example for others, or allow our own children to go astray.

It has been said that the first question that God will ask every parent is: "Where are your children?" If we can't give a good answer to that question, we are in trouble. Jesus said: "But whoso shall offend one of these little ones which believe in me, it were better for him if a millstone were hanged about his neck, and that he were drowned in the depth of the sea." (Matt. 18:6) That kind of life shows a tremendous loss.

We are also trifling with God's important law of responsibility when we say that it doesn't matter any more what we believe or what we do. We are being seriously irresponsible when we say that God is dead or that we ourselves are not answerable for what we do. In so many ways we put ourselves into spiritual bankruptcy by our unwarranted surmises and irresponsible guesses. Most religious leaders are relying too much on their own wisdom. Everyone shows a loss when we live by the loose, permissive attitude of our age where we say that we may do as we please. That philosophy soon sends us into bankruptcy, especially when we are so pleased to do wrong. Our age has developed some enormous appetites for evil, and our senses are frequently misled by our perverted tastes. There are some who feel that they are perfectly free to choose hippyism, hoodlumism, labor racketeering, domination by racial minorities, or educational gangsterism. One of the reasons why so many people must be confined in jails, reform schools, and mental institutions is because they are so pleased with all kinds of mental and moral perversions. All the while these so-called freedoms are running up skyhigh deficits and showing returns that are below sea level.

Sin has never been permanently profitable, and we can easily bankrupt ourselves by setting each other an example in atheism, immorality, and drunkenness. There are many people on whom even God loses money. No thoughtful person could actually believe that evil was good, but we have dope peddlers, murderers, adulterers, and other types of criminals merely because of an overwhelming ungodly lust to do as we please. Those who are recruiting members for hippie organizations are doing as they please. The pushers of venereal disease, and the pushers of venereal attitudes, venereal faiths, and venereal education are doing as they please. At the same time they are pushing up the high cost of living and seriously reducing its return.

I know of a man who has a good income, a fine education, a wonderful wife, and four intelligent children, and yet he makes life a hell on earth for them. He has developed what might be called a sadistic personality. He is always needlessly torturing his wife by his unkindness. He makes her beg for money and crawl to obtain his favor. If she wants to get their children a few simple presents for Christmas or their birthdays, she has to leave the home and earn the money herself. His selfish, unprofitable egotism makes him a miserable tyrant, an inconsiderate husband, and an irresponsible human being.

He is also guilty of a serious kind of murder, as he has killed his wife's love of life and her interest in the things around her. He might even have his own suicide charged against him, as he is destroying in himself those godly traits with which he was endowed by the Creator. In his despotic role he becomes a kind of Satan and locks his wife up in a little private social hell where he is depriving her of life's natural pleasures and the happy life meanings that God intended her to enjoy.

A rubber company manufacturing new heels for men's shoes had an advertisement which read: "Come in and see America's No. 1 heel," and at the bottom of the poster had been written in a female hand, "Sorry, brother, I married him." How unprofitable it can be to produce these destructive emotions in the hearts of other people!

In describing some unprofitable lives, Jesus drew a simile from a scene in a graveyard. He described the clean-looking, well-polished exterior beauty of a tomb and then pointed out that within it was filled with contamination, dead men's bones, and all kinds of uncleanness. Then slightly changing the simile he said: "Woe unto you, scribes and Pharisees, hypocrites! for ye make clean the outside of the cup and of the platter, but within they are full of extortion and excess." (Matt. 23:25)

The losses in our society are presently threatening our entire civilization with destruction. It is bad enough to suffer these serious financial losses, but we just cannot afford the tremendous moral and spiritual destructions with which we are threatening ourselves. Jesus compared the value of one soul to the wealth of the entire earth. What would be a proper return on such an investment? And how disappointing it would be to waste this great resource and make God and everyone else poorer because of us. It is probable that our most important calling in life is to lower life's costs and increase its profits.

Hollow Men

MANY YEARS AGO, T. S. Eliot wrote a poem entitled "The Hollow Men." It has great significance for the many people of our time whose lives are empty of purpose. When one lacks real inwardness he fails to receive the satisfactions that come to those who have great moral and spiritual resources. Hollowness presents one of our most serious general problems. An empty sack cannot stand upright. And our lives droop and sag under the heavy weights of living when our lives are filled with the blankness, boredom, confusion, and frustration that is caused by emptiness. Many of life's most serious failures can be described by the degree of their hollowness. What could be worse than that devastating feeling of one who has nothing important to believe in, or to live by, or to fight for, or to be devoted to?

One memorable night in Babylon many centuries ago, the fingers of a man's hand appeared on the wall of King Belshazzar's palace and left a message, saying to the monarch: ". . . God hath numbered thy kingdom, and finished it. . . . Thou art weighed in the balances and art found wanting. Thy kingdom is divided, and given to the Medes and the Persians." (Dan. 6:26-28) When weighed on God's scales the vacuum in Belshazzar's faith made him a lightweight. Because of a shortage in his good works Belshazzar became one of the world's most famous hollow men. It is sometimes a great advantage to lose weight physically, but we bring on serious consequences when we begin losing our moral and spiritual substance. Even to correctly feed our bodies doesn't help us very much if our spirits are weakened by the malnutrition that causes hollowness. One of the things that most incites our pity is to see someone whose body doesn't grow or whose mind doesn't develop. However, these particular problems can be corrected in the resurrection, but what can be done for those who have no moral vitality and always remain infantile in their spirituality?

The reason that no suitable place could be found in Bethlehem for Jesus to be born was because all of the available space had already been taken up. And as we pack our lives full of evil they more or less automatically become empty of good. Among the chief characteristics of emptiness are our regrets, our despair, and that awful sense of vacancy that one feels when life itself seems not to be worthwhile. The feelings of boredom, depression, unworthiness, and disobedience are the typical emotions of hollow men, whereas the purpose of life is to have a feeling of real joy and an earned sense of being worthwhile.

Life can only reach its maximum in profitableness when we are genuinely happy and are approved by God. The feeling of fulfillment and the sense of satisfaction that come when our lives are worthwhile are among our most satisfying emotions. The right kind of food in our stomachs produces a very pleasant sensation of fullness by relieving us of those awful gnawing hunger pains that accompany emptiness. As the stomach becomes empty it shrinks and causes unpleasant feelings, but so does the mind and so does the soul. Jesus was trying to help us avoid the pains of eternal emptiness when he said: "And blessed are all they who do hunger and thirst after righteousness, for they shall be filled with the Holy Ghost." (III Nephi 12:6)

And when we are filled with the Holy Ghost, we are also filled with happiness and purpose and interest and an enthusiasm for life. Physically, we are what we eat; mentally, we are what we think; and spiritually, we are what we do. A good reading program can fill our minds with the most inspiring ideas and the greatest ambitions. A good program of religious activities can give our spirits that pleasant feeling of being worthwhile. In describing the success of the Prophet Daniel, the Old Testament says that he had an excellent spirit in him. An excellent spirit is a dependable guarantee against all of the diseases of hollowness.

The story is told of three medical students working in their laboratory. They were trying to balance a cadaver up against the wall on his own feet in order to study him more effectively. But each time, just as they thought they had him properly balanced, he would slump down onto the floor again. Finally, one of the students said: "I know what is the matter with this dummy, he hasn't any spirit in him."

When we lose our spirit, some kind of a slumping process is always bound to take place. Whether we lose the spirit of accomplishment or the spirit of righteousness or the spirit of progress or the spirit of happiness, some kind of an emptiness is always the result. Every time that we fail to use any of our physical muscles or our spiritual talents, they tend to shrink.

When we disobey God we lose his spirit. When we tolerate even a few sins or a little apathy in ourselves some of our substance is lost and we become less than we previously were. One bad attitude can empty life of much of its good in very short order. To some extent each of us is like a water cask full of potential leaks. Every evil that we commit causes a leak in our faith. Our inactivity empties us of our ability. Indifference drains us of our accomplishments, and sloth reduces the strength and the size of our mental muscles. As we cease to strive we lose our ambition, and as we fail to honor our ideals they also soon disappear.

But even that very serious tragedy of a spiritual death does not come about by any kind of a sudden blowout; it usually takes place by just a series of slow leaks. If we tolerate a little thoughtlessness, a little carelessness, a little forgetfulness, a little disobedience, a little sin, then almost before we know it, we may have lost an eternal life.

We constantly worry about the possibility that our civilization might someday be destroyed by an atomic holocaust or that our earth might be made empty of its people by a poisonous fallout. We fervently pray that these things may never happen, and yet millions of lives are actually falling prey to influences that from an eternal point of view are even more serious. Many lives are presently being emptied spiritually by the explosion of sin and the fallout of hate, lust, and selfishness. There are other moral problems that destroy our character, drain off our happiness, and leave us to live through the horrors of hollowness.

To forsake God makes us hollow men, and so does forgetting our duties. The scriptures and reason are always reminding us that we should continuously keep some important ideas active in our muscles as well as in our minds. To do this we must remember the Sabbath day, and our marriage vows, and the covenants of our faith. Leaks in our memories are very dangerous because we are largely unconscious of them when they are taking place. The moment of forgetting, like the moment of birth, is an unconscious moment. At the time one is being born, he is actually not aware of what is happening. He does not discover that he has been born until several months later. In contrast the moment of learning is a conscious moment and we are stimulated and made happy by our new acquisitions of knowledge.

But because we are unaware that we are forgetting, we are also frequently unconcerned. We often lose our ideas, our ideals, and our ambitions without regret or without even knowing that they are gone. At this very moment, some of our faith and our righteousness and our enthusiasm may be slipping into oblivion through our forgetfulness. We can also destroy our faith by our sins or cause our ambition to wither and disappear because they are either misused or abused. Thus by several processes we frequently become hollow men without knowing it.

Mr. Eliot wrote another poem referring to the deterioration that sometimes takes place in human lives, which he called "The Wastelands." This may also be difficult for us to comprehend. It is easy to understand the wastelands of the deserts, the wastelands of the swamps, the arctic wastelands of ice and snow and what damage they may cause, but Mr. Eliot pictures those more devastating human wastelands where such things as mental depression and spiritual desolation may be destroying our eternal accomplishment without our being aware of it. Think of our alcoholic wastelands and how easily they come about. Or think of those areas wherein our finest human values are being laid waste by immorality.

Tragically enough we create some serious wastelands in our souls when we have no faith to live by, or no ideals to aspire to, or no godly standards to bolster up our performance. We are aware that something is presently happening in our world that is actually tending to make it empty and desolate of certain very valuable human qualities. There are some general changes that are taking place in our attitudes that are destroying our business morality, emptying our churches, and cheapening our outlook on life.

After World War II, a group of displaced, discouraged men were referred to as "the beat generation." It is thought that our own trend toward emptiness may be even more serious, inasmuch as we are abandoning our religious attitudes, weakening our faith, and reducing our righteous industry. We are losing our national gold supply through a draining-off process, but we are also losing much of our intestinal fortitude, our national morality, and our spiritual integrity because they are also being drained off, and in their places we are tending to fill ourselves with a harmful national hollowness. Growing out of this emptiness in our national life we are producing too many Hells Angels, Devils Disciples, hippies, and nothings. We have noted the disturbing increases taking place in crime, psychosomatic illnesses, mental diseases, and spiritual decay. But probably the central neurosis of our times is emptiness. This hollowness is indicated in many ways. We have increasing numbers of slackers from duty, deserters from reason, objectors to industry, and haters of righteousness. Our horrible race riots, our fantastic booze consumption, our pathetic dope addiction, our wasteful dropouts from religion, and the dreadful destruction caused by iniquity all put an unquestioned odor of spiritual death in the air.

A vast hollow place has been left in the communist countries from which God has been banished, but a vacuum also grows in our own personal lives when we let go of our faith or fall down in our ideals or forsake God. There are many religious ministers who are emptying the lives of other people by filling them with "the new morality" and persuading them that God is dead and that it doesn't matter any more what we believe or do. A great army of marchers and advocates of rebellion and strife are tending to make our world empty by promoting their own particular brands of irresponsibility. Certainly we are not increasing our weight on God's scales when we glorify liquor and tobacco, glamorize immorality, and allow thousands of dope pushers to move freely among our children. Large crowds of hippies are gathering in our cities to live in idleness and uselessness. With their unattractive clothes, their disorderly persons, their destructive morals, and their lust for unearned attention, they are generally breaking down our society and destroying its value. We might wonder how God can look upon our unsightly sins and our intolerable disobedience without being sick at his stomach as well as in his heart.

In one single airport each day over 20,000 books are sold that glamorize illicit sex, encourage violence, promote crime, and corrupt the general population. As we run these millions of evil thoughts through our minds, we tend to increase the percentage of wrong that makes up our activities. Then as the space for good becomes less, our nation becomes more hollow.

The scriptures refer to our days as "the fullness of times." There are many kinds of fullness that are abundantly available to us. The scripture speaks of a possible fullness of joy. A fullness of faith will lead us to a fullness of the glory of God. Through Isaiah, the Lord said: "I will put my spirit into their inward parts." We can also be filled with the Holy Ghost.

We can adopt the spirit of the finest literature, and we can develop the most worthwhile devotion. We can enjoy the most uplifting personal experiences, and we can absorb the best from the greatest biographies, the most stimulating poems, the finest philosophies, the most ennobling plays, and the most important holy scriptures.

Socrates said: "As water can be made to run by means of a syphon from the fuller to the emptier cask, so wisdom can be made to run from the greater to the less among men." And wisdom can be made to run into us from a thousand sources if we reserve enough space that has not already been filled with evil.

As we look beyond the distractions of the present, we should discover that the future rewards of righteousness are perfectly sure. Eternity is not a shadowy, misty place. Heaven is real. God is real. His program for our eternal exaltation is real. The Son of God is a real person, who, like his Eternal Father, has a resurrected body of flesh and bones as tangible as ours. It is the universal decree of God that all of us shall someday be resurrected and each will be rewarded according to his works. If we live a full life, our futures will be filled with happiness and joy, and we will be real people living a real life in a real heaven. We will have real abilities, some real work to do, and some real people to love and associate with.

God has ordained happiness as the purpose of our lives. He desires that we have every blessing. He has given us the privilege of helping bring them about by banishing our hollowness and filling our lives with faith, good works, and godliness, that we may live with him forever in a fullness of joy.

The Hymns

WE HAVE MANY THINGS to make our lives interesting. The other day I was impressed with the pleasure that one man takes from the ownership of some fine horses. Another friend has great joy in a prized coin collection. Other people take pride in their collections of beautiful tapestries, paintings, or flower gardens on which their souls seem to feed. I have always been impressed with our large, modern, well-ordered supermarkets, where the finest fruits and vegetables are assembled in thousands of colors, tastes, and varieties. In addition to their beauty, they serve our needs by delighting our appetites, supplying us with the vitamins necessary to maintain the health of our bodies, furnishing us fuel for our minds, and making possible the logic of our reason, the inspiration of our spirits, and the beauty of our personalities.

From our food we get the ability to work, to play, to communicate, to laugh, to solve our problems, and to live at our best. It can be a great joy on a summer day to walk through a supermarket and see ice-cold watermelons and every other kind of interesting food and drink in an endless variety. These things impress themselves upon our minds because of their utility and the pleasant past experience that we have had with them. While we couldn't possibly make use of even a small part of them at one time personally, they all make a friendly appeal to our senses and assure us of their help when our need arises. Then we may purchase and carry away with us whatever our heart desires.

We can have a similar experience when we go into a large bookstore and browse around among the great volumes filled with the most interesting variety of mental foods and spiritual stimulants. Here are available the most interesting ideas that can be run through our hungry minds to produce as much satisfaction as can be had from the finest Sunday dinner. From the bookstore, we may carry away those volumes that will produce in us the most exciting and satisfying of all human experiences. From the available books we may learn how to make a living, have fun, build a character, and eternally glorify our souls. From the bookstore we may get books on drama, history, theology, biography, business, fiction, satire, and humor to our heart's content.

But sometimes we may hunger for a more elegant expression, or need a more powerful language than can be had from mere prose. Then we do with words and ideas what they do in the supermarkets to upgrade the attractiveness of their products when they are graded for color, size, quality, and then displayed in such a way as to make the strongest possible appeal to our appetites. Some designers of expression serve us as architects of speech and engineers of sound. We call them poets, philosophers, and musicians. They are special people who have been endowed with great imaginative, emotional, or intuitive powers and are capable of expressing their conceptions or emotions in language that is especially pleasing to us because of its meaning and beauty.

The poet fashions his phrases from thoughts that have been measured, weighed, matched, tailored, and harmonized. Then their marching order is given a particular cadence in rhyme and music. The metre, harmony, power, and beauty of great poetry sometimes affects our minds like wine. As the great poems are effectively run through our personalities, they produce soul raptures; they quicken emotions and excite ambitions, all of which can raise the level of our lives.

There is an extraordinary form of poem that has been set to music that we refer to as a hymn. Hymns are a kind of food for our souls. A hymn is an ode with a particular spirit. It is a song of praise, a prayer of gratitude, a poem of love, or a lesson of faith. Hymns are a common part of our most lofty expression wherein we worship God and extol his goodness by a musical rhythm coming from our hearts.

A hymn is not only a sentiment that is given power in our souls, but in its turn it also charges our minds and hearts with greater meaning. A hymn is an elated composition that is marked by such artistry and beauty that it furnishes the most favorable climate in which a person may effectively approach his Maker. The Lord himself has said: "My soul delighteth in the song of the heart; yea, the song of the righteous is a prayer unto me, and it shall be answered with a blessing upon their heads." (D&C

25:12) There are many reasons why we ought to sing a lot more than we do.

There are many hymns for many occasions. Suppose that out of the depths of our souls we sing the hymn called "Abide with Me" in which we address God and say from our hearts:

> Abide with me, 'tis eventide!
> The day is past and gone;
> The shadows of the evening fall;
> The night is coming on!
> Within my heart a welcome guest,
> Within my home abide;
> O Savior, stay this night with me;
> Behold, 'tis eventide!
>
> Abide with me, 'tis eventide!
> Thy walk today with me
> Has made my heart within me burn,
> As I communed with Thee.
> Thy earnest words have filled my soul
> And kept me near thy side;
> O Savior, stay this night with me;
> Behold 'tis eventide!
>
> Abide with me, 'tis eventide!
> And lone will be the night,
> If I cannot commune with thee,
> Nor find in thee my light.
> The darkness of the world, I fear,
> Would in my home abide;
> O Savior, stay this night with me;
> Behold 'tis eventide!

What a great delight it is to have whole volumes of hymns written in every age and coming from every land for every occasion to help us satisfy our souls!

Annie Malin has written a sacramental hymn saying:

> God, our Father, hear us pray;
> Send thy grace this holy day;
> As we take of emblems blest,
> On our Savior's love we rest.
>
> Grant us, Father, grace divine;
> May thy smile upon us shine;

As we eat the broken bread,
Thine approval on us shed.

As we drink the water clear,
Let Thy Spirit linger near;
Pardon faults, O Lord, we pray;
Bless our efforts day by day.

Parley P. Pratt has written a hymn that keeps us looking forward to one of the greatest events in our earth's future history as well as our own. He says:

Come, O thou King of Kings;
We've waited long for thee,
With healing in thy wings
To set thy people free;
Come, thou desire of nations, come;
Let Israel now be gathered home.

Come, make an end to sin
And cleanse the earth by fire,
And righteousness bring in,
That saints may tune the lyre
With songs of joy, a happier strain,
To welcome in thy peaceful reign.

Hosannas now shall sound
From all the ransomed throng,
And glory echo round
A new triumphal song;
The wide expanse of heaven fill
With anthems sweet from Zion's hill.

Hail! Prince of life and peace!
Thrice welcome to thy throne;
While all the chosen race
Their Lord and Savior own.
The heathen nations bow the knee,
And ev'ry tongue sounds praise to thee.

President John Taylor was charged with the responsibility of directing the missionaries in carrying the message of the restored gospel to the nations of the earth. He wrote this stimulating missionary hymn, saying:

Go ye messengers of glory;
Run ye legates of the skies;

Go and tell the pleasing story
That a glorious angel flies,
Great and mighty, great and mighty,
With a message from the skies.

Go to every tribe and nation;
Visit every land and clime;
Sound to all the proclamation;
Tell to all the truth sublime:
That the gospel, that the gospel
Does in ancient glory shine.

Go, to all the gospel carry,
Let the joyful news abound;
Go till every nation hear you,
Jew and Gentile greet the sound.
Let the gospel, let the gospel
Echo all the earth around.

Bearing seed of heavenly virtue,
Scatter it o'er all the earth;
Go! Jehovah will support you;
Gather all the sheaves of worth.
Then, with Jesus, then, with Jesus,
Reign in glory on the earth.

Eliza R. Snow, a great poetess of the latter days, was inspired to write one of the immortal classics of truth for our time. It is a worshipful hymn entitled "O My Father." As we need inspired composers we also need an inspired understanding and expression as we sing:

O my Father, thou that dwellest
In the high and glorious place;
When shall I regain thy presence,
And again behold thy face?
In thy holy habitation,
Did my spirit once reside?
In my first primeval childhood,
Was I nurtured near thy side?

For a wise and glorious purpose
Thou hast placed me here on earth,
And withheld the recollection
Of my former friends and birth.
Yet oft-times a secret something
Whispered, "You're a stranger here."

And I felt that I had wandered
From a more exalted sphere.

I had learned to call thee Father,
Through thy spirit from on high;
But until the key of knowledge
Was restored, I knew not why.
In the heavens are parents single?
No, the thought makes reason stare!
Truth is reason; truth eternal
Tells me I've a mother there.

When I leave this frail existence,
When I lay this mortal by,
Father, Mother, may I meet you
In your royal courts on high?
Then at length when I've completed
All you sent me forth to do,
With your mutual approbation
Let me come and dwell with you.

We remember with gratitude and should express with a
holy passion the soul-stirring poem of Phillips Brooks:

O little town of Bethlehem,
How still we see thee lie.
Above thy deep and dreamless sleep
The silent stars go by;
Yet in the dark streets shineth
The everlasting Light.
The hopes and fears of all the years
Are met in thee tonight.

For Christ is born of Mary;
And gathered all above,
While mortals sleep, the angels keep
Their watch of wondering love.
O morning stars, together
Proclaim the holy birth;
And praises sing to God the King,
And peace to men on earth.

How silently, how silently,
The wondrous gift is giv'n!
So God imparts to human hearts
The blessings of his heaven.

No ear may hear his coming,
But in this world of sin,
Where meek souls will receive him, still
The dear Christ enters in.

And William Fowler commemorates the great blessings of
the final gospel dispensation in which we join to sing:

We thank thee, O God, for a prophet
To guide us in these latter days.
We thank thee for sending the gospel
To lighten our minds with its rays.
We thank thee for every blessing
Bestowed by thy bounteous hand.
We feel it a pleasure to serve thee
And love to obey thy command.

When dark clouds of trouble hang o'er us
And threaten our peace to destroy,
There is hope smiling brightly before us,
And we know that deliverance is nigh.
We doubt not the Lord nor his goodness.
We've proved him in days that are past.
The wicked who fight against Zion
Will surely be smitten at last.

We'll sing of his goodness and mercy.
We'll praise him by day and by night,
Rejoice in his glorious gospel,
And bask in its life-giving light.
Then on to eternal perfection
The honest and faithful will go.
While they who reject this glad message
Shall never such happiness know.

One of the greatest of our hymns centers in our own homes:

There is beauty all around
    When there's love at home;
There is joy in every sound
    When there's love at home.
Peace and plenty here abide,
Smiling sweet on every side.
Time doth softly, sweetly glide
    When there's love at home.

In the cottage there is joy
    When there's love at home.
Hate and envy ne'er annoy
    When there's love at home.
Roses bloom beneath our feet;
All the earth's a garden sweet,
Making life a bliss complete
    When there's love at home.

Kindly heaven smiles above
    When there's love at home;
All the world is filled with love
    When there's love at home.
Sweeter sings the brooklet by;
Brighter beams the azure sky;
Oh, there's one who smiles on high
    When there's love at home.

How gracious God has been to make possible for us an
eternal success! We may attain the highest glory by following
his direction. We ought to memorize both the words and the
music of many great hymns. And then in appreciation, we sing:

How firm a foundation, ye saints of the Lord,
Is laid for your faith in his excellent word!
What more can he say than to you he hath said,
You who unto Jesus for refuge have fled.

In every condition, in sickness, in health,
In poverty's vale or abounding in wealth,
At home or abroad, on the land or the sea,
As thy days may demand, so thy succor shall be.

Fear not, I am with thee, O be not dismayed,
For I am thy God and will still give thee aid.
I'll strengthen thee, help thee, and cause thee to stand
Upheld by my righteous, omnipotent hand.

When through the deep waters I call thee to go,
The rivers of sorrow shall not thee o'erflow,
For I will be with thee, thy troubles to bless,
And sanctify to thee, thy deepest distress.

When through fiery trials thy pathway shall lie,
My grace, all sufficient, shall be thy supply.
The flame shall not hurt thee, I only design
Thy dross to consume and thy gold to refine.

And then we have a hymn of farewell and blessing, in which we sing:

> God be with you till we meet again;
> By his counsels guide, uphold you;
> With his sheep securely fold you;
> God be with you till we meet again.
>
> God be with you till we meet again;
> When life's perils thick confound you,
> Put his arms unfailing round you;
> God be with you till we meet again.
>
> God be with you till we meet again;
> Keep love's banner floating o'er you;
> Smite death's threatening wave before you;
> God be with you till we meet again.
>
> Till we meet, till we meet, till we meet at Jesus' feet.
> God be with you till we meet again.

What a hope to look forward to the time when we may all meet at the feet of him whom it is our present privilege to worship and serve!

I Will Return

IN 1941, THE UNITED STATES and Japan were having some disagreements over points of national policy. On December 7, while Japanese diplomats were in Washington, presumably trying to settle their differences, their military forces made a surprise attack on our outpost in Hawaii.

At 7:55 a.m. on that fateful morning a wave of 189 Japanese air planes darkened our skies and dropped their deadly cargo on our air installations and then went on to attack the fleet stationed at Pearl Harbor. At 8:50 a.m. a second wave consisting of 171 additional enemy planes came in from the sea to finish the job of destruction. After an hour's assault, our great bastion in the Pacific was a smoking shambles. On this one day, which President Roosevelt said would live in infamy, practically all of our airplanes and ships were either destroyed or disabled, and 2,323 of our servicemen were left dead.

Following this sneak attack, the Japanese had many swift and far-reaching victories. In fact, the war was almost lost in the first few months while we were getting ready to fight. In the following few weeks the Japanese successfully attacked many of the far-flung possessions of both England and the United States. They launched a seaborne invasion of Hong Kong, Malaya, and the Philippines. Guam, a lonely American outpost in the Marianas, fell to the Japanese on December 11, 1941; Wake Island on December 23; and Hong Kong on Christmas Day. By the end of December, large Japanese forces were poised in Malaya and the Philippines ready to strike at Borneo, the Celebes, and New Guinea.

On February 15, 1942, Singapore, the great British naval base in the Far East, surrendered to a Japanese force that came down from the north. Most of Burma fell in March and April, 1942, while Ceylon and India were threatened by the large Japanese naval force that controlled the Indian Ocean and the Bay of Bengal.

By the end of March, 1942, the Japanese were in possession of the East Indies; they had also pushed into New Britain and the Solomon Islands and were in a position to strike at Port Moresby, the Allied stronghold in southern New Guinea, and even Australia itself was threatened.

In the Philippines, General Douglas MacArthur, with a force of 19,000 American regulars, 12,000 Philippine scouts, and 100,000 soldiers of the new Philippine army, fought a desperate delaying action. As Japanese troops threatened Manila, MacArthur withdrew his men into the Bataan Peninsula for a hopeless but gallant stand. When it was decided that the American cause was hopeless in the Philippines, General MacArthur took his wife and son and left for Australia, under cover of darkness. There he hoped to reorganize his command to dispossess the Japanese of their evil gains.

His successor, General Jonathan Wainwright, withdrew his men to Corregidor on the tip of the peninsula and there held out until disease, starvation, and superior enemy forces made further resistance impossible. On May 6, General Wainwright surrendered his force of 11,574 men. The 37,000 troops that had been left on the peninsula to cover his withdrawal had surrendered on April 9. The Americans had been beaten, but their leaders hadn't the slightest intention of allowing the Japanese to permanently win the war. In bidding farewell to those who looked to him for leadership and victory, General MacArthur gave them a solemn promise of future liberation, saying, "I will return!"

The following 40 months were torturous ones for many Americans. Because of the early advantages won by Japanese treachery, many of our people were required to live under conditions that imposed the most severe hardships and suffering. Under the domination of the Japanese many Americans lost their lives; others lost their wealth and their health. Many were forced to endure the severe privation of concentration camps.

But these sufferers were not forgotten, and as fast as possible the armed power of America was using these difficult months to prepare for an overwhelming future victory. Soon the course of war began to change, and the major losses were being transferred to the Japanese. Finally, in mid-July, 1945, the "Big Three," including President Truman, Prime Minister Churchill, and Joseph Stalin met in conference at Potsdam. By this time the atomic bomb had become a reality, and it now became necessary to decide whether or not this fantastic new weapon should be used to stop the continued spilling of blood. On July 26, what was known as the Potsdam Declaration was issued, calling upon Japan to surrender or face "the utter devastation of the Japanese homeland." The Japanese government leaders in Tokyo favored accepting the terms of the Potsdam Declaration, but the generals wanted to continue the war. Finally President Truman and his advisors decided to use the awful means in their hands to end the fighting.

Accordingly, on August 6, 1945, a lone B-29 flew over Hiroshima and dropped the first atomic bomb. It leveled 4.4 square miles of the city and killed between 70,000 and 80,000 people. Even then the Japanese army leaders continued to hold out, and so on August 9 another bomb was dropped on Nagasaki. The following day the Emperor made the decision for peace, and the Japanese cabinet informed Washington that it would accept the Potsdam terms.

September 2, 1945, became one of the historic days in our generation as the Allied fleet entered Tokyo Bay. Then on the decks of the battleship *Missouri* the representatives of the Japanese Imperial general staff signed the Articles of Surrender. This action brought the end of the war and the liberation of prisoners began.

General MacArthur had kept his word, and those surviving the starvation and terror of the war had restored to them those important God-given privileges of life, liberty, and the pursuit of happiness.

This event is now past history. Since then the war criminals have been punished, and many of the others involved have long since passed away. Even the hardships and suffering of the survivors have now become mere memories, but this important event in our history might remind us of another "I will return" promise, which is still pending in the world of our future.

As a part of the great plan of salvation, God created this earth as the most suitable place for his children to work out their eternal salvation before him. This earth was made ideal as a place for us to receive our mortal bodies, organize our families, and learn to walk a little way by faith. Our first parents were given the instruction to multiply and replenish the earth and teach their children to live the kind of lives that would ultimately qualify them to become like their eternal, heavenly parents. We were born into a world of opposites where we could see good and evil side by side. We were all endowed with a conscience and the ability to choose the right and reject the wrong. Our world's history has not been without other infamies. Enough evil has been let loose in the world to do more damage to our success and happiness in a day than was done by the Japanese in the entire war. We have not been very careful about following divine instructions, and the forces of evil have piled up many victories. In our infamous disregard of truth and right some of our people have gone over to the enemy as they have loved the works of Satan more than those of God. Some of those whom God has counted on have become murderers, criminals, adulterers, disbelievers, and rebels. And all of this has taken place on an earth that was built for good.

In an attempt to set things right the Son of God came in the Meridian of Time to redeem his people from sin and to set all earthly inhabitants a close-up example of the kind of lives that we are expected to live. After a short ministry of three years our tendency toward infamy brought about betrayals and false accusations and led to the crucifixion of Christ by the very people whom he had come to save. Following his death, those whom he had appointed to carry on his work were also compelled to suffer indignities, imprisonments, and violent deaths. In addition, the doctrines that he was so particular about were changed, and the evils that have been running rampant have caused many men and women to be placed under the bondage of Satan and confined in the concentration camps of sin. Our infamy has caused enough suffering to make the misery of Bataan and Corregidor seem like a Sunday School picnic.

Even the killing of the Son of God did not give a permanent victory to the forces of evil. This earth has a glorious destiny and, like Pearl Harbor, even the tragedy of Calvary was only temporary. Even with his death and the evil that has followed it, the Son of God has never given up, and righteousness is destined for an eventual triumph. While Satan is now largely in control and is functioning as the king of this world, yet the great Redeemer has also said, "I will return!" He has given us many of the details of just what his second coming is going to be like.

This important event is now thought to be almost in our immediate future. Throughout the entire history of the world it has been one of our most talked-of events. We know that the Son of God is coming back to cleanse the earth of its sins, punish the wrong-doers, free the captives, destroy the concentration camps of sin, bind the arch-enemy, Satan, and destroy his power. This destruction will also involve a kind of super-bomb-atomic-finish on a world-wide scale. In speaking of this event the Psalmist said: "Our God shall come, and shall not keep silence: a fire shall devour before him, and it shall be very tempestuous round about him. He shall call to the heavens from above, and to the earth, that he may judge his people. Gather my saints together unto me; those that have made a covenant with me by sacrifice." (Psa. 50:3-7)

The world of evil is now face to face with a kind of Potsdam Declaration from the big three of heaven. It has been made perfectly clear that either we must repent or we will face a destruction more awful than a thousand Hiroshimas and Nagasakis. Imagine what was meant when, through Malachi, the Lord said: "For, behold, the day cometh, that shall burn as an oven; and all the proud, yea, and all that do wickedly, shall be stubble: and the day that cometh shall burn them up, saith the Lord of hosts, that it shall leave them neither root nor branch." (Mal. 4:1)

For over 1,900 years the great privilege of repentance has been held out before us. We have been promised forgiveness of our sins if we will forsake our evil and throw off our sinful bondage, but we have failed to follow counsel. In fact, we have been so heedless of God that our crime waves have been getting worse. Our atheism has been increasing. Even now our immorality is becoming more flagrant and shameful. But all of this does not change the Lord's declaration that he will return to set things right. Jesus said: "For the Son of man shall come in the glory of his Father with his angels; and then he shall reward every man according to his works." (Matt. 16:27)

In describing this event the Prophet Joel said: "The sun and the moon shall be darkened, and the stars shall withdraw their shining. The Lord also shall roar out of Zion, and utter his voice from Jerusalem; and the heavens and the earth shall shake: but the Lord will be the hope of his people, and the strength of the children of Israel." (Joel 3:15-16)

Paul said: "And to you who are troubled rest with us, when the Lord Jesus shall be revealed from heaven with his mighty angels, in flaming fire taking vengeance on them that know not God, and that obey not the gospel of our Lord Jesus Christ." (II Thess. 1:7-8)

In speaking of the signs that would signal his second coming, the Lord told of the wars and rumors of wars by which the people of the earth would bring suffering upon themselves. He compared our conduct with that of the people of Noah's day and indicated that there should be great iniquity and hate in the world where many false teachers would lead many people away from God. After giving all of these signs Jesus said: "Now learn a parable of the fig tree; When his branch is yet tender, and putteth forth leaves, ye know that summer is nigh: So likewise ye, when ye shall see all these things, know that it is near, even at the doors." (Matt. 24:32-33)

In spite of the mess that we have made of our tremendous opportunities, our earth was created for good, and woe to those whose houses are in disarray when he returns!

The Moslem Mosque of Saint Sophia in Istanbul is a transformed Christian church. It was once one of the most beautiful Christian churches in the world. When it was taken over by the Moslems, all of the Christian inscriptions and symbols were painted out. Over the years the Moslem paint has been wearing off. One day an American was standing under the great dome and through the worn paint he could faintly make out the picture of Christ ascending from Mount Olivet with outstretched arms, pronouncing a blessing upon the people. The picture's inscription was quoting the angels of the ascension, who said, "Ye men of Galilee, why stand ye gazing up into heaven? this same Jesus, which is taken up from you into heaven, shall so come in like manner as ye have seen him go into heaven." (Acts 1:11)

Enthusiastically the American pointed out the reappearing Christ on the church's walls and said to his friend: "He is coming back!" And so he is! He is not dead. He does not sleep. He has not lost his power to reveal himself; neither has he lost his interest in the world which he created. Certainly all of the sin and wickedness even of our own day will never be able to blot him out permanently. The accretions of sins and the daubs of disobedience that have caused so much suffering through the centuries have only temporarily hidden him from view. The covering is growing thin and he is coming back. Soon he will reign in righteousness upon the earth as King of kings and Lord of lords, for the earth and the fullness thereof is still the Lord's, and its brilliant future belongs to him.

A small boy, who had seen Holman Hunt's great picture where Jesus was knocking at the door, said to his father: "Daddy, why doesn't someone let him in?" Then he thoughtfully added: "Maybe it is because they live in the basement and can't hear him knock." Too frequently we live in the basement of life below the level of understanding, or it may be that some of us can't hear because we are in the beer tavern with our hearing aids turned off, or it may be because our minds are so strongly centered on evil that the still small voice can't get through to us. Of this we may be absolutely certain, that he is coming back. He said: "I will return!" And what a great day it will be for us if we can go out to meet him with clean hands, pure hearts, and great enthusiasm!

Incognito

THERE ARE MANY very interesting words in the dictionary. One of them is the word *incognito*. It comes from an Italian word meaning unknown, and it identifies a condition where one wears a disguise, or by some other means one's name, character, rank, etc., are kept concealed. A prince may travel incognito to avoid the crowds, or the annoyance, or the ceremonies that may be involved. Of course, different people have different reasons for wanting to remain unknown. The reasons why a bank robber or a betrayer of his country would want to keep his identity a secret are obvious. For other reasons writers frequently use an assumed name to keep their identity hidden.

Benjamin Franklin was a printer and he created a fictitious person by the name of Richard Saunders in order to have someone's name to attach to his own ideas. Some 2,500 years ago Mr. Aesop wrote a lot of fables in which he gave animals and trees the qualities of human beings and let them act out their experiences for our benefit without completely exposing our human weaknesses to ourselves.

All of us wear disguises in one form or another. For various reasons no one ever seems to get very well acquainted with anyone else. Many husbands and wives, parents and children live very close to each other for a long time without really learning very much about the hopes, dreams, ambitions, and needs of each other. A great many women even like to keep their ages a secret. Then with cosmetics, special hairdos, and other cover-up devices they put disguises on their eyes, their cheeks, and their lips. We pad our clothing to give ourselves the kind of representation that we would like to have, but all the time we keep our real selves more or less of a secret.

In talking with people about their marital problems, men frequently say, "My wife doesn't understand me." Wives say, "My husband doesn't appreciate me." Children say, "I can't get close to my parents," and parents say, "I am afraid of my children." One wife indicated that she had lived with her hus-

band for thirty years and had never discovered whether he loved
her or not. She was not much more certain about what her attitude was toward him. We not only disguise ourselves physically,
but we also disguise ourselves mentally and spiritually. We
hide our successes, our intentions, and our weaknesses from
other people. We disguise our speech and cover up our motives;
we are ashamed to show our true emotions, and we misrepresent
our feelings to the point where we are strangers to everyone,
including God and ourselves. This tendency to keep to ourselves
a secret is one of many big problems.

It has been said that everyone needs a discoverer. Each year
Hollywood sends a great many talent scouts out all over the
world trying to find those people on whom they can lavish $3,000
per week. Very frequently they settle on someone who hasn't
any idea that he is possessed of those valuable traits that the
world so much seeks. Life itself is a giant talent hunt. We are
always searching for someone or something. We are searching
for wealth and position. We are looking for wives, employees,
political candidates, and personal friends. We are searching for
talents, opportunities, occupations, and pleasures. Sometimes
we think we have found what we are looking for only to be disappointed or to find that we have been deceived or betrayed.
That is, we haven't properly penetrated the disguise or we are
misled by some alias or false front.

We probably have more trouble in properly identifying our
real selves than almost any other thing. We sometimes get ourselves so loaded down with inferiority complexes or feelings
of guilt or mistaken judgment that we find ourselves making
more serious errors. We know more about our own weaknesses
than others do, and we are likely to sell ourselves short because
of them. Or we load ourselves down with discouragement, lethargy, and sloth. Because of our self-concealment and self-decep-
tion we not only need to discover ourselves, but we also need
someone to wake us up, educate us, inspire us, and motivate
us to be somebody. We also need someone to call us to repentance, to help us appreciate life, and to teach us how to be
successful in reaching our own objectives.

We remember that ancient scene when Adam and Eve hid
from God among the trees of the Garden of Eden. In a general
way we have been doing that same thing ever since. As a result
of hiding from God most of us never get to know him very well,

whereas Jesus said: "And this is life eternal, that they might know thee the only true God, and Jesus Christ, whom thou hast sent." (John 17:3) He has told us that if we do his will we shall know of his doctrine; and if we live as we should we may always have his Spirit to attend us.

Along with knowing God, we should also get a lot better acquainted with ourselves. Certainly one of our greatest opportunities is indicated by the Socratic injunction which says: "Know thyself." We ought to know why we do as we do and how we can do a little better. Isn't it interesting that the thing that we know less about than anything else in the world is our own individual selves? We can ask ourselves questions about science, invention, politics, or history and get fairly good answers, but if we try to figure ourselves out, or if we sit down and try and write out an analysis of ourselves and explain our mind and soul qualities, we may not get very good answers We are also confused when we try to understand why we do as we do when we believe as we believe. Or why is it that we can control about everything except ourselves? We have fairly good control over our hands and feet, but sometimes very little over our brains, our tongues, our emotions, or our ambitions.

If we should really get acquainted with ourselves, we would find that everything that we seek we already have. That is, every man carries within himself the very things that he searches for. If we seek faith, we need only look within ourselves, as God has already implanted within us the seeds of faith, waiting only for us to make them grow. If we need courage, we need only to develop that which we already have. Greatness is not in London or in New York or in Paris or in San Francisco; it is in ourselves. It is very interesting that the greatest values of our world are in people, even though we may not understand them.

Actually there are no ordinary people, if we could just get under their disguises. Or association is somewhat like the association we have in attending a masquerade ball. There we never really know who we are dancing with until everyone takes off their masks during the last dance. When the veils of our mortality are drawn aside, we may discover a lot of things even about ourselves that we are not presently aware of. Those people whom we now consider to be the most ordinary may be the kind of people that we will feel like falling down and worshipping.

Suppose that we had seen Abraham as he herded his sheep out on the deserts of Palestine. It is probable that we may not have been particularly impressed, but we would likely have felt differently if we could have seen him as he stood with God among the noble and great in the Council of Heaven, or suppose you could visit with him now as he serves with the Creator in his heavenly kingdom.

Many of those with whom we presently associate during our mortal probation were also among the noble and great in the Council of Heaven. Gods, angels, spirits, and men are all of the same species in different stages of development and different degrees of righteousness. Many of them were also like unto God.

It has been said that of all the scientists who have ever lived upon the earth 80 percent of them are alive today. But it may also be that 80 percent of those who stood with God among the noble and great may be alive today. If God reserved most of his greatest inventors, scientists, and other leaders to live in this greatest of all dispensations, it would not be reasonable that he would reserve a bunch of spiritual scrubs to come here when the gospel should be restored and the greatest events of earth's history should take place.

Every day among earth's present inhabitants we are probably talking to and walking among many others of those noble and great who stood with God in the council of heaven. We should be very thoughtful in our treatment of them. The Apostle Paul said that we should be careful how we entertain strangers, as many people have entertained angels unawares. Probably in more than one way that is also true of us.

The scripture says that God made man "a little lower than the angels and has crowned him with honor and glory." One translation of this verse says that God made man *for a little while* lower than the angels. In some things even Jesus was made a little lower than the angels for a little while, but in his mortal disguise this condition was only temporary for him, and it is only temporary for us. Not very long ago all of us were in the spirit world. Then we walked by sight. We have all seen God. He is our Father. We lived with him. But we must learn to walk a little way by faith in our mortal disguise. However, if we make the most of our possibilities, after the last dance of our masquerade ball, when we take off our masks, we may find that the offspring of God have the potentialities of their eternal parents. We are told that God is such a glorious person that no one in his natural state can stand in his presence and live, and this is the kind of person that we may become if we are faithful.

Actually none of us have ever seen a mere mortal. Governments are mortal and businesses are mortal. but those people that we shake hands with, talk to, smile at, bear our testimonies to, teach, marry, snub, ignore, and love are all immortal. They will all live on forever and they will carry with them those marks that were acquired by our association. If it is bad business to be forgetful in entertaining strangers, it is also bad business to fail in our fellowship with our friends. We should love and be helpful to our enemies and go out of our way to set a good example to everyone, as we will sometime find out that we have actually been associating with gods masquerading in this mortal disguise. Someone once said that he tried to be very friendly to those whom he passed on his climb up to success, as he may pass them again on his way down. Life would assume a new and vastly greater importance if we knew who we were. Someone once said to his friend: "Who do you think you are?" And he whispered quietly to himself, "I wish I knew." Some day we will discover that we are the actual children of God, formed in his image, endowed with his attributes, and heirs to his glory. Being the children of God we might sometime be seriously embarrassed if we go through our mortality acting like delinquents, atheists, sinners, and the sons of Satan. None of those that we presently meet either in or out of the church are perfect, and yet they are all wonderfully important people. What a great thrill it ought to be to fellowship with them, work with them, and assist them to learn the best of life's lessons! It has been a great blessing to many people to have befriended the great and mighty when they were poor and struggling. What a joy it ought to be each Sabbath day to take our contemporaries by the hand, look into their faces, enjoy their companionship, and call them "brother" or "sister"! As we realize their potentialities as the children of God we should also try to make a contribution to their eternal destiny.

We remember that even the Savior of the world was not recognized by many people for what he actually was. It is also very interesting to try to imagine the kind of person that Mary of Nazareth must have been in the Grand Council of Heaven to have been selected to be the mother of the Son of God in her mortality. We might try to understand her present beauty and magnificence in that heavenly home. The scriptures proclaim that many were selected and ordained in heaven for their ministry here. This was true of the Redeemer; it was true of Abraham; it was true of Jeremiah; it was true of Mary; and it is true of us. The Prophet Joseph Smith said: "Every man who has a calling to minister to the inhabitants of this earth was ordained to that very purpose in the Grand Council of Heaven before the earth was." Henry Van Dyke has said: "No one is ever born into the world whose work is not born with him." Every person born into the world is an individual of great importance, and we should manifest that greatness in everything that we do. We should make the best and the most of our own lives so that when we take off our masks during the last dance, we will be satisfied with who we are and what we have done.

Loyalty

ONE OF THE TRAITS that has an extraordinary influence upon human success and happiness is loyalty. Loyalty symbolizes quality. It stands for constancy and integrity. It adds beauty, luster, and greatness to every life that will give it domicile. The dictionary describes loyalty as a faithful allegiance. One who is loyal is devoted and true to those things to which he owes fidelity. He honors his obligations to his country, his church, his family, and his friends. He manifests his devotions to the causes he espouses, to the ideals he believes in, and to the thoughts that hold him true to his purpose. Loyalty acts like a compass and always sees to it that we are pointing directly toward our star.

The state of Kansas has adopted the sunflower as its state emblem. The sunflower is also the symbol of loyalty. All flowers welcome the sun but only the sunflower follows it.

A moving picture showed a ship that had been torpedoed at sea. The lifeboats had been launched and all but two of the passengers had abandoned the sinking ship. The captain who had been blinded by the explosion had made known his intention to be true to the tradition of the sea and go down with his ship. His loyal assistant and faithful friend had supervised the loading of the lifeboats, and when they were all safely launched he had come to stand by the side of his blind master. The captain was urging his friend to save himself, but the servant was telling his blind master the story of the sunflower, the symbol of loyalty.

The sunflower follows the sun, not only in the early morning hours when the day is young, but it continues throughout the zenith of the day when the heat is great. The sunflower looks directly into the face of the sun in the morning and is constant and steadfast throughout the long afternoon. As the sun declines in the west it still looks directly into the face of the sunflower. Until the sun disappears into the sea, the sunflower follows the sun, and the next morning when the sun rises in the east, it is greeted by the ever loyal face of the sunflower.

The two men were standing in the captain's cabin as the water rose from their ankles, to their knees, to their waists, and just before the great ship gave up its life to sink to the bottom of the ocean the servant said to the master: "The sunflower follows the sun. You go down with your ship, I go down with you." That is loyalty.

There is another factor involved in loyalty. When any captain comes to the end of his voyage, he likes to meet this greatest of all crises dressed in his smartest uniform and with all of his personality qualities functioning at their best, in full loyalty to his ship. Out of loyalty to one's family, his country, himself, and his God, everyone should always keep himself dressed in his finest soul qualities. Then he radiates enthusiasm. The qualities of devotion and patriotism light up his entire personality and make his soul radioactive. They put sparkle in his eyes, a light in his expression, conviction in his voice, and success in his blood stream.

When one wants to add a little color to his personality nothing could be more appropriate than to put in some of the true blue of loyalty. It provides a far greater incentive for accomplishment than money. To know extreme happiness and to inspire the greatest confidence in others, one should be loyal and constant to every trust. The weathercock was not chosen to symbolize loyalty because his allegiance changes with every passing breeze. The chameleon was also passed by, because he shows a different color in every environment. Loyalty is always loyal. It is always true blue, and no quality in human life seems quite so beautiful and worthwhile as a satisfying, solid, dependable, uplifting, comfortable loyalty.

We remember Benedict Arnold as a traitor. He was a general in the early colonial army. In some ways he was considered to be a stronger officer than Washington, but his interests were self-centered and he was easily offended. He had a changeable disposition that depended upon the circumstances rather than upon what was right. In order to avenge an imagined slight, he bargained with the enemy to sell West Point to the British. Even though his country's future had been designed by God and was built upon the solid foundation of Christian principles, as an American general he was willing to betray his country and turn the interests of his countrymen over to their enemies to satisfy his own wounded pride.

In contrast to this ugly trait we see one of Benedict Arnold's contemporaries, with a much lesser rank, named Nathan Hale. He was captured by the enemy and sentenced to be hanged. Before the noose was put around his neck he was asked if he had anything to say. He said: "I regret that I have but one life to give for my country."

On the night of Arnold's betrayal there was great confusion at army headquarters. No one knew just how far the treason had gone, or how many people were involved. And in appointing the father of Daniel Webster to stand guard through the balance of that long, awful night General Washington said: "Captain Webster, I can trust you." There is no greater compliment than this.

We are still living in the country established by God to be the citadel of liberty with its divine mission to keep freedom, righteousness, and human dignity alive in the world, and the jewel of loyalty shines just as brightly in our lives now as it did in theirs then and it is just as hard to find.

Everyone who is born heir to the great blessings of this land is also born subject to carrying a full share of the responsibilities for its welfare. When anyone has a part in fostering his country's crime waves, condoning its rebellions, taking part in its strikes, giving comfort to its enemies, or increasing its weaknesses and sins, he is *betraying* his country. At the same time he is also being disloyal to God under whose thoughtful direction this nation was established. One of the crimes that we should shun the most is any conscious or unconscious disloyalty, unfaithfulness, or tendency to betray our country. There are many human beings who for a few dollars or a sense of notoriety can be induced to foment internal strife, tear down our national strength, and furnish helpful information to our enemies. As we allow strikers to throw people out of work by closing down our industries or permitting racial riots, we are helping destroy our country.

Again and again our communist enemies have vowed to destroy America and bury her people. We know that their procedures are never honest and never out in the open. They try to get people fighting among themselves. They stir up race riots at home and incite national quarrels abroad. Instead of the Christian doctrine of peace on earth, good will among men, they cause trouble in every place they can.

America was built on Christian principles. These are the principles of free agency, order, and obedience to those laws that we have made to govern ourselves. To be truly loyal we should also have in our hearts a genuine obedience to the laws of God and a willingness to labor wholeheartedly to bring about his purposes in the earth. When we insist on being idle, becoming dope addicts, spreading venereal disease, burning draft cards, and trying to incite people against the laws, we are being disloyal. And when we try to influence each other by threats, or demands, or marches, or bypassing our duly elected officers, we are tearing down those divinely established institutions that have made America great.

One of our most serious sins is disloyalty, and by this process we become traitors to America, traitors to God, and traitors to our own best interests. Many are still sponsoring that spirit that caused the war in heaven. Satan not only rebelled against God and the spirit majority, but he drew away one-third of all those heavenly hosts after him. Because of their disobedience they were cast out of heaven, but their Satanic doctrines are still being carried on under the inspiration of the Devil.

In Russia, as a part of their national policy, the communists have officially banished God. They recognize no higher power than their own, and they base their national program on force, deceit, and intimidation. They forbid the practice of religion and are inducing many people to forsake their Christian principles and go over to the enemy.

In this connection, we remember the case history of Judas Iscariot. Before he succumbed to this miserable weakness of disloyalty, Judas was a member of the Church of Jesus Christ in good standing. He occupied the high office of an apostle and was a member of the Quorum of the Twelve that Jesus had organized to carry on his work. But he allowed the spirit of disloyalty to get into his thinking. When an opportunity presented itself, he said to his master's enemies: "What will ye give me, and I will deliver him unto you?" He made a bargain with them for 30 pieces of silver. Then with a kiss he betrayed the very one who had appointed him to his high office.

Over and over again in different ways, we are practicing this same deadly sin of disloyalty and betrayal. In our ignorance and weakness, we betray God. We betray him with our subterfuges, our rationalizings, and our deceits. We betray him with our curses and our sins. We join with the enemy of all righteousness, and by our opposition and our non-support we try to tear down the Church that he has established. We destroy the effectiveness of the Church's doctrines and make its members weak and sinful by setting them an example in alcoholism, dope addiction, atheism, and immorality.

Occasionally we should check up on ourselves to determine how we are doing in carrying forward the work of the Lord. Jesus said: "He that is not with me is against me; and he that gathereth not with me scattereth abroad." (Matt. 12:30) He also said: ". . . every . . . house divided against itself shall not stand." (Matt. 12:25) We ought to keep in mind who we are helping when we absent ourselves from church, or break the Word of Wisdom, or help to foster weaknesses and sins in others. One of the greatest of all possible strengths would be to create within ourselves this great virtue of loyalty — loyalty to our country, loyalty to our family, loyalty to our God, and loyalty to ourselves.

Elbert Hubbard once said: "If you are going to work for a man, in heaven's name work for him. Be true to his purposes, advance his interests, like him, cooperate with him and be loyal to him." If we can't do those things then we have no business posing as his employee, identifying with him, and accepting his compensation. When one can't be loyal to America, he has no business living in America or posing as an American citizen.

I know of one man who for many years has been employed as a salesman of a fine company. To those on the outside this man seems to be a fine employee, but he fosters trouble. He criticizes his fellow employees. He can always find something to make fun of or to gossip about. He likes to make slighting, belittling remarks about others. Of course, everyone has faults. Even the presidents of the United States have vulnerable spots and places where they may be attacked if someone so desires. Over this man's years as an employee he has seriously lowered the morale of his own organization and reduced its prestige in the minds of many people. Instead of getting on the team and trying to help lift everyone up, he causes them to become discouraged and lose heart. Four of his fellow salesmen have quit their jobs because of him. He gets some kind of a false sense of pride from the fact that he is able to make others fail while he stays on. This quiet underground sabotage that is always being carried on by him is very costly to his employer who has a big investment in the education and training of all his employees. Yet, think of the damage that can be done by one man almost without anyone being aware of it himself.

I know of another man who is thought of as a good American. He belongs to a Christian church. He has a fine wife and family, and yet he is thoroughly disloyal to every one of them. Every day he reduces his wife's confidence in human beings. He makes his children ashamed of him by setting them such a bad example. His wife worked in order to send him through school, enabling him to get a good job, but he is completely unfaithful and disloyal to her. He has not only broken her heart but makes it almost impossible for her to live. The distractions caused by his disloyalty and sins have made it difficult for him to keep pace in his profession and in his ignorance he betrays those clients who place their trust in him. He makes this dreadful word seem even more awful as he goes about being disloyal to his country, to his church, to his family, to God, and to himself.

As the sunflower follows the sun, may we effectively foster this great gem of loyalty in our own souls.

Meat That Ye Know Not Of

THE SCRIPTURES are a great source of strength to many people for many different reasons. In the parables we are furnished with some excellent comparisons for our own lives. We also have the great commandments restraining us from evil with their motivating and authoritative "thou shalt nots." Then we have the constructive philosophies that can effectively help us mold our own success. One of the most important values of the scriptures is the personal example and motivation of those individuals by whom the scriptures were inspired and written.

Of course by long odds the central figure of the scriptures and our greatest benefactor is Jesus of Nazareth, the Son of God and Savior of the world. Once as Jesus and his followers were making their way from Judea into Galilee, their route took them through Samaria and they stopped to rest at Jacob's well near the Samaritan city of Sychar. They arrived at the well at about noon and inasmuch as they were naturally a little travel weary, they decided to stop to rest and to recharge their strength. Appropriately the disciples were sent into the city to get food. While Jesus was resting he asked a Samaritan woman, who had come to the well, to give him a drink. Then after an interesting conversation, the woman left her water pots and went into the city to tell the people about this prophet who tarried at their well on his way through Samaria. Soon a large audience came out from the city to hear Jesus. By this time the disciples had returned and were urging Jesus to eat the food that they had brought for him. Jesus now had more important things to do. The disciples were concerned as to why he didn't seem hungry any more. In answer to their questions he said: "I have meat to eat that ye know not of." Those to whom he spoke didn't understand, and they wondered if while they were away someone else may have given him food. Jesus explained to them and said; "My meat is to do the will of him that sent me, and to finish his work." (See John 4:8-34) Greater strength always comes when we are doing the things that we ought to be doing.

The human digestive system is one of the wonders of the universe. We put into it all kinds of grains, fruits, flesh, herbs, and liquids, and then by some miracle that no one understands, these materials are converted into energy, friendship, vision, wisdom, personality, understanding, bone and tissue, and dozens of other abilities which enable us to live profitably and to effectively carry on our share of the work of the world.

There is something even more spectacular that takes place when we feed the spirit or cultivate our ambitions or motivate our wills. There are some important miracle foods that enrich and enliven our souls. They can have a more powerful effect upon our strength than does our physical food. More than almost anything else we need to understand the source of our own success and how to increase it. Jesus made an important declaration that man does not live by bread alone. We need a good big dose of inspiration occasionally. We need to wind up our enthusiasm, strengthen our faith, and invigorate our minds.

In his book *The Masque of Kings*, Maxwell Anderson says: "If you'll go stop three tradesmen on the street and ask the three what it is they live by, they will reply at once, 'bread, meat, and drink,' and they'll be certain of it. Victuals and drink, like the rhyme in Mother Goose, make up their diet. Nothing will be said of faith in things unseen, or of following the gleam. Just bread and meat and a can of wine to wash it down. But if you know them well, if you know them better than they do, behind the fish eyes, and the bellies, each one burns candles at some altar of his mind in secret, secret often from himself; each is a priest to some dim mystery by which he lives. Strip him of that and bread and meat and wine won't nourish him; without this hidden faith he dies and goes to dust."

Men have often done impossible things when they have been set on fire with the zeal of some holy purpose. It was said that when George Washington was fighting for his country he seemed like a man possessed by a supernatural power. Washington fed on patriotism and success and a love of freedom and the consciousness of a righteous cause.

Martin Treptow was killed in the Battle of Chatteau Thierry in 1918. In the diary found on his body he had written these words: "I will work, I will save, I will sacrifice, I will endure. I will fight cheerfully and do my utmost as though the entire conflict depended upon me alone." That kind of philosophy and that spirit of determination give us a more powerful kind of energy than ever comes from bread alone.

During the first World War, it was discovered that men could sleep in the mud, eat moldy bread, and actually enjoy it if they believed in what they were doing and had faith that their efforts would bring them victory.

An amateur athlete feeds on a particular kind of mental and emotional diet that enables him to exert himself to the very limit of his capacity in order to win for the school. This kind of spiritual food makes his teammates seem to him like brothers. Their success becomes quite as important to him as does his own. Then he often plays over his head because he is stronger than himself.

The apostle Paul fed on a special kind of diet that enabled him to endure every kind of hardship without murmur, complaint, or weariness. He said: ". . . in labours more abundant, in stripes above measure, in prisons more frequent, in deaths oft. Of the Jews five times received I forty stripes save one. Thrice was I beaten with rods, once was I stoned, thrice I suffered shipwreck, a night and a day I have been in the deep. In journeyings often, in perils of waters, in perils of robbers, in perils by mine own countrymen, in perils by the heathen, in perils in the city, in perils in the wilderness, in perils in the sea, in perils among false brethren; in weariness and painfulness, in watchings often, in hunger and thirst, in fastings often, in cold and nakedness. Beside those things that are without, that which cometh upon me daily, the care of all the churches." (II Cor. 11:23-28)

With all his problems Paul was able to glory in his difficulties and get satisfactions from his persecutions. Paul did not live by bread alone. Many years before, he had received a commission to carry the message of the gospel, and no amount of opposition could turn him back. Paul mentions that he also had some personal problems. He says that his bodily presence was weak and his speech contemptible. He mentions that he had a thorn in the flesh. But men can get along without money, without title, name, or influence. One's appearance may be poor and his speech may be faulty, but all of these may be as nothing if he knows where he is going and is on fire with conviction.

At the end of Paul's life he was able to summarize his difficulties with enthusiasm. And to the Hebrews he said: "For ye had compassion of me in my bonds, and took joyfully the spoiling of your goods, knowing in yourselves that ye have in heaven a better and an enduring substance." (Heb. 10:34) Then of himself he said: "For I am now ready to be offered, and the time of my departure is at hand. I have fought a good fight, I have finished my course, I have kept the faith: Henceforth there is laid up for me a crown of righteousness, which the Lord, the righteous judge, shall give me at that day: and not to me only, but unto them also that love his appearing." (II Tim. 4:6-8)

In speaking of a diet that has given strength, we remember the funny-paper story of Popeye the Sailor. In this fantasy Popeye had found a food that gave him herculean strength. Whenever he needed super strength, he merely ate a required amount of spinach and then no labor was too difficult for him to perform. This idea is not so far-fetched as we might imagine. There are many mental and spiritual foods that can give us strength for the most difficult accomplishments.

I have a friend who has a number of large looseleaf notebooks in which he keeps his literary treasures. He selects and writes down those things that give him courage, enthusiasm, and faith. A great many of these he memorizes and then he reruns these motivating emotions and ideas through his mind to produce just about any desired attitude, as well as the strength that goes with it.

We can absorb a certain kind of spirit by going to a funeral. When we fully participate in the spirit of a football game we get another kind of attitude and another kind of power. If we feed ourselves on a certain kind of emotional food we get angry. Other things make us sad, depressed, discouraged, and weak. Some people can't hear certain music or read certain poems without crying. However, there are other kinds of foods that make people jump for joy and give them ambition and power.

The apostle Paul lived on a kind of food that had prepared him to make any kind of effort or endure any kind of hardship with joy. With his books of literary treasures my friend can put himself in just about any mood by running these philosophies of courage and faith and ambition through his mind, and through his spirit and muscles. These emotions can now regulate his life. These treasured poems, songs, and bits of wisdom have now become a part of him, and they always carry with them a particular spirit that is nourishing and vitalizing. It is as though he has a great supply of especially selected foods loaded with the particular vitamins required to meet his particular needs. He has taken Popeye's story out of fantasy and made it a part of his own reality. He has provided his own cans filled with the spinach of courage, the spinach of industry, the spinach of enthusiasm, and the spinach of good cheer. There are other cans loaded with faith, conviction, determination, and a great devotion to his ideals. With such a supply of foods at his immediate call there are then not very many accomplishments that lie beyond his easy reach.

Jesus indicated that his own source of power came from doing the will of his Eternal Father and in a very literal, practical way that can be the greatest of all known sources of power, and it can be readily utilized by us. Solomon said: "As a man thinketh in his heart, so is he." Demosthenes once said: "No one can have a high and noble calling while engaged in petty and mean employment, for whatever the pursuits of men are, their characters will be similar."

When one understands that he is engaged in that work in which God himself spends his entire time, he will begin doing the things and thinking the thoughts that will give him tremendous strength. The earth itself was organized as a place where the members of God's family could work out their eternal exaltation in the most advantageous way. When we get the spirit of God in our hearts, the fire of faith in our minds, and a righteous ambition in our muscles, then we don't tire or fail very easily. Neither do we go stale or get discouraged. A strong testimony of the truth of the gospel will give one more strength than eating his lunch.

The prophet Job had a source of strength that was unavailable to others when he said. ". . . while my breath is in me, and the spirit of God is in my nostrils; my lips shall not speak wickedness nor my tongue utter deceit . . . till I die I will not remove mine integrity from me." (Job 27:3-5)

We need a lot more of this kind of faith and a better supply of godliness to bring our performance up to where it ought to be.

We should also get a little more excited about our work. Edward Everett Hale has said that "the best education is to be perpetually thrilled by life." We need greater challenge; we need something hard to do.

Before the earth itself was organized Jesus was chosen to come here and redeem mankind from death. His mission was also to teach us the principles of life, explain the doctrines of salvation, and set some goals of accomplishment for us to reach. We may also make it our meat and our drink to do the will of him that sent us and to finish his work. We may get enough righteousness in our minds and enough of the love of God in our hearts that we may become like him. This ambition should be to us like food and drink. Jesus received his strength from the fact that he did his Father's work so effectively. What a great stimulant this idea can be for us to build up the kingdom as well as to benefit from this great power in our own lives!

The Miracles of Christmas

N EAR THE END OF each calendar year we set aside a special period that we commemorate as Christmas. It is usually thought of as the high point of the year. It is a kind of yearly sabbath when we meditate upon the many facets of the birth of the Son of God into our world. This is the time when we relive those wonderful traditions connected with the stable in Bethlehem and the new star that arose out of the east. We rehearse the account of the wise men and the shepherds, and to celebrate the occasion we light up our homes, sing Christmas anthems, and give presents to each other. Among the most important wonders of Christmas are the Christmas miracles.

The dictionary says that a miracle is an accomplishment that lies beyond human capability. We usually think of miracles as deviations from the laws of nature as we know them. The first miracle in the ministry of Jesus took place at Cana when he turned the water into wine. When other people produced wine they planted the vine and cared for the fruit until the grapes were ripe and ready for the wine press, but greater intelligence enabled Jesus to bring these elements together in quicker order.

He did many even more wonderful things; he made the blind to see, the lame to walk, and restored the dead to life. At age twelve he taught the wise men in the temple. He fed the multitude with five loaves and two fishes. He taught principles of righteousness, which, if followed, would not only make the people of our present world successful and happy but would also save our souls. One of the most significant miracles of Jesus took place when he broke the bands of death and initiated the universal bodily resurrection.

With justifiable pride we refer to that part of our knowledge explosion, which took place on July 20, 1969, when we landed two American citizens upon the face of the moon. This event was hailed by one great American as the greatest event that has ever taken place since the creation. Certainly it is no small thing to have two mortal men travel through space to reach another heavenly body, but this twenty-four-billion-dollar American miracle that enabled Mr. Armstrong and Mr. Aldrin to spend two hours and fourteen minutes on the moon pales into insignificance when compared to the fact that the Son of God spent some 33 years upon our earth.

From the time of the miraculous immaculate conception until he arose from the dead, his life was surrounded with miracles. Even the space travel of that first Christmas far surpasses our present abilities in that field. The important pre-Christmas wonders began to take place when an angel appeared to Zacharias and told him that he was to become the father of John the Baptist who would be the Lord's forerunner. Then, in introducing himself, the angel said: "I am Gabriel, that stand in the presence of God; and am sent to speak unto thee, and to shew thee these glad tidings." (Luke 1:19) A few months later the same angel Gabriel was sent to a young woman in the city of Nazareth by the name of Mary, and among other things he said to her: "The Holy Ghost shall come upon thee, and the power of the Highest shall overshadow thee: therefore also the holy thing which shall be born of thee shall be called the Son of God." (Luke 1:35)

To understand this one fact alone that Jesus Christ was and is the literal Son of God has already worked untold miracles in the lives of many people. To be worthy of God's presence would be far more exciting than any trip to the moon could possibly be. In our age of wonders it took twenty-four billion dollars and many years of work by our greatest scientists to put two men on the moon, and even then they had to take with them the very air that they breathed. A whole multitude of heavenly beings came a much greater distance to sing heavenly anthems to the newborn king, and they came without the benefit of flying machines or space suits.

Luke gave us an account of this interesting event when he said:

"And there were in the same country shepherds abiding in the field, keeping watch over their flock by night. And, lo, the angel of the Lord came upon them, and the glory of the Lord shone round about them: and they were sore afraid.

"And the angel said unto them, Fear not: for, behold, I bring you good tidings of great joy, which shall be to all people.

"For unto you is born this day in the city of David a saviour, which is Christ the Lord.

"And this shall be a sign unto you; Ye shall find the babe wrapped in swaddling clothes, lying in a manger.

"And suddenly there was with the angel a multitude of the heavenly host praising God, and saying,

"Glory to God in the highest, and on earth peace, good will toward men.

"And it came to pass, as the angels were gone away from them into heaven, the shepherds said one to another, Let us now go even unto Bethlehem, and see this thing which is come to pass, which the Lord hath made known unto us.

"And they came with haste, and found Mary, and Joseph, and the babe lying in a manger.

"And when they had seen it, they made known abroad the saying which was told them concerning this child." (Luke 2:8-17)

What a wonderful good fortune for us that, out of all of the planets in the vast domains of God, our earth should be honored by having the Son of God born here! Not only was he born upon the earth but he came here in his official capacity as the world's Savior, and had been appointed in the Grand Council of heaven many years previously to be the Redeemer of all the earth's inhabitants on condition of their obedience. It is also significant that God's only Begotten Son in the flesh was like us in form and appearance, and we know that he was also like God, his Eternal Father.

A divine revelation says that "God has created worlds without number," and he has peopled them with his own children, but his first begotten and most capable Son in the spirit who assisted God in these creations was ordained to be our Savior, example, and Redeemer. In foretelling his birth Isaiah said: "For unto us a child is born, unto us a son is given; and the government shall be upon his shoulder: and his name shall be called Wonderful, Counseller, the mighty God, The everlasting Father, The Prince of Peace. Of the increase of his government and peace there shall be no end. . . ." (Isa. 9:6-7)

The poet said:

> There was no other good enough to pay the price of sin,
> He only could unlock the gates of heaven and let us in.

One of the greatest Christmas presents that we can conceive is that he has atoned for our sins on condition of our obedience. It should also substantially raise the value of our earth in our eyes to know that his own future as its Redeemer is also connected with it. We think of our earth as a pretty good place just as it is, but since the Fall of Adam it has existed in its telestial or fallen state.

The Lord has told us many things about the glorious future of our earth. The time will soon come when the Son of God will again come to the earth. This time he will be accompanied by his mighty angels, and they will come in flaming fire to cleanse the earth and to inaugurate his millennial reign of a thousand years upon it. Then we will all know firsthand much more about peace and good will of which the angels sang on that first Christmas night so long ago. When he comes to rule, our earth will be raised in its status and will become a terrestrial earth. Then the paradisiacal beauty of its Garden of Eden days will be restored. To get acquainted with the moon should also increase our appreciation of the earth. The moon has no fertile topsoil, no life-giving atmosphere, no rainfall, no rivers, no plant or animal life. The moon was appointed to give its beautiful light to our earth by night. (See Gen. 1:16-18)

In contrast to the moon, think of the care God exercised in preparing this earth as a place of human habitation. He gave it its laws, its beauty, its material abundance, and ordained its glorious future. After the Millennium our earth will again have an increase in status. It will then become a celestial sphere, and those who qualify for the celestial order of God will live upon it forever. If our earth is good enough that the Son of God should want to live here, then it must be pretty good, and certainly we should make the most of our own opportunity to live here eternally.

The greatest gift that we could give ourselves at Christmas time might be our own list of all the Christmas miracles we have to be thankful for. Of course, we still regret that there was no room found in the inn where he could be born, but it will be a much greater tragedy if there is no room for us on our celestialized earth because we have made no room in our lives for his love, his righteousness, and his obedience.

At Christmas time we love to think about the great new star that guided the wise men across the desert and enabled them to lay their treasures at the feet of the Prince of Peace and the King of kings. His life was also intended to be our guide, and the great scriptures were likewise given for that purpose.

In the same chapter in which Luke tells of the visit of the angels from heaven, he also tells of the earth growth made by Jesus as our example. Luke says: "And Jesus increased in wisdom and stature, and in favour with God and man." (Luke 2:52) He increased in wisdom that represents his great mental developments. He increased in stature, indicating his magnificent physical growth. He increased in his favor with God that represents an important religious development, and he increased in his favor with man that signifies his outstanding social progress. This four-fold program should also be a constant inspiration for us to follow. Among the greatest of the miracles are the miracles of growth. By some mysterious process acorns can become oak trees. We get many wonders out of seeds. Human foreheads can grow broader, hearts can get bigger, vision can become more perceptive, spirituality can become more intense, and righteousness can become more all inclusive. God has made it possible that a thousand giant redwoods can come from an ounce of redwood seed, but the Creator's most serious concern was not about the welfare of redwoods. He was far more interested in having his offspring develop to become like their eternal parents.

One of the greatest Christmas thoughts is that we are the children of God formed in his image and in possession of his potentialities. We know that God, angels, spirits, and men are all of the same species in different stages of development and in different degrees of righteousness. Jesus grew up without sin unto salvation and then said: "Follow me." He organized his Church upon the earth and indicated that we should belong to it. He taught the great principles of truth and outlined the means by which our eternal exaltation could be brought about. In giving the apostles their final instructions before his ascension he said: "Go ye therefore, and teach all nations, baptizing them in the name of the Father, and of the Son, and of the Holy Ghost: Teaching them to observe all things whatsoever I have commanded you: and, lo, I am with you alway, even unto the end of the world." (Matt. 28:19-20)

Jesus announced his own interest in us by saying: ". . . I am come that they might have life, and that they might have it more abundantly." (John 10:10) To increase the abundance of our lives is also one of the greatest of our own opportunities. We can get a good start in the right direction by getting the miracles of Christmas into our lives. Obedience to God is one of the wonder drugs of the spirit to increase our faith and vitalize our industry. We make some of our most dramatic and profitable responses to life at Christmas time.

Former President Hadley of Yale University once said: "The most important thing that anyone ever gets out of college is the college spirit." Then one begins to play for the school. Then his teammates become his brothers, and their success becomes quite as important to him as his own. It is likely that one of the most important things we can get out of Christmas is the spirit of Christ growing in our hearts. That is the spirit of "peace on earth, good will toward men." It is that spirit of love and righteousness that re-performs the miracles of Christmas in us.

In summarizing the accomplishments of his life, Mr. J. A. Francis makes a thrilling and accurate appraisal of the influence that Christ has had in our world. He said: "Since then nineteen wide centuries have come and gone and today he is the very center of the human race. I am well within the mark when I say that all the armies that ever marched, and all of the navies that were ever built, and all of the parliaments that ever sat, and all of the kings that ever reigned put together have not affected the life of man upon this earth as powerfully as has this one solitary life."

May we take full advantage of his wonderful Christmas miracles.

The Mortician's Handbook

SOME TIME AGO I was permitted to examine a mortician's handbook. I was particularly intrigued by one chapter that was entitled "Five Ways to Tell a Dead Man." In trying to help a mortician do his job properly, the handbook said that if no mist appeared on a mirror when placed under the subject's nostril, or if he didn't bleed when pricked with a pin, he was dead.

This task of recognizing death is not just the job of morticians. The problems involved are not always as simple as they may appear at first thought. The situation becomes even more complicated because there are so many forms of death. Death comes in several degrees. The dictionary says that death is that state of being where the organs of motion and the faculties of life have ceased to perform their functions. In most cases this cessation comes upon us a little bit at a time. Frequently one may continue for a long period in a state where animation is so near to a total suspension that it is difficult to tell which side of death's zero one may be on.

We hear of people falling into "a dead faint," or one may lose himself in "a dead sleep." Sometimes disease may reduce one to a point where any evidences of life are difficult to discover. For obvious reasons it is very important for the mortician to be completely accurate in his diagnosis. An accurate diagnosis is just as important to us in our spiritual, mental, and social lives. Life is the most important commodity in the universe and everyone is interested in its many manifestations. Some aspects of our lives may be even more important to us than their physical forms. Our spiritual lives, our social lives, our occupational lives, and our moral lives are all subject to some kind of degree of death. Usually death doesn't come all at once on a 100 percent basis.

In the parable of the Good Samaritan the Bible says that certain thieves left the man from Jerico "half dead." (See Luke 10:30) Death also has other sizes in its fractions. We are aware of the fact that the government properly measures disability in percentages. Everyone isn't equally disabled. Therefore the government makes its payments on the basis that one person is 90 percent disabled, while another is 50 percent disabled, and a third may be only 10 percent disabled. In many of their various manifestations life and death may also be measured as a percentage because everyone is not equally dead.

Paul speaks of the children of disobedience who were dead in trespasses and sins. (See Eph. 2:1-2) He points out that death had overtaken the faith of some because of their "dead works." (Heb. 11:13) He said to the Hebrews that some of them were "as good as dead." (Heb. 11:12) Many living and many dead people are very close together on death's percentage chart and have about the same practical value.

Recently I saw death manifest itself in many different degrees among the trees of a neglected fruit orchard. Some trees were completely bare and totally dead, while with some other trees one-half of their branches were dead and the other half were still alive. A few branches were afflicted with blight, where all their leaves had the color of death, and diseased fruit was sickly and scrubby. Almost all of these trees were possessed by some fraction of death, but a very similar situation frequently applies to us. Sometimes we get a diseased and sickly look when the deadly blight of sin stamps out our spiritual health. What a miserable, fractional death we suffer when our ambition dies, or our hope dies, or our interest in life dies, or our morality dies! The blight of a 90 percent death is frequently brought upon us when our faith dies, or our happiness dies, or our industry dies. We can't be buried because there is still a physical mist on the mirror.

Some time ago I talked with a woman who had tried to commit suicide. She seemed to have lost all her interest in life. She remained alive so far as pain and regret were concerned, but she was dead to those beautiful joys that she should have had. When one dies intellectually, spiritually, or morally, there may not be very much reason left to live on physically. On the tombstone of one person someone had carved his epitaph, saying, "Died at 30, buried at 65." Sometimes a great sorrow, a tragic disappointment, or some serious sins can destroy one's desire and one's will to live. Then there are also several kinds of living death where one dies over and over again.

Shakespeare said: "Cowards die a thousand times before their death; the brave man never tastes of death but once." In some ways we are like the cat having nine lives. Where one has more than one life he is eligible to more than one death. The drunken, the immoral, and the unfaithful also die many times before their deaths, and they may also die many times after their deaths as well.

The scripture speaks of living deaths and eternal deaths. How much is there left to live for when one is dead to truth and dead to God and dead to righteousness? When death gets a sufficient majority in our lives we soon pass the point of no return. Those who continue to follow Satan will eventually be enslaved by him. When they lose their power of choice they are compelled to share his fate. John the Revelator saw the eternal destiny of those who had surrendered a majority fraction of their lives to evil. It was said to them: ". . . and he which is filthy, let him be filthy still: and he that is righteous, let him be righteous still. . . ." (Rev. 22:11)

Think what it would be like to be completely turned over to unrighteousness. Some think it is all right to sow a few wild oats or go on some kind of an excursion into evil, providing they can get back, but sin acts as a kind of dope and we are not usually aware that we are going too far. When we can't get back we must live with evil forever. When the fraction of evil gets too large, the remaining good is strangled and dies, and then we reach that terrible destination of being 100 percent dead so far as the things of righteousness are concerned. Satan is the father of sin. He is "pure" evil and he seeks that all men might be miserable like unto himself. It would be a great idea if we had a kind of life's handbook to keep us informed as to our accumulated fraction of righteousness. It would be helpful if we had a kind of thermostat that would set off an alarm if our percentage of death went beyond a certain point.

The story is told of a man whose plane had been wrecked while flying over the wastes of the Arctic. He knew that there was a native village beyond the hills a few miles away. However, it was bitter cold, and progress through the snow would be very difficult, but his only chance to avoid death was to reach the village. Therefore, he set out for his destination where he knew he would find food, warmth, and life. After walking a few miles through the snow he became very tired. As he stopped to rest he began to get drowsy. He decided that if he could take a short nap in the snow he could rebuild enough energy to enable him to reach the village. As he lay there in the soft snow he thought how warm and restful he now felt, but just as he was about to drop off to sleep he was struck by the awful thought that he was freezing to death. He was so shaken by the idea that he jumped to his feet and began to run as fast as he could toward the village. He realized that he was running for his life. As he ran he began getting his life back. Soon his mind was fully aroused and the great surge of blood churning through his arteries gave his body a feeling of new strength. He knew that as long as he could maintain his effort he was safe. With his spirit working at its maximum he soon arrived at his destination where food, rest, and care placed him beyond danger. He had been 95 percent dead, but now he was 95 percent alive. In only a slightly different sense all of us are running for our lives.

Dorothea Brande once wrote a stimulating book with a provocative title called *Wake Up and Live*. Mrs. Brande points out some ways in which we can put more life into our living. When one dies physically he completely loses his warmth, fervor, energy, and spirit. He also loses the ability to serve. In some fraction these same things happen to us spiritually, morally, and mentally. When one's ambition ceases to function effectively, his success gets cold and his interest in his work becomes listless and apathetic. To wake up and live is a more pleasant objective than to lie down and die. It is a great idea that we can have life in a much greater fraction. Mrs. Brande's book is a good one and it can be very helpful, but Deity himself has written the best "Wake Up and Live" books.

The Son of God announced his own mission by saying: ". . . I am come that they might have life, and that they might have it more abundantly." (John 10:10) God did not create us in his image with the expectation that we should merely be one-half alive. He does not want us to let a devastating blight make those great faculties and senses look like a half-dead fruit orchard or like the earlier condition of the prodigal son when the father said: "This my son was dead and is alive again." God wants us to live again on a glorious, eternal basis. A significant statement was made about Jesus when it was said: "In him was life and the life was the light of men." What a great day when that can also be said of each of us!

The scriptures say that God has life in himself. He has given the Son to have life in himself, and if we keep ourselves alive to the end of our mortality we will then be given life in ourselves. This will be an eternal life, the kind of life that God has. In order to have a 100 percent eternal life with God in heaven we should put a lot of life into the things that we do here. Because the body is dead without the spirit, God has ordained a glorious resurrection. Only with the spirit and the body inseparably connected can we receive a fullness of joy. What an exciting prospect to have the possibility of living eternally on a 100 percent basis, to be able to feel life in our minds, our spirits, our personalities, our hearts, and our glorious, resurrected, celestialized bodies! And what a disappointment it would be to have to live throughout eternity with a lot of dead, unsightly, unpleasant branches. What gratitude we should show to God for this privilege of having an abundant, eternal life! Of course, we should remember that everything has its opposites and as an eternal life is the greatest of all objectives, so an everlasting death is the most dreadful of all fates. The loss of even a small part of eternal life would be a tragedy. Jesus said: "And fear not them which kill the body . . . but rather fear him which is able to destroy both soul and body in hell." (Matt. 10:28)

It has been said that no one ever loses eternal life by a blowout; it is always just a series of slow leaks, a little thoughtlessness, a little disobedience, a little procrastination, a little sin, and before we know it we have lost eternal life. It would be the height of folly to so much dread to lose mortal life all at once and then to deliberately throw away an eternal life a little bit at a time. A few wrong thoughts and a little carelessness may mean some dead branches throughout eternity. The physical body is made up of what it eats. The mind is made up of what it thinks. A little evil may start us on our way down hill.

We don't have to lose very much of the spirit of success to make our lives difficult by giving failure more than a working majority of influence. When we fall down in our works just a little, we begin weakening our faith so that it tires more easily and begins to die. Then little by little the good in our lives may lose its voting power. When godliness has only a minority interest in our lives, our enthusiasm dies, our righteousness dies, and we may soon find ourselves under the full control of evil. To head off this change we should wake up now and start run-

ning for our lives. Many people have passed the point of no
return without knowing it. Evil can soon make redemption
improbable and finally impossible. As the Savior has said: "My
blood will not cleanse them if they hear me not." If we lose
the will to repent we have lost the saving power of the atonement and have lost our eternal lives.

When no mist appears on the mirrors of our activity, we
had better wake up and start living. When our industry doesn't
respond to the pricking of our conscience, we had better start
running for our lives. When our religious enthusiasm begins
getting cold and our devotion starts getting sleepy, we had better
turn on our works and get them churning up our faith. When
our moral food doesn't taste good, it is a pretty good sign that
we are sick. When we find ourselves building bars in our homes
instead of altars, or when we can feel more excitement over a
horse race or a prize fight than the prospect of the Celestial Kingdom, we should know that we have a problem needing immediate
attention. When our religious enthusiasm starts slowing down,
it means that our faith is starting to die a little bit at a time.
When we think the Ten Commandments are out of date and
no longer apply to us, and when we half believe that God is
dead, we have already lost a lot of ground in our quest for life.
When we don't like to say our prayers, or read the scriptures,
we had better start checking the steam on the mirror. Or if by
some chance we are identifying with those strange people who
dislike work, hold illicit love-ins, and take part in glue-sniffing
and dope addiction, then we had better stick a few pins into
our spirits and find out what is happening. We ought to increase
our interest in some great "wake up and live" scriptures and
in some great "wake up and live" activities. We should wake up
and think, wake up and worship, wake up and get going. It is
very stimulating to wake up and start running. We should
remember that we are running for our lives — our eternal lives!
We need to be fully alive if we are to reach our goal in safety
and on time. Someone once wrote a book entitled. *How to Stay
Alive the Rest of Your Life.* That would be a good title for all
of us to write under.

Oak Trees

N ONE OF SOLOMON'S most provocative proverbs he said: "Where there is no vision the people perish." This wise statement has some interesting applications in every department of life. The railroad engineer is able to provide more protection for his sleeping passengers because a giant headlight projects a mile-long shaft of light down the tracks. As the locomotive rushes through the darkness the light is extended at an equal rate so that the train may travel safely across an entire continent on a single mile of advance lighting. Human beings can provide their own safety as they learn to project their own headlights along the rails of life. However, there are several differences between these two situations. The railroad engine is provided with a light that is all ready to turn on, whereas more or less, each human being must manufacture his own vision for himself.

There are many divine gifts that are bestowed upon us in an undeveloped state. At birth, we receive a perfect pair of eyes, but they cannot discern objects. We have ears that cannot distinguish sounds. Our legs are perfectly fashioned but are unable to bear the weight of the body, much less walk. Our excellent brains lack reason, and even our hands are helpless. According to what we do, these faculties may acquire some almost godlike powers or they may lie dormant forever. It was full-grown adults to whom Jesus referred, when he spoke of eyes that couldn't see, and he had in mind that we don't see far enough or soon enough or clearly enough. In a completely unique gift, God has provided man with two creators: one is God and the other is man himself. It has been said that in this important partnership, looking toward man's development, God furnishes the capital and it is required that man himself must supply the labor and the supervision. In the personal ministry of Jesus he gave sight to the blind, restored hearing to the deaf, imparted understanding to the thoughtless, and brought the dead back to life.

We are given the responsibility for performing these same miracles for our own benefit. It is our most important job to teach our own weak eyes to see and to replace our blindness with a full measure of sight. Vision is much more than merely a function of the eyes; it is also the concern of the mind. We supply our vision with its greatest candlepower as we teach ourselves to think, evaluate, reason, understand, believe, and do. We should be aware that nothing is ever born fully developed, and growth is one of the most difficult mysteries to understand or to believe in or to bring about. The job is made still more complicated, inasmuch as among all of God's creations man is not only the most helpless creature at birth, but he has the longest period of infancy. A dragonfly acquires the fully developed powers of an adult in a few hours. His flying skills, food-getting techniques, reproduction abilities, and parental excellences are all in the package to begin with. Without any apparent instruction he knows who his natural enemies are, how to avoid dangers, and how to make a living. It is an interesting fact that the further up life's scale one goes, the longer the period of infancy becomes. Even among the highest forms of life — next to man himself — the period of infancy is very short. All of God's creatures below man behave in their sphere in a way that leaves little to be desired. At one year of age, a mother bird is a model of faithful performance. She never loses her way. She never deserts her young, she never has an inferiority complex, and she never gets drunk.

Many of these forms have completed their life's span before a human being even starts to school. It is sometimes 30 years before many human beings are able to effectively carry on their chosen life's work and fully provide for a family. Even in fifty years, many husbands never learn to get along with their wives, and even later than this, some are still wrestling with such problems as alcoholism, nicotine addiction, and sloth that would never cause even the most retarded animal the slightest difficulty. Even though our natural endowments are vastly superior, as our own creators, we sometimes never mature more than a small percentage of our physical, mental, or spiritual potentiality.

Ralph Waldo Emerson once said: "I have never seen a whole man." What he meant was that he had never seen a man as perfect as the man he could imagine. There are dozens of perfect birds and there are hundreds of animals and thousands of plants that fill the purpose of their creation in a way that leaves nothing to be desired. Very few human beings ever get very close to the degree of perfection intended for them. God has never once found it necessary to give the animal creation any such commandments as those given from Mount Sinai saying, "Thou shalt not."

One of our most serious problems seems to be our difficulty to see. We are so prone to join with the fool who said in his heart, "There is no God." Instead of accepting God and being guided by his wisdom we continue our contests to reach new heights of crime, liquor addiction, and those things that are causing our problems, and so frequently we are unable to believe even in ourselves or in our own futures. God has tried to teach us the advantages of developing greater character qualities and more worthwhile abilities in ourselves, but we can't seem to see ahead far enough, either to understand our own needs or to materialize our own potentialities. It is primarily our lack of vision that makes us unwilling to accept divine guidance or to invest the necessary effort to bring about our own eternal destiny, and we therefore bring upon ourselves a kind of arrested development so that sometimes we just never grow up. Accordingly we put on our midget suits and become dropouts and sinners and ne'er-do-wells.

When one takes a stand against maturity, it is hard to see the advantages of getting thoroughly prepared for an occupation, or for marriage, or for parenthood, or even for our eternal lives. Because these important events often lie beyond the short range of our imagination's headlights, we see them only as shadowy, misty, ghost-like shapes. Without a clear vision our discernment fails and we become hazy and confused about values. One's judgment is never any better than his information. Lacking clear vision also makes us unable to compensate for that deception of perspective that makes everything close by look large and important, while everything in the distance seems of small consequence.

We not only become dropouts from education but we become dropouts from religion and from success and from eternal glory. As our vision decreases, our discouragement, failure, sin, and errors increase. Then we go blind concerning our possibilities and become dropouts from eternal happiness. When we indulge in too much negative thinking, our pigmy attitudes become dominant in the personality, and there is little chance to realize our potential — mentally, morally, spiritually, socially, or financially. We place a serious handicap upon ourselves when we insist on looking at our possibilities through the belittling end of the telescope and increase the world's most widespread disease, which is the deadly inferiority complex.

A resourceful inventor is one who can see possibilities in advance. A good architect first builds the cathedral in his mind before the people can be summoned to worship. To improve our own success we should prelive our possibilities and thereby get on a more intimate basis with that progress which we haven't yet made.

One of our most magnificent abilities is to comprehend the possibility that foreheads can get broader, and hearts can get bigger, and muscles can get tougher, ambitions can reach greater goals, enthusiasms can become more meaningful, and that a more effective industry can bring about greater accomplishments. Our midget instincts always tend to set in operation those processes of rationalizing, alibiing, and offering excuses that reduce our possibilities. It is our midget inclinations that say: "I was not cut out to be such and such, or I was born wrong, or I am what I am and there is nothing I can do about it." If tolerated very long these inclinations will cut off our hopes, cause our faith to grow weaker and our souls to shrivel up. Pigmy talents always tend to immobilize our courage, kill our industry, and prevent our eternal progression, but growth is probably the greatest invention of God, and we strengthen our abilities primarily by its use.

If you would like to have a good growth exercise for your imagination, suppose that you were an acorn, trying to believe in your ultimate possibilities as an oak tree. Suppose that you had never seen an acorn become an oak tree, and you have no past experience for understanding the growing process. There are so many difficulties involved where even an appeal to the reason or an examination of your assets may not help very much.

To begin with, an acorn is smaller than the end of your thumb. Inside it is made up of an unimpressive mealy substance, which, even under a microscope or in face of the most scientific examination, gives no evidence of its miraculous power. An acorn has no self-starters, no gadgets, no engine, no thermostats, and no written directions on how to proceed, and yet if you plant this little seed in the soil and leave it all alone in the dark, it has the ability to become a giant oak tree — this in spite of the fact that it has no one to counsel it or help it along. By the exercise of this miraculous power that God has placed inside it, it can actually reach its destiny and multiply the original investment by a million times, and its wood, branches, leaves, and roots will all be completely unlike the original acorn from which they all came.

I don't know anyone who professes to understand this miracle, but I do know that acorns can become oak trees. And I have no inclination to question the divine pronouncement that under the right conditions the offspring of God may eventually become like the parent. It may have been to keep us humble that someone wrote:

> Don't worry if your job is small
> And your rewards are few.
> Remember that the mighty oak
> Was once a nut like you.

God has not only endowed us with his own potentialities but he has also left a full set of instructions on how to proceed. We know that all happiness and all success is conditioned upon our personal righteousness and obedience to his laws. The rewards of good and the consequences of evil have been fully explained to us, but we continue to have difficulty in believing. Almost no one believed that the flood would come as foretold. Even the Savior himself was not accepted. The word of the Lord tells us that most of the really important events in our lives are still ahead of us. However, there are very few people who actually believe the hundreds of prophecies announcing the glorious second coming of Christ to cleanse the earth of sin. Few have any clear picture of the establishment of Christ's millennial reign upon the earth. We have many prophecies foretelling the literal bodily resurrection. We know about the final judgment, the various degrees of glory, and the eternity of the family unit, but because our faith can't see these future events very clearly they never seem to us very real or very believable, and consequently we miss the motivation of their power.

We don't even believe in our personal possibilities, and so like the antediluvians we just go along insisting on business as usual, making such unreasonable responses to life as: "God is dead," or "Everybody's doing it," or "We are not responsible." As long as these important events are still a little way down the track our ailing vision says, "What difference does it make anyway?"

The story is told of a young man being apprehended while stealing a watermelon. Someone said to him: "Bill, if you take that watermelon now, you will have to pay for it in eternity." Bill said, "If I can have that much time, I'll take two."

Any penalty or any reward seems very unimportant if it is placed far enough in the future. However, no matter how near or how far, the price of sin and the penalty for disbelief have always been extremely high. Esau traded off his entire birthright for a mess of pottage. Like so many of us he was cheated by the deception in his own shortsightedness. We are also made poorer by our undeveloped discernment and the inaccurate judgment of those values that lie down the tracks ahead of us. Because we think it can't happen to us our false reasoning may so far divorce us from reality as to make us lose the greatest blessings of our lives. Our greatest opportunity is to develop the kind of vision necessary to reach our eternal objectives; and even though we may now seem to be only as acorns, we may someday become giant oak trees.

Poetry

SOME OF LIFE'S greatest pleasures and many of its most important meanings come from language. It would be difficult to visualize our lives or imagine our satisfactions without the ability to express ourselves. Language takes several forms and it may be written, spoken, heard, or thought. Included in our language we have all kinds of persuasion, conversation, debate, religious discussion, and political declarations. Then there is an extra-special kind of language that we call "poetry." Poetry has a little more elegance and a little greater punch than ordinary language.

Someone has said that "poetry is language dressed up in its best clothes." It is one form of speech that is a little more refined. It has a little more spirit, a little more music, and a little more beauty than regular forms of literature. Poetry can sometimes say more and say it with greater effectiveness. It adds perception to life, widens our horizons, sharpens our spiritual contacts, elevates our spirits, raises the temperature of our enthusiasms, and increases the joy content of our experiences.

Poetry fills an important inspirational need and helps us to live more fully with a greater awareness of life's values. It provides a motivation which enables us to get greater performance from ourselves. The poet assembles from many sources what has been felt, observed, learned, or imagined. Then he selects, combines, reorganizes and refines them in such a way that he may create some brand new experiences which appropriately stimulate and satisfy us. A poet may develop a greater insight so that he can pass on to us a better understanding of our world and a finer appreciation of its people. Charles Elliot Norton has recommended that whatever our occupation may be and however crowded with affairs our hours are, we should not fail to spend a few minutes each day in refreshing our inner lives with a bit of poetry.

Ezra Pound defined great literature as that language which has been charged with meaning to the utmost possible degree. This definition might also serve as a good description of our poetry. We may enjoy the refined thoughts of others without investing the time or becoming involved in the expense or risk that we would need to put into our actual experience.

Someone has said that every day we ought to think a good thought, read a great poem, listen to some inspiring music, absorb a great scripture, and do a noble act. We have a daily need for something to encourage us, raise our sights, wind up our faith, and fill our ambitions with power. And it has been pointed out that in their ability to upgrade our lives, the poets stand next to the prophets.

I have an interesting little book entitled *101 Famous Poems*. It is like a supermarket with 101 products that should be memorized, loved, and lived with. In one of these poems, written under the title of "The Present Crisis," James Russell Lowell says:

Once to every man and nation comes the moment to decide,
In the strife of Truth with Falsehood, for the good or evil side;
Some great cause, God's new Messiah, offering each the bloom or
     blight,
Parts the goats upon the left hand and the sheep upon the right,
And the choice goes by forever 'twixt the darkness and the light.

Careless seems the great Avenger; history's pages but record
One death-grapple in the darkness 'twixt old systems and the Word;
Truth forever on the scaffold, Wrong forever on the throne, —
Yet that scaffold sways the future, and, behind the dim unknown,
Standeth God within the shadow, keeping watch above his own.

Then to side with Truth is noble when we share her wretched crust,
Ere her cause bring fame and profit, and 'tis prosperous to be just;
Then it is the brave man chooses, while the coward stands aside,
Doubting in his abject spirit, till his Lord is crucified,
And the multitude makes virtue of the faith they had denied.

Walt Whitman points out that "to have great poets we must also have great audiences." He says that the Greeks were great during their golden age because their audiences yearned for poetry. Certainly every inspired book needs an inspired reader. In our day we have such a great collection of fine poetry, and from these poems we may select the inspiration and imagination about our exalted human concepts and the high ideals of life as they are presented in their most beautiful forms.

Anciently one who was thought to be worthy of bearing the laurel or wearing the crown of the muse of poetry was given the title of poet laureate. Later this title was used to honor other eminent poets. It has also been conferred by some universities on poets of noted ability. In England, an outstanding poet was appointed by the sovereign to be a member of the royal household. And his duty as poet laureate of England was to compose odes and poems for national occasions and for the inspiration of members of the court. A poet is not bound to write poems only about those things which have actually happened. He is free to exercise his imagination over the entire range of his emotional powers so as to touch all of the fundamental principles of truth. This may include all of the useful truth that has been expressed in fables, parables, history, or fantasy. And by the integrity of his treatment, the details of all of these fundamental avenues of truth are made available to us in dynamic form to uplift us by their strength and beauty. Someone once said that the poetry of Coleridge is the blossom and flagrance of the greatest human thoughts and passions translated into the language of the emotions.

The values in great ideas may be more easily incorporated in our ambitions when they are dressed in beautiful, rhythmical, poetical language. Great poetry is characterized by harmony and by those emotional qualities that appeal to the feelings and stimulate the imagination. Wordsworth spoke of the vocal raptures of poetry. Keats said, "I will fly to thee on the wings of poetry." John Milton said, "He who would do laudable things ought to be a true poem in himself." Every life is supplied with a poetic vein, but we must learn to command the shaft by which the gold is withdrawn. Of course, many of the most excellent poets have never versified. But everyone should develop those qualities of harmony, expressiveness, artistry, and an ability to elevate the spirit that is said to belong to poetry. Even by reading and memorizing poetry we may train ourselves to feel extra beauty, develop more music in our hearts, and acquire the spirit of a more effective expression. When we feel the harmony and music of poetry, we can improve our lives and make these extra virtues a permanent part of us.

Of course, great prose too can step up the intensity of our reactions and increase the range of our vicarious experiences. In its various forms, our language is almost all-important to our success. It can help in clarifying life's meanings and give our emotions greater power.

Language is the instrument of persuasion; it is the chief ingredient in all kinds of advertisements, propaganda, bulletins, sermons, and political declarations. But that special language called "poetry" can also be used as a kind of sugar-coated, nice-tasting pill by which some wholesome truths can often be made more palatable. Language, like people, affects us more powerfully when dressed up in a significant attire that is pretty and colorful. Like other forms of literature, poetry has an interest in every kind of human experience, whether it is beautiful or ugly, strange or common, noble or ignoble, actual or imaginary. And when such ideas are artfully transmitted, the various uplifting ideas can be made to serve our best interests more effectively.

Even such experiences as sickness, death, pain, and suffering, which in real life may be unpleasant, can be made to seem both pleasurable and profitable through fine poetic thoughts. In real life, getting soaked in a rainstorm may not be very pleasant, but in poetry it can become a happy occasion. Sometimes when we cry in actual life it means that we are unhappy, but many people cry while reading a great poem as a manifestation of their joy. Ordinarily, we don't like to be frightened in real life, whereas sometimes we go to the movies or read a book with that very purpose in mind. Even righteous wars can give us joy when we read about them in elevated language afterward. We sometimes go to a great lecture to receive a challenge that we are unable to give ourselves.

Sometimes when we are dull, bored, unperceptive and lifeless we can be made responsive and brought back to life by the music and driving power of a great poem. Poetry may help us to focus our attention and organize our experience in such a way as to get greater understanding and produce more satisfactions.

To understand success is one of the first steps toward attaining it. Here again, poetry can be helpful as the most condensed and concentrated form of literature. Poetry can usually say the most in the fewest number of words. Elevated thoughts cannot be adequately expressed in degraded language. One may read poetry while lying in a hammock sipping a cool drink, while low music is playing in the background. But while engaged with great ideas his mind should never assume that attitude. Poetry may soothe and relax, but its primary function is to arouse and awaken.

Sometimes an idea can be used to shock us into activity. Poetry might serve as a substitute for a sedative, but it fills a greater need while maintaining us in a state of animation. Poetry is the language of love. And to get the greatest amount of good out of poetry, one should fall in love with love's spirit and language. Then everything around him seems more beautiful and worthwhile. Then even the most trivial things can seem of great consequence.

When one person loves another person, the importance of the beloved is greatly increased in the mind of the lover. Great truths and great ideals also are magnified by feelings of love. Poetry has a greater power to move us because it is able to make the maximum use of the music and emotion of language. A good poet chooses his words for their sound, their meter, their cadence and their music to reinforce their meaning.

Edgar Allan Poe describes poetry as music combined with a pleasurable idea. Some people may disagree on the amount of attention that poetry deserves, but certainly our success can be helped by getting a love of rhythm and the beauty of meter more deeply rooted in us. Rhythm is related to the beat of our hearts, the pulsations of our blood, the intake and outgo of air in our lungs. Everything that we do naturally and gracefully, we do rhythmically. There is a rhyme in the way we swim, the way we ride a horse, the way we swing a golf club or use a baseball bat. The term *rhythm* refers to any wave-like recurrence of motion or sound. In speech it is the natural rise and fall of language. All language is to some degree rhythmical, for all language involves some kind of alternation between accented and unaccented syllables. We need some kind of a rhythm in our lives that we can tap our foot to, so to speak.

In every word of more than one syllable, one syllable is accented or stressed by giving it more prominence in pronunciation than the others. The word *meter* comes from the word meaning measure. The rhythm and the sound of language can be harmonized to produce the music of poetry. Not only is this music enjoyable in itself, but it also reinforces meaning and intensifies our finest communications.

Poetry engages the responses of the whole man in his senses, his imaginations, his intellectual powers. It does not merely touch him on the side of his nature. The mission of great poetry is not merely to entertain its devotees but to inspire more measure and help them reach greater accomplishments. With great poetry, we can get some fresh insights and a renewal of life itself into our human experience, and a person can develop a broader and a deeper understanding of his fellowmen as well as of himself by the music that good poetry can put into his soul. A study of poetry delights our hearts, ornaments our lives, supplies us with information, and increases our success ability.

Prisoners

ONE OF THE SIGNIFICANT institutions in our society is its prisons. At the present time in the United States we have over 750,000 people who are confined in federal, state, or local penitentiaries. In addition, there are approximately 500,000 younger people who are being detained in reform schools and detention homes.

In earlier times prisoners were often confined in underground windowless dungeons. Very frequently a cave or a pit served as the place of imprisonment, and the prisoners were often bound with cords or placed in irons.

Freling Foster tells us about one of America's cruelest jail sentences. A young 16-year-old Boston boy by the name of Jesse H. Pomeroy was convicted of murder in 1876. There were some who wanted him executed, but he was sentenced to life imprisonment in solitary confinement as a compromise. For the next fifty-six years until his death in 1932 he was kept in complete isolation, always within the dark confines of prison walls. It is a horrible thought to try and imagine what the life of this human being must have been like. What did he think about? What were the emotions that filled his heart?

It is interesting to remember that there are some other kinds of prisons, some of which are even more horrible. Many of us serve as slaves of our own bad habits and our own attitudes of irresponsibility. Many people are imprisoned by dope, alcohol, and evil thinking. We become prisoners of hate, greed, and lust.

Sir Rabindranath Tagore, the Hindu poet who won the 1913 Nobel Prize in literature, once said: "Prisoner, tell me who it was that bound you." "It was my master," said the prisoner. "As I amassed my wealth an unusual sleep overcame me, and upon waking up I found that I was a prisoner in my own treasure house." "Prisoner, tell me who it was that wrought this unbreakable chain." Said the prisoner, "It was I who carefully forged my prison fetters! I thought that my invincible power would hold the world captive, leaving me with freedom undisturbed. Thus night and day I worked at the chain with huge fires and cruel hard strokes. When at last the work was done and the links were complete and unbreakable, I found that it held me in its grasp."

Some people must be locked up as protection to society. Some have to be confined as a protection to themselves. Imprisonment is also frequently used as a punishment for wrong-doing and a means of reformation. We are also punished for our sins to help us develop a more healthy point of view for the future. Sometimes this punishment is very great, as we are punished by our sins as well as for our sins. Sometimes punishment incites enough fear in us that we turn away from evil.

The apostle Peter tells us of the fate of that group of people who were disobedient to God in the days of Noah. First they paid with their lives by being drowned in the flood, and upon arrival in the spirit world they were sent to an eternal prison house to serve out a much longer sentence. We feel bad about the long fifty-six-year sentence of Jesse Pomeroy, but the ante-diluvians suffered an additional confinement of at least 23 centuries.

The flood took place about 2,300 years, B.C., and the scripture tells us that while the body of Christ lay in the tomb, his spirit went to the prison house to visit the confined prisoners and to organize the work of preaching the gospel of redemption to them with the prospect of releasing those who showed themselves to be deserving. Peter said: "For Christ also hath once suffered for sins, the just for the unjust, that he might bring us to God, being put to death in the flesh, but quickened by the spirit; by which also he went and preached unto the spirits in prison; Which sometime were disobedient, when once the long suffering of God waited in the days of Noah, while the ark was a preparing, wherein few, that is, eight souls were saved by water." (I Peter 3:18-20)

Peter tells us why this mission was necessary when he said: ". . . for this cause was the gospel preached also to them that are dead, that they might be judged according to men in the flesh, but live according to God in the spirit." (I Peter 4:6) All people must be judged according to the law, and because some have disobeyed the law or have not had an adequate chance to know it, under the program of a merciful and just God that opportunity is given in the spirit world to those who are entitled to it.

The scripture is clear about the fact that an important part of the mission of Jesus was that of releasing the prisoners from their bondage by teaching them the truths of the gospel and by getting them to accept the atonement by their righteousness. Christ's atonement makes possible our release from an everlasting imprisonment. When Jesus inaugurated the resurrection, he made it possible for our bodies to be released from the grave and our minds be released from ignorance and sin. Suffering can serve a very good purpose. Under some conditions it can have a purifying effect. In our interests God runs an eternal prison house on a far more extensive and productive basis than that of our federal and state governments. In speaking of disobedient spirits Isaiah said: "And they shall be gathered together, as prisoners are gathered in a pit, and shall be shut up in prison, and after many days they shall be visited." (Isa. 24:22)

Isaiah describes the mission of the Savior of the world by saying that it was "To open the blind eyes, to bring out the prisoners from the prison, and them that sit in darkness out of the prison house." (Isa. 42:7)

Unlike many of the prisons with which we are familiar we must reform before we can be released from the eternal prison house. As Jesus said: "Verily I say unto thee, Thou shalt by no means come out thence, till thou hast paid the uttermost farthing." (Matt. 5:26) The Son of God took upon himself our sins on condition of our repentance. If we are to be saved at all we must either repent or suffer. Jesus has said: "My blood will not cleanse them if they hear me not." And in one of the great scriptures of all time it was said: "For behold, I, God have suffered these things for all, that they might not suffer if they will repent; but if they will not repent they must suffer even as I; which suffering caused myself, even God, the greatest of all, to tremble because of pain, and to bleed at every pore . . . and would that I might not drink the bitter cup, and shrink." (D&C 19:16-18)

Sin is a terrible offense to the order of heaven, and every account must be settled in full. Jesus probably talked about hell as much as he did about heaven. Hell is a divine institution and it serves many sets of prisoners in different ways.

The permanent occupants of hell are made up of those who
rebelled against God in the antemortal life. They were expelled
from heaven and are forever denied future progress. To these
are added the most evil of those who live upon the earth. This
is according to the great law of consequences. This segregation
is also a protection for those who live righteously. Freedom-
loving, righteous, peaceful citizens would not like to live in a
society where gangsters, murderers, robbers, traitors, plunderers,
and vandals were a constant threat and were given a free hand
to do as they pleased. The scripture says that "God cannot
look upon sin with the least degree of allowance." He has decreed that no sin and no unreformed and unforgiven sinner will
ever be permitted into his presence. What would heaven be
like if drunks, dope addicts, murderers, and trouble-makers were
given membership? Some of hell's temporary inmates who have
not passed the point of no return will be educated and reformed,
and when they are worthy they will finally be given their freedom. We must seek our freedom in the right way, which is
repentance, reformation, and restitution. There would be no
point in trying to scale the fences of the eternal prison house,
or tunnel under the walls, or overpower the guards, or bribe
the judge.

During Christ's mortal ministry he organized his Church
and placed in it the appropriate officers and leaders to carry
on his work. He gave us the idea of celestial glory as the goal
to work toward. He has given us a set of written commandments
and scriptural directions to guide us in our conduct. One of
the tremendous advantages of righteousness is that it keeps
us out of the prisons and enables us to avoid the natural punishments of sorrows and sufferings. Immediately we should begin
freeing ourselves from the prisons of fear, the prisons of hate,
the prisons of ignorance, and the prisons of sin. Think of the
millions who are slaves to alcohol and the other millions who
are in bondage to immorality. Dope addicts are not free to
do as they please, and these fetters that we are presently placing
upon ourselves may continue to bind us throughout eternity.

In Dickens' *Christmas Carol*, Ebenezer Scrooge and Jacob
Marley were business partners. Several years after Marley's
death he paid a visit to Scrooge, dragging behind him a long
burden of fetters. By way of explanation Marley said to Scrooge:
"I wear the chains I forged in life." And so do we all.

The story is told that the great Michelangelo once saw a misshapen block of rough marble that a student had spoiled. He was told that the marble was useless, but Michelangelo said: "It is not useless, send it over to my studio. There is an angel imprisoned in it which I must set free."

Our primary job is to set our minds and our spirits free, for both here and hereafter. In either place imprisonment is a very heavy burden. The ruthless regimentation requires the loss of personal power and the disgrace of our sins destroys happiness and sentences us to a life of misery. The person imprisoned is not the only one who suffers. Families, friends, and associates must all bear a part of the disgrace and penalty. All prisoners long for their day of deliverance. They count the months and the days until they will once more be free. They vow that they will so conduct their future lives in such a way that never again will confinement be necessary for them.

We cannot understand how anyone who thinks about freedom would ever be willing to deliberately forfeit it, and yet great numbers of men and women are presently self-imprisoned. They have built their own prison walls, forged their own chains, and determined the severity of their own bondage. God's primary gift to man is his own freedom, and it is very displeasing to him when we allow it to be destroyed for any reason.

The greatest of all wars was the one that was fought during our antemortal existence to determine whether or not men and women should be free. The human soul was not created to live in chains. Many of God's lesser creations get sick and die when they are confined. Even birds were not supposed to live in cages. It was planned by the Creator that birds should scratch in the earth, soar in the sky, and sing the beautiful songs of freedom. When they are put in cages an important part of their nature is destroyed. This is also true of caged animals and caged human beings.

The worst kinds of imprisonment are not in state and federal penitentiaries. The chief obstacles to escape are not in iron bars but in our tendencies to continue our evil ways. One of the chief problems of dope addicts, atheists, and moral perverts is that they love the substances out of which their cages are made. The longer one stays in any prison cell, the harder it is to get away, as day by day the fetters are growing stronger. The poet has said:

> Oh, doom beyond the saddest guess,
> As the long years of God unroll;
> To make thy dreary selfishness
> A prison of the soul.

There are many disadvantages to being placed in bonds, and if we are to be free at all we must set ourselves free. The first steps toward freedom are a thorough knowledge of truth and a strong desire to be free. Jesus said: "Ye shall know the truth and the truth shall make you free."

The Prophet Job

ONE OF LIFE'S greatest delights is the study of biography. It is also one of the least expensive. Life is that primal element out of which all experiences are formed. Every man has some wonderful physical equipment. He has a miraculous brain, a potentially magnificent personality, a godly spirit, and the greatest of all future possibilities. Nothing is more productive than to turn the spotlight of our attention on the many facets of our God-given human nature and study the interesting interplay of human experience as it reacts upon itself.

One of the most interesting classifications of human beings is that small group of men called the prophets. They are selected by God to assist him in carrying forward the enterprise of human salvation; yet they are interesting in their own right. Each has some fine capability, and they are assigned to serve as God's watchmen, messengers, motivators, teachers, and judges. They also serve as our patterns, as we usually don't do very well when we have no better model to go by than ourselves. The Holy Scriptures are important because of the great religious doctrines and their guidance in our human behavior. The values of the scriptures have been especially enriched by the great biographies that they contain. The scripture is a kind of God's "Who's Who" and is a divine catalog of those men and women who are important to God.

One of these great men is the Prophet Job. It has been said that the Old Testament Book of Job furnishes us with the finest expression of the poetic genius of the Hebrews. It has also been accorded a leading place among the greatest masterpieces of world literature.

Job was an Edomite of outstanding piety, and the theme of his book centers in that eternal question concerning the purpose of human suffering, either merited or not merited. Left to themselves, most men are by nature morally frail, and one of the purposes of our lives is to be tested, proven, tried, and strengthened. We watch Job as he goes through the wringer of trial, and even after all of these centuries we still speak of "the patience of Job." We are made stronger by that fortitude with which he met the severe suffering that he did not understand. While Christ himself is our greatest example of innocent suffering, yet in his day Job stood pretty well at the top of the list. Patience is one of the traits in shortest supply in our own day. It is the natural disposition of most people to rebel when events are not to their liking. Instead of a manifestation of love and forebearance, our feelings frequently turn to hate, bitterness, disobedience, and evil. By this process of mishandling our sufferings many of our greatest blessings are frequently lost. In describing one of the great traits of Jesus the scripture says: "Though he was a Son, yet learned he obedience by the things which he suffered; and being made perfect he became the author of eternal salvation unto all them that obey him." (Heb. 5:8-9) If it were possible for Christ to be made perfect through suffering, then we should probably know a little more about how to handle this great power in our own lives.

There are also many other important issues raised in the Book of Job that we need to find some answers to. Some of these are: "If a man die, shall he live again. . . ." (Job 14:14) "Canst thou by searching find out God. . . ." (Job 11:7)

There is another very important question asked in the Book of Job which says: "Can a man be profitable unto God, as he that is wise may be profitable unto himself? Is it any pleasure to the Almighty, that thou art righteous? or is it a gain to him, that thou makest thy ways perfect?" (Job 22:2-3)

If man does the right things, he can be very profitable unto himself, and he can be very profitable to God. God has said: ". . . this is my work and my glory — to bring to pass the immortality and eternal life of man." (Moses 1:39) God's love is centered in us and he is made happy and prosperous when we are successful. We might try to imagine the joy and profit that Job brought to God, as even among the luminaries that light up the pages of the Holy Scriptures, Job stands out like a great beacon, and he passed all his tests with flying colors. We are introduced to Job in the first chapter when the record says:

"There was a man in the land of Uz, whose name was Job; and that man was perfect and upright, and one that feared God, and eschewed evil.

"And there were born unto him seven sons and three daughters.

"His substance also was seven thousand sheep, and three thousand camels, and five hundred yoke of oxen, and five hundred she asses, and a very great household; so that this man was the greatest of all the men of the east." (Job 1:1-3)

That sounds pretty good for a starter. Job gets some recommendation from the fact that he had done well financially and had been succssful with his family. The scripture also gives him a top rating in his human relations when it says that "he was the greatest of all the men of the east." However, Job's greatest credit comes from the fact that he stood well with God. Again the record says:

"Now there was a day when the sons of God came to present themselves before the Lord, and Satan came also among them.

"And the Lord said unto Satan, Whence comest thou? Then Satan answered the Lord, and said, From going to and fro in the earth, and from walking up and down in it.

"And the Lord said unto Satan, Hast thou considered my servant Job, that there is none like him in the earth, a perfect and an upright man, one that feareth God, and escheweth evil?

"Then Satan answered the Lord, and said, Doth Job fear God for nought?

"Hast not thou made an hedge about him, and about his house, and about all that he hath on every side? thou hast blessed the work of his hands, and his substance is increased in the land." (Job 1:6-10)

This "hedging-about" process based on our obedience seems to be one of the characteristics of God's relations with us. If we keep his laws of health, we have strong bodies and clear minds. If we pay our tithing, do our planning, and practice our industry, the Lord blesses us with material abundance. If we keep ourselves mentally, physically, and religiously strong, a great multitude of benefits are showered upon us. In other words, if we follow his instructions, he usually hedges all of us about on every side. However, Satan argued that it was easy for one to be faithful when everything is going well. But said he: ". . . put forth thine hand now, and touch all that he hath, and he will curse thee to thy face." (Job 1:11)

This involves our program of testing, and this is frequently the place where so many of us fall down. However, in every field, it seems that problems and challenges are necessary to bring out the genuineness and sincerity of our characters. Satan was inferring that Job's piety depended upon his prosperity. Satan said that Job didn't serve God for nothing, and the intimation was that Job's religion was mere selfishness. Many people actually do behave in that way. To them a good religious attitude is merely a profitable business asset. Satan was suggesting that if God were to withhold his blessings, he would see such a different kind of attitude manifest itself in Job that he would curse God to his face.

Actually we see this doctrine of weakness manifesting itself every day. The wealthy, powerful nations of our own time, including our own, are trying to buy friendship and cooperation with money. We give out many benefits in order to get other nations on our side. Many individuals, old and young, must be bribed, or they will rebel and join ranks with those who will make their loyalty more profitable. Satan was accusing God of having a kind of a Marshall Plan for keeping on the good side of Job. In any event, Satan obtained permission to put Job's loyalty to the test: "And the Lord said unto Satan, Behold, all that he hath is in thy power; only upon himself put not forth thine hand. . . ." (Job 1:12)

From the height of his prosperity and happiness, Job was suddenly plunged into the depths of misery and gloom. He lost all of his property, his children were cut off from life by violent deaths, and while Job was profoundly grieved, he never wavered but clung reverently to the will of God. Satan concluded that the test was not severe enough, and he received permission to afflict Job's person to the limit. Job was smitten with a loathsome disease, calculated to make him an outcast and an object of abhorrence to other people. Still Job was obedient to God and his faith remained unbroken. Within himself Job reasoned as follows: "Shall we receive only good at the hand of God?" Apparently Job felt that he should be willing to bear his share of the problems and suffering, as well as enjoy the blessings.

God must have been very proud of Job when it was proven that he could stand up to the worst hardships under the most trying adversity that even Satan could devise. Job was content; he said: "Naked came I [into the world] and naked shall I return thither: the Lord gave, and the Lord taketh away; blessed be the name of the Lord." (Job 1:21)

Some of Job's friends argued with him, and even his wife got discouraged and seemed about ready to give up. She suggested the formula frequently followed by many people in trouble when she said to her husband: ". . . curse God and die." (Job 2:9) Job didn't understand God but he was not a quitter. If God had decreed that he should suffer, that was God's business and he probably had some good reasons for doing as he did. Job himself was solid and steadfast. He said: "Though he slay me, yet will I trust in him. . . ." (Job 13:15) No matter what the circumstances, Job would continue to do the best he could.

Frequently problems and suffering serve the best purposes in our lives. In every way Job trusted God and naturally God trusted Job. He had already said that Job was an upright man, and Job proved that God did not have him overrated. In the midst of these serious troubles, Job made a magnificent speech to himslf. He said: "All the while my breath is in me, and the spirit of God is in my nostrils; My lips shall not speak wickedness, nor my tongue utter deceit . . . till I die I will not remove mine integrity from me. My righteousness I hold fast, and will not let it go: my heart shall not reproach me so long as I live." (Job 27:3-6) We might shout: "Hurrah for Job!" Then we might try to imagine what a tremendous boost our world would get if we had about 3½ billion people just like him. Any such man would be very profitable to himself. He would be profitable to God and profitable to his fellowmen. With Job's attitude we could also answer the prayer of Jesus when he said: "Thy Kingdom come thy will be done on earth as it is in Heaven." Job held on to his integrity, but he also held on to his consistency. Speaking of God, he said: "He also shall be my salvation: for an hypocrite shall not come before him." (Job 13:16) Job not only had strong personal convictions within himself, but he was also anxious to get some of these convictions into other people for their own benefit. Answering the question, "If a man die shall he live again?" Job said:

"Oh that my words were now written! oh that they were printed in a book!

"That they were graven with an iron pen and lead in the rock for ever!

"For I know that my redeemer liveth, and that he shall stand at the latter day upon the earth:

"And though after my skin worms destroy this body, yet in my flesh shall I see God:

"Whom I shall see for myself, and mine eyes shall behold, and not another; though my reins be consumed within me." (Job 19:23-27)

Job knew a great deal about God's plan for our eternal salvation. He also knew a great deal about God and about himself. He said: "But there is a spirit in man: and the inspiration of the Almighty giveth them understanding." He knew that we are all likely to err unless we follow instructions. He said: "Great men are not always wise: neither do the aged understand judgment." (Job 32:8-9)

Job was a great man and he knew what some of us may not know — that all of our human wisdom is pretty weak as compared to the wisdom of God. However, God talked with Job about some pretty important things. He said to Job:

"Gird up now thy loins like a man; for I will demand of thee, and answer thou me.

"Where wast thou when I laid the foundations of the earth? declare, if thou hast understanding.

"Who hath laid the measures thereof, if thou knowest? or who hath stretched the line upon it?

"Whereupon are the foundations thereof fastened? or who laid the corner stone thereof;

"When the morning stars sang together, and all the sons of God shouted for joy?" (Job 38:3-7)

As human beings, we have great antiquity; many divine revelations have indicated that as God's spirit children we saw the foundations of this earth being laid. We knew that we were going to have the privilege of coming here and living upon it. Then we walked by sight. We have all seen God; he is our Father. We had a voice in formulating the plan for our own exaltation and eternal progress. In the Council of Heaven we knew that this would be a place to which we would come and take upon ourselves these beautiful, wonderful bodies, build our characters, develop our personalities, vitalize our spirits, and be tested and proven in doing the will of God. We were all present and approved of the action "when the morning stars sang together, and all the sons of God shouted for joy."

Job had great faith in God. He said: "I know that thou canst do everything, and that no thought can be withholden from thee." (Job 42:2) What a great idea that we can follow Job in his faith! After Job had passed all his tests, he was given twice as much as he had had before. The record says: "So the Lord blessed the latter end of Job more than his beginning. . . ." (Job 42:12) And God will similarly bless us if we are equally faithful.

Psychosclerosis

I N 1967 DR. NORMAN VINCENT PEALE wrote a very interesting book entitled *Enthusiasm Makes the Difference*. This great word *enthusiasm* comes from some interesting Greek words meaning "God in us." Enthusiasm is that impassioned emotion that gets into people's hearts when they have an inspired interest in some particular thing. More than almost anything else it is enthusiasm that gives us an ardent zeal to accomplish. It is made up of a kind of religious fervor causing an exaltation in our feelings. In his meaningful book, Dr. Peale discusses the importance that a well-directed, intelligent enthusiasm can have in both our material and spiritual success. He also points out some of the many problems that arise when we are not enthusiastic about the right things. When we don't have a sufficient amount of this positive vital quality in our lives, some of the less valuable negative traits always rush in to fill up the vacuum.

Dr. Peale tells of one occasion when he had an interesting experience with a cab driver in New York City who was lacking something in his enthusiasm for life. As Dr. Peale and two of his friends entered this man's taxi to go to an appointment, they greeted the driver very affably and commented on what a wonderful day they thought it was. They asked the driver what he thought about the weather. They inquired about his health and they asked him how his business was getting along. To each of these very genial inquiries, the driver responded with a glum and depressing grunt. It seems that although he was only 35, he had acquired a rather dismal attitude about life generally. It was obvious that he was in a very depressed and pessimistic frame of mind which was also reflected in his face and had apparently been stamped into his soul.

This situation was naturally very interesting to Dr. Peale, inasmuch as this is the field of one of his special interests. As the conversation progressed among the driver's three passengers there were several occasions when Reverend Peale's friends addressed him as "doctor." This seemed to touch an area of interest in the driver. He logically concluded that he had a medical doctor in his cab and that the occasion provided him with a good opportunity to get a little free medical counsel. Therefore, when a lull in the conversation gave him the chance he was waiting for, he said: "Doc, I wonder if you'd give me a little advice?"

Dr. Peale replied: "Certainly. What kind of advice do you want?" The driver said, "Well, I haven't been feeling so well lately. I've got a pain in my back, and another one in my side. I don't sleep so good, and I'm always tired. What do you suppose is the matter with me? Do you know of anything that you can give me that will make me feel better?"

Dr. Peale is always interested in these kinds of human experiences, so going along with the driver's assumption that he was a physician, he said: "My friend, I seldom practice my profession in taxicabs or give out prescriptions while going along the highway; but since we're both here, I will be glad to give you the best advice I can." He continued: "Of course, you can understand the disadvantages of making an off-the-cuff diagnosis, but it seems to me that you have all the symptoms of psychosclerosis."

This shocking pronouncement so startled the cab driver that he almost ran off the road. It sounded to him as though he had a very extraordinary and formidable disease. With considerable concern and apparent apprehension, he said, "What is this psychosclerosis?" Dr. Peale said, "Have you ever heard of arteriosclerosis?" The driver was not certain that he had, but in any case he indicated that he didn't know what it was. Dr. Peale explained that arteriosclerosis is a hardening of the arteries, and that any other kind of sclerosis indicated that some hardening process is taking place; that many people have hardening of the arteries, some have a hardening of the nervous system, others have a hardening of the heart. "But," said Dr. Peale, "what you seem to have is psychosclerosis. That is where the hardening takes place in the thoughts and attitudes."

That is probably what is bothering a lot of us. It is pretty easy to lose our flexibility, not only in our arteries but in several other places. Some people are suffering from a hardening in their faith or a hardening of their ambition. Sometimes we get hardened in our sins, and hardened in our atheism. The doctor doesn't always put the true cause of death on the death certifi-

cate, and many people actually die because of some hardening
that takes place in their point of view.

The taxicab driver was beginning to crack up at this early
age in his life because he had lost his enthusiasm. His negative
outlook was getting set like concrete, and he had a hardening
in his mental attitudes. But out of this taxicab diagnosis Dr.
Peale coined a great big, imposing, ten-dollar word which might
well represent a disease for which more of us should be taking
some treatments.

Psychosclerosis is not of recent origin. In one form or
another it has been bothering us for a long time. We remember
the large number of references made in the Bible to those diseases
that bothered the Egyptian Pharaoh and brought eleven serious
plagues upon his people. Many times Pharaoh hardened his heart
while the Lord was trying to get the children of Israel out of
Egypt. When the pressure was on, Pharaoh would agree to let
the Israelites leave Egypt; but when the expediency was relaxed
his unrighteous second thoughts caused a hardening of his heart.
The thought of losing this great labor force not only made the
Pharaoh change his mind, it also changed his attitudes and put
hardness into his heart.

There seems to be a lot of connection between what is in
our minds and the condition of our hearts. Sometimes when we
get our minds set on the wrong things, it hardens our hearts
toward God and prevents us from doing the right things. But
the Lord has his own ways of practicing medicine and he knows
how to go about softening us up. And one thing that can help
us change our minds and become a little more soft-hearted is to
have some real trouble wherein we undergo some serious suffering. Therefore when Pharaoh hardened his heart and refused
to let the Israelites go, the Lord sent a plague upon Egypt in
which the rivers and the other waters were turned to blood.
This awful problem caused the Pharaoh to relent for a little while,
but apparently the medicine was not strong enough for a permanent cure; and before the Hebrews could get out of the country,
Pharaoh had hardened his heart again.

Then, in succession, the Lord sent a total of eleven plagues
upon the Pharaoh and the country that he ruled. Besides the
blood, they had plagues of frogs, lice, flies, murrain, boils and
blains, pestilence, hail, locusts, a plague of heavy darkness, and

finally the firstborn in every Egyptian family died. Because of Pharaoh's hardheadedness and hardheartedness, much of his country was destroyed. He also lost a very large percentage of his people.

But what about us? By the hardness and obstinacy in our activities, we have brought upon ourselves more than eleven plagues and we are suffering for about the same reasons that the Egyptians did. On February 27, 1833, the Lord gave us his law of health that we refer to as the Word of Wisdom. And because we have set our minds and hardened our hearts against it, we have brought upon ourselves the plagues of alcoholism, lung cancer, encephalitis, etc., which have taken many times more lives than all of the plagues of Egypt put together. We have also worked up some caffeine plagues, some dope plagues, some hippie plagues, some plagues of draft-card-burners and slogan-marchers. We have a plague of sub-reasonable, hard-boiled people trying to force their beliefs onto others. Because so many have hardened their hearts against obeying the law, we are presently suffering some plagues of crime, plagues of vandalism, and plagues of delinquency. We have a tax plague inflicted upon us to pay for the wars and soul sicknesses that desolate our land because we are too hardheaded and too hardhearted to obey either God or our own reason.

When we disobey the laws of God our spirituality gets rigid and brittle and we get mean. Then we become involved with a far worse case of psychosclerosis than the negative taxicab driver had.

The dictionary says that one who is hardhearted is unsympathetic and unfeeling. The newspapers tell of people who have become callous, cruel and pitiless without even knowing it. The divorce courts tell of people who have become stubborn, wilful and selfish. And the scriptures also refer to stiffneckedness, ungodliness and disobedience, which are all varieties of hardheartedness.

Steel manufacturers harden iron by alloying it with other metals. And many of our lives become hard because we alloy them with cynicism, atheism, crime and sin. When one's life has been alloyed with evil, the hardness is also stamped in his face and set in his soul. Anyone becomes hard to live with when he is unsympathetic and lacks feeling for the better things in life. Bitterness, immorality, and atheism cause a hardness that can destroy us.

We don't like water that has been hardened by too many impurities. And God doesn't like that hardness in men that makes us incorrigible, inflexible, disobedient, and unloving. The heard heart of Pharaoh brought on the Egyptian plagues, which caused Pharaoh and his people to suffer some very hard times. Likewise our hardness brings hard times upon us. When we have hard hearts, it is hard for us to believe the gospel. And when it is hard to believe the gospel, it is hard to live properly. When it is hard for us to go to church and hard to think right and hard to behave ourselves, it is hard to be enthusiastic or happy or successful. A bad case of psychosclerosis makes us mentally and spiritually gloomy and depressed, and probably does us more general damage than any of the other dread diseases.

A man recently sought psychiatric help who was complaining that the tensions of life were driving him crazy. He was approaching a state of mental imbalance and was not far from a state of hysteria. He kept referring to what he called life's "rat race," and he didn't think that he could endure the tensions of this "dog-eat-dog" world very much longer. He suggested that he felt that he would have to leave town for a while and get away from the tensions that were bringing on his mental breakdown. He had problems in his business, he had marital problems, family problems, financial problems, and personal problems. He felt as though the "breaks" were all going against him. He said that even the air of his town was filled with tensions.

The psychiatrist tried to help him to understand that the tensions were not in the air, but in his own mind, heart, attitudes, and nervous system. If one took into the laboratory for scientific analysis and study a sampling of the air from this man's community, it would be found to be absolutely pure so far as any tensions were concerned. It may have a lot of dirt in it or it may have the fumes from airplanes and automobiles. There may even be a little poisonous fallout from our atomic explosions, but not even a speck of tension would be found.

There is no tension in the air but there is a lot in the people who breathe the air. And we can only have good mental health as we un-tense ourselves and de-confuse ourselves and un-harden ourselves. When the scripture says, "Physician, heal thyself," it means that we should get the hardness out of our lives.

The Pharaoh could have saved himself from eleven destructive plagues if he had softened his heart and gotten rid of his psychosclerosis. And the most important part of any of our problems is to get our thinking straightened out so that the right kind of attitudes — faith, industry, and righteousness — can flourish in our lives.

When God created us in his image, he also endowed us with a set of his attributes and potentialities. He planted in us all of the seeds of enthusiasm, joy, industry, ambition and spirituality. And all that we need to do is just to nourish them and make them grow. Normal children have a happy childhood, and if they grow up properly their lives will be filled with a healthy excitement and interest in the glory of life. But if we allow too many of the alloys of cynicism, evil or disobedience into our lives, our viewpoint begins to harden. Huxley once said that the secret of genius is to carry the spirit of childhood over into maturity. That is, it is important to preserve our natural God-given enthusiasm. Jesus said it this way: ". . . except ye . . . become as little children, ye shall not enter into the kingdom of heaven." (Matt. 18:3).

Too often we lose unnecessarily this natural enthusiasm for life which is one of the finest elements of our human nature. If we begin picking up the destructive alloys of selfishness, sin, and disobedience to God, then we start getting psychosclerosis, we become tense and suffer those harmful depressions of the spirit that make troubles hard to endure, success hard to attain, and life hard to live.

Many people die of arteriosclerosis and a lot more die from the broken hearts, disappointments, gloomy attitudes, and sins that don't get mentioned on the death certificates. A water softener may be a great convenience if we have hard water. But the philosophy of the scriptures and the Spirit of the Lord will soften up our lives and make us better husbands, better wives, better citizens, and better candidates for eternal life. They will help us to develop our natural God-given enthusiasm for straight thinking and faithful activities, which will result in health, wealth, happiness, and eternal glory.

Radiation

OUR WORLD HAS A recorded history of some 5,970 years. Four thousand of these passed before the birth of Christ, and 1,970 others have passed since. Among the very interesting events in our history are the discoveries that have been made, most of which have come in comparatively recent times. Even the western continent was only discovered 478 years ago. We didn't know that the world was round until about that time. Even with our recent knowledge explosion we strongly suspect that many of the most important things have not yet been discovered. Newton compared himself to a boy standing on the seashore with a few pebbles of knowledge at his feet and an ocean of truth lying before him unexplored.

We don't know very much about gravity, or light, or heat, or what makes the grass grow. We didn't even discover the circulation of our own blood until Harvey's time a little over 300 years ago.

One of these comparatively unexplored subjects that has attracted our attention in recent years is that of radiation. While we see it in operation all about us, we don't know very much about it. In the process of the internal changes taking place in some substances, various kinds of energy are emitted and propelled through space in a way that we know little about. After years of heartbreaking experimentation Pierre and Marie Curie announced the discovery of the wonderful chemical element called radium. This has an enormous amount of radioactivity, and as these rays are thrown off they may be used for many purposes, including the curing of various kinds of diseases. They can also exert a deadly influence, and Marie Curie herself died from the burns received from the rays of the powerful element that she had discovered.

Of course, the lives of all of us are dependent upon various kinds of radiation. For example, we do not live on an independent earth. If the sun's rays were turned off for just a few hours, no life could exist in our world. Every day God is sending us energy, food, light, and life itself from the great general store-house of our universe, which is the sun. The sun's rays pass through millions of miles of cold, dead space, carrying all of those things necessary to sustain our lives, and they only release their valuable load when they strike our atmosphere.

Our knowledge of radiation has been increased by our dis-covery of nuclear fission. When an atomic explosion takes place a vast amount of energy is released into the air, and the deadly "fallout" that follows can be very injurious to any kind of life or growth.

It is reported that some of those people who were not killed in the atomic explosions over Hiroshima and Nagasaki were so badly burned and deformed by the radiation and the resulting fallout that many of them died later or lived as deformed cripples. However, it is probable that the most helpful, as well as the most destructive, forms of radiation emanate from human beings. We don't yet know very much about those important fields that we refer to as inspiration, revelation, mental telepathy, or the radioactivity of our own enthusiasm. We do know that large quantities of energy are emitted from some people that find lodgement in others. In order to communicate with someone you don't always need to fashion your ideas into sounds or write them out in words. People in your presence can feel your ideas and attitudes. If you love someone very much there is a mysterious radiation that carries that message to those occupying the space around you.

The life of everyone is radioactive and the power thus gen-erated may be used for either good or evil. When we generate the evil traits of hate, fear, dread, or any kind of spiritual depres-sion within ourselves, they are usually broadcast more or less automatically into the surrounding territory, and their effect is only limited by the amount of power that we have developed. On the other hand when we build up those great quantities of faith, spirituality, and enthusiasm, they radiate out to animate other people for good.

Out of India comes the idea of the aura. In substance, this idea is to the effect that everyone is enveloped in a kind of radioactive zone that goes with him everywhere he goes like a great cloud that affects others with some degree of light or darkness, good or bad.

Before a child is old enough to understand any verbal discourse he can feel his mother's love. As adults develop effectively these rays are given greater range and more power. Even a dog lying on the front porch knows when you are afraid of him and when he should be afraid of you. These human traits operate through a kind of personal broadcasting station. We also have a kind of reception center that has been installed in us and that is continually receiving the messages of others. An employer can do a better job in hiring an employee if he gets inside the prospect's aura and has a personal interview, instead of doing it by mail or even over the telephone.

While at the house of Caiaphas the High Priest, Peter denied that he knew Jesus on three different occasions, but he didn't deceive anyone. Even the servant girl knew of the truth and she said to him: "Thy speech betrayeth thee." There are many of these personal influences that continually betray us.

Emerson once said: "I cannot hear what you are saying when what you are is thundering in my ears." Because we do not always understand how these things operate does not make them any less real. I have no conception of how millions of tons of foodstuffs, energy, and vitamins are sent through space in one form to be changed upon arrival to what exactly suits our needs. Neither can I understand how musical symphonies and television pictures can pass around us unheard and unseen, until they strike a radio or television set; nor is it clear to me how the influence of an individual reaches out beyond his own personal boundaries to change the lives of other people. And yet I know that all of these events regularly take place.

Recently the *Reader's Digest* printed an article in which it was said that if you press a block of silver against a block of gold, the molecular action causes each substance to throw flecks of itself across its own boundaries to become a part of the substance that is placed next to it. This is also about what happens with human beings. Tennyson once said: "I am a part of all that I have met." Emerson said: "I can no more remember the books I have read than the meals that I have eaten, yet each is a part of all that I am."

Every time we come within the magnetic range of someone else an interchange takes place that modifies us so that neither party will ever be the same again. Each of us is a kind of human mosaic made up of those parts that we have picked up from others.

It was said that the mere *presence* of Napoleon on the battlefield was the equivalent of a reinforcement of a hundred thousand additional troops. The great qualities of courage, industry, and military skill that Napoleon had developed in himself became imbedded in his soldiers. How deep this goes is indicated by one of Napoleon's soldiers who was about to undergo a chest operation for the removal of some shrapnel. He said to the surgeon: "If you'll cut a little deeper you'll find the emperor." Napoleon was not only in the soldiers' hearts, but he was also in their minds and muscles, attitudes and skills.

This might be a part of the phenomenon that takes place when one person falls in love with someone else. It has been said that the soul of the lover lives in the body of his beloved, and this human interchange takes place in every department of life. Some have so built up these traits of influence that in any interchange they can often carry the field before them without even the necessity of words being spoken. It was said that George Washington won the independence of the American states, not so much by what he did as by what he was.

Jesus spoke as one having authority. His words, attitudes, skills, and convictions radiated to other people where they found lodgement and acceptance. The people explained the strength of the apostles by saying that "they had been with Jesus." They had been the beneficiaries of his fallout. It is one of the attributes of God that his spirit extends throughout the immensity of space to bear witness of the truth, to testify of God, and to inspire the lives of all deserving people, although they may be actually separated from him by millions of miles.

Like the rays of the sun this divine Spirit brings with it the light that enlightens every person who is born into the world. Jesus said: "But the Comforter, which is the Holy Ghost, whom the Father will send in my name, he shall teach you all things, and bring all things to your remembrance, whatsoever I have said unto you." (John 14:26) Another function of the Holy Ghost is to "reprove the world of sin." (See John 16:8) While we don't know much about how conscience or the still small voice or inspiration operates, by some kind of process the Spirit of God reaches out throughout the universe to uplift and benefit all mankind. This idea of sending out messages is also a program that God has designed for his offspring to put into operation. Men were not only created in the image of God, but they were endowed with a set of his attributes and potentialities. Men and women can not only receive inspiration, but they can also give inspiration, and certainly if the offspring of God are ever to become like the eternal parent, we must learn more about this process of beneficial radiation.

I know of one who ministers in religion and who, while he is speaking, is also sending out thoughts of love and goodwill to all the members of his audience. Everywhere he goes he blesses people and sends out prayers in their behalf. The people always seem to pick up these energized rays and are uplifted by these flecks of good that come to them from him. His cheer, faith, and love actually sustain and uplift many people. While in a particular presence, one is a different kind of individual than he is when he is left to himself. We can supplement this God-given ability by the effective cultivation of the voice, the personality, the faith, the appearance, the spirit, and every other God-given resource. Of course we must make sure that these energized particles have the right effect upon those of whom they become a part.

Some time ago I saw a man with a severe sunburn. Those warm, invisible rays had felt so pleasant and gentle on his skin, but the exposure had been too harsh and too long, and the accumulated consequences had sent him to the hospital with severe burns. We may also be unaware that sometimes we are sending out injurious energy. Rays of hate, scorn, lust, and fear can destroy our personalities and burn into our souls, or the souls of those to whom they are directed within our magnetic range.

Almost everyone as a boy has had something to do with what we used to call burning glasses. One can take the amount of sunlight that falls harmlessly on the back of his hand and by concentrating it through a convex lens into a pinpoint of light, can develop enough heat to start a forest fire that can destroy millions of dollars worth of valuable property. The wrong traits concentrated through this radiation process can also destroy success and deform souls.

I heard a man say about his wife: "She burns me up." That was exactly what was happening. Recently a home was broken up because some harsh rays of unkindness from the husband had so dominated the wife that her happiness had been killed and her stimulating personality had receded and dried up. The Lord wants us to be loving and kind and has indicated that to exercise any degree of unrighteous dominion or compulsion over others is wrong.

Sometimes the rays of censure, scorn, hate, ridicule, or just plain criticism can be harsh enough to kill. Great suffering can be induced by humiliation and condemnation. By this burning-glass process our own "fallout" can give inferiority and guilt complexes and be as poisonous as that which comes from an atomic explosion. The radiation from our sins may deform, mutilate, twist, or even destroy its victims. God has given us the privilege of helping others, but we do not have the right to contaminate others with spiritual or mental leprosy.

The success, reputation, peace of mind, and happiness that people build up in their lives may be worth a billion dollars to them, and no one has the right to detract from or destroy it. One of the most vicious possible sins is to be a character assassin or a destroyer of the reputations of others. To implant one unworthy idea in someone's mind may keep a psychiatrist digging for the rest of his life to uproot it. As it is difficult to get ink stains out of one's white shirt, so it is difficult to get alcohol out of one's appetite, or bad attitudes out of his mind, or uncleanness out of his soul.

There is an old proverb that says: "Your influence like your shadow may fall where you yourself will never go," and this influence for good that we may send in all directions represents one of our greatest opportunities. These wonderful little energized particles of ambition, faith, courage, and spirituality will embed themselves in others to change their nature for good. There is a beneficial fallout from faith, and from courage, and from kindness that is highly radioactive. To some extent everyone resembles the sun. Everyone is capable of sending out these helpful rays with their great ability to do good, and we may help God to fill our world with the sunshine of faith and righteousness.

Rebellion

THERE IS A destructive moral problem that is presently raging through our world, which is called rebellion. This is not a new disease, but it presently seems to be attaining epidemic proportions with corresponding changes being made in our personal lives. Certainly this is one of the important influences that must be reckoned with in our new decade. It is obvious that certain kinds of rebellion serve a good purpose. It is very commendable when we rebel against such things as weakness, irresponsibility, idleness and sin in ourselves, but much of this present plague of rebellion is made up of "pure" evil.

There are so many people who are presently rebelling against law and order. Great numbers of young people are rebelling against their parents, education, and decency. Some are rebelling against beauty in their dress, in their language, in their appearance, and in their behavior. A rebellious streak operating in a group of lives can destroy faith, love, progress, and happiness faster than about any other thing. Sometimes people may become so inflamed by rebellion that the most sound logic and the toughest laws are unable to change their course. An unreasonable desire to "kick the establishment" has been an important factor in our wide-scale hippyism, dope addiction, national disloyalty, atheism, venereal disease, and our general mediocrity.

After a barber had cut a young man's hair, he said: "Your mother will like this haircut." The young man replied: "If she does, I won't."

The fact that God said "Thou shalt not commit adultery" is used by some people as an excuse to plunge head over heels into various forms of the new morality. Many people actually boast of their sex exploits, take pride in wearing hideous clothing, having smelly bodies and degrading attitudes. Instead of taking pride in themselves, apparently it sometimes seems smart to fill their tissues with booze, their lungs with nicotine, their minds with disloyalty, and their flesh with venereal disease. There are rebellions going on against education, against religion, and against excellence. It is reported that a high school student with an "A" on her report card was concerned about the possible bad effect that it might have on her social acceptance. Her friend said: "It won't hurt you if you just don't let it get spread around."

Our day's gigantic increases in crime and delinquency act as a barometer of our rebellion against law and order, and the rise in the sin content of our lives marks the progress of our rebellion against God and good.

It is interesting to recall something about the origin of this evil force and to identify those who are presently supplying its vigorous sponsorship. The first example we have of the exercise of this evil power took place in the antemortal Council in Heaven when Satan rebelled against God. At that time, Satan was known as Lucifer, the light bearer, the brilliant son of the morning. In spite of his great intelligence and power, he allowed this ugly trait to turn him against the wisest and most righteous being in the universe. God is the literal Father of our spirits. The firstborn and most capable of his spirit children was known as Jehovah, who was chosen in that antemortal period to be the Redeemer of men and the Savior of our world on condition of our repentance and obedience. Lucifer contested the Savior's appointment and opposed God's plan of salvation. When he was overruled, Satan rebelled and led away one-third of all the hosts of heaven after him. As a consequence he was cast out of heaven, his followers were cast out with him, and they became the devil and his angels. This is the most serious crime that was ever committed and it drew the most serious punishment. Rebellion is still going on and its punishment is still very great. In our own day the Lord has said: "And the rebellious shall be pierced with much sorrow; for their iniquities shall be spoken upon the housetops, and their secret acts shall be revealed." (D&C 1:3)

On any list of crimes we think of such sins as rebellion, treason, and betrayal as being at the top of the list. Disloyalty to God is the greatest sin. It is closely followed by disloyalty to righteousness, disloyalty to country, disloyalty to our families, and disloyalty to ourselves. We are reminded that the very serious problems of Cain, Judas, and Benedict Arnold came in this category. Cain made an unacceptable offering, and when it was rejected, instead of repenting, he completely rebelled against God, took an oath, and made a special covenant henceforth to serve Satan. Judas turned his master over to his enemies to be crucified. During the Revolutionary War, Benedict Arnold tried to sell West Point to the British. On a little different scale these same great crimes are being re-enacted by us every day. Just think of the people who, like Lucifer, are still rebelling against God and leading people away from him. The United States and many other nations are presently filled with people who, if they had the opportunity, would be just as disloyal as Benedict Arnold was. Many men are disloyal to their wives. An increasing number of children are proving disloyal to their parents and are following Satan.

The vigor of Satan's nefarious warfare is increasing because Satan knows that his time is short. Those who are not keeping the commandments of God are assisting Satan. Jesus said: "He that is not with me is against me; and he that gathereth not with me scattereth abroad." (Matt. 12:30) The evil forces of communism have officially outlawed God in their countries. They have everywhere turned against the religion of Christ and are using some variety of force and intimidation that has always characterized the work of Satan. The chief effort of our world rebellion is centered in opposition to God and in doing those things that he has forbidden. This is in spite of the fact that God has always been our best friend. He is also the best friend of the communists and of all criminals and sinners.

The specific mission of Jesus was to save sinners, and if we permit him to do so, he will bring about our greatest possible success and happiness. Our antagonism to God would be a little bit more understandable if he were our enemy, but God wants to help us. He is all wise, all good, and all powerful. In addition, rebellion is always so unprofitable. Whether we are communists, or devils, or sinners, to rebel against God or to rebel against good is like committing suicide. It would be much wiser for us to accept his righteousness, be governed by his wisdom, and hold ourselves responsible for carrying out our part of his program.

The dictionary says that a rebel is one who opposes authority. Instead of using reasonable means of bringing about reform, a rebel fosters force and practices intimidation. Some forms of rebellion consist in burning the property of others, and in opposition to constituted authority people often lie, steal, and kill. Many religious rebels are proud of their unorthodoxy. They seem at perfect ease in violating church standards and destroying human faith. Sometimes we indulge in immoral practices, merely to satisfy a Satanic lust for rebellion.

The gangster is a rebel against society. He has a destructive spirit that is often completely divorced from both reason and morality. We sometimes turn against parents with little consideration being given as to what is right or wrong. Many people turn against law and order, courts and schools, governments and churches, without having any substitute with which to replace them.

One woman is presently conducting a campaign against God. Her husband was killed in a drunken-driving accident. She blames God for letting it happen. Then to vent her disapproval, she has stopped going to church and has forbidden her children to take any part in any religious activity. Her behavior is now intemperate and immoral, and she does many other things that she thinks would offend God. She seems very pleased to think that she is punishing him.

We don't always remember that government and God and parents are not wrong merely because we are against them. Who can figure out a better way to get born than by having parents, or a better way to grow up than in a family organization, or how can we live more profitably than under a democratic government, or where can we get a more dependable power to run our solar system than God? Even so there are always better ways to make changes than by launching a rebellion, or having a trial by marches, or getting someone to come around to our point of view by burning his house down. Governments and families were established by God, and anyone who attempts to bring about their overthrow is evil.

The devil is not just the instigator of rebellion; he is also its present primary sponsoring power. Jesus once pointed out that Satan was the father of lies (see John 8:44), and he is also the father of crime, sin, vandalism, treason, arson, and rebellion. Everyone who supports him in any degree will hurt themselves here and will suffer the most serious consequences in the world to come. It would seem reasonable that even Satan would hesitate to go against a wisdom, experience, and power that is so much superior to his own.

Just as Satan has continued to be a liar, so he has continued to be a rebel, and he is still stirring up a maximum of trouble and hate among other people.

Recently a dejected young man came to talk about some of the problems of his marriage. While he had been trying to persuade his prospective wife to marry him, she had expressed serious concern about whether their marriage could survive his bad habits. She knew that marriage, like any other relationship, could only be successful and happy when founded upon righteousness and governed by correct principles. She knew that their chances for success would be greatly improved if he could live the kind of life that would entitle them to be married in the temple. But the idea of righteousness was oppressive to the young man, and he objected to doing his personal housecleaning that she expected before their marriage. However, he faithfully promised that if she would marry him now, he would discontinue his transgressions. But their marriage was never able to get off the ground because her husband disregarded all of his promises. When his wife began to remind him about what had been agreed upon, he became resentful. Then he tried to get his own way by launching a counterattack against her. He thought that she would give the whole thing up, rather than go through all of this unpleasantness.

He set himself against righteousness and his own promises. He said: "The more she pushed me, the more I fought back." Because there can be no happy coexistence with evil, a serious antagonism developed between them. They have now become natural spiritual enemies. They are about like God and Satan; everything that she is for he is against. This is particularly bad for him, inasmuch as she is so far ahead of him in character qualities, and their love can't live very long while this unholy rebellion is going on. Because he is so deeply engrossed in his sin, she must either abandon her own way of life or abandon him.

Inasmuch as his lies and rebellion have already completely killed her respect, she is now in the process of getting a divorce. Now when he is faced with this loss and now that it is too late, he wants to patch things up and start all over again, but all that he has to offer is what he offered originally — a set of worthless promises. It's pretty hard to be enthusiastic in starting one's life over again when you know that your partner is spiritually bankrupt and that there is no reasonable basis for any hope. By this man's rebellion he has lost his wife, his family, his job, the esteem of his friends, and his own self-respect; and even if he could use his worthless promises to get another wife and another job, his new spouse and his new employer may not be able to tolerate his evil any better than the others did. His basic problem is that instead of love and cooperation he has only rebellion to offer. He prefers to indulge his own weakness instead of doing what is right. His method of justifying himself by attacking others attempts to bring everyone down to his own level.

The rebel is destructive. He kicks the establishment, he tears down, he bites the hand that feeds him, he kills the goose that lays the golden eggs. He turns against righteousness and fights those virtues that would guarantee him a life of happiness and success. He spits against the wind. He kills the love that would make him happy, and he never thinks of locking the barn door until after the horse has gone.

The way of life adopted by the rebel is a manifestation of the awful sin of irresponsibility, and it does not harmonize with logic or reason. With faith, love, righteous industry, and worship in our hearts, we can attract to ourselves the greatest blessings of God. Rebellion is the opposite of attraction, and it is the opposite of good. Many of our worst errors of rebellion are found in the religious areas of our lives. Thomas Carlyle once said that a man's religion is the most important thing about him; that is what he believes in and thinks about and works at and fights for and lives by. When two married people are antagonistic in their religious principles, trouble is already on its way. Happiness cannot prosper when people are pulling in opposite directions, and rebellion makes any kind of peaceful coexistence impossible.

Sometimes people develop immoral inclinations as a rebellion against their wives or parents. One uses something obnoxious to the other to beat him or her into conforming to his evil. Many children quit school or move away from home as a rebellion against their parents. We rebel against the Church and against God to make our own evil seem justified. Rebellion has its greatest use as an instrument of Satan. If we feel that we have to rebel, we should rebel against weakness and evil and error in ourselves. We can do that best by developing those godly traits of loyalty, honor, faith, and righteousness. If we want to be problem-solvers we will have gone a long way when we have solved our rebellions.

Red Spectacles

A LITTLE GIRL ONCE reported that her grandfather always wore his red glasses when he ate cherries, because they made the cherries look so much bigger and redder than they were before. This idea represents a pretty good success technique and has several important applications to our progress and happiness. We used to sing a song about "Looking at the World Through Rose-Colored Glasses," and we can also make our world look better when we see it through bigger plans, more inspiring hopes, firmer faith, and greater ambitions. On the other hand we can start some harmful downdrafts when we look at the world through our fears, our doubts, our glooms, and our evil imaginations. A destructive emphasis can be given to life by looking at it through the belittling end of life's telescope. We frequently use the small end through which to view our own futures and possibilities, but we sometimes turn the magnifying end on our problems and discouragements.

It is said that an optimist is one who sees opportunities in his obstacles while the pessimist sees obstacles in his opportunities. If we look at our blessings through the big end of life's telescope, it makes everything seem interesting, important, and wonderful. By how they look at things, some people actually train themselves to be miserable, and the small end of the telescope can teach us to take a kind of doleful delight in failure, gloom, and unhappiness. With a kind of trifocal vision we sometimes see our bowl of cherries as sour, green, and wormy. By using the other end we can make dishonesty seem profitable and sin seem advisable.

Abraham Lincoln once said: "We are only about as happy as we make up our minds to be." And we are only about as faithful and as diligent and as successful as we make up our minds to be.

On one occasion an Arabian prince was examining his dinner of figs under a microscope. With this magnifying glass on his eyes he beheld a great army of little microbes that were also feeding upon his dinner. While these little creaures may actually be beneficial, they can sometimes ruin even a prince's appetite.

Sometimes we put on the magnifying glasses of criticism that show us all kinds of faults and failings so that our friends appear like the prince's figs with microbes crawling all over them. Our point of view frequently makes life seem like the funhouse in a recreation resort where the mirrors show us with all kinds of distortions. Sometimes we are too fat and sometimes we are too lean; sometimes we are too short and sometimes we are too tall. We also see others as deformed, inferior, and filled with guilt.

Someone has said: "I looked at my brother through the microscope of hate and said: 'How small my brother is.' I looked at my brother through the telescope of scorn and said: 'How low my brother is.' Then I looked at my brother in the mirror of truth and said: 'How like me my brother is.' "

Shakespeare tells us that his purpose in writing his plays was to hold the mirror of truth up to life, to show virtue her own image and scorn her own likeness. He said to his readers: "I your looking glass will be and will modestly discover to yourself qualities that you yourself know not of."

Certainly we need to know a great deal more about ourselves. Goethe once said: "I have in me the germ of every crime." We also have within us the seeds of divinity and it is how much we see in ourselves that determines what our futures will be. We need some good spiritual spectacles through which to look at our own destinies. Jesus was holding the mirror of truth up before us when he said: "The Kingdom of God is within you." A note in the King James' version says that he meant the Kingdom of God is among you. That may be what he did mean. The phrase "the Kingdom of God" has at least three meanings. It may be used to indicate a place, or an organization, or a condition. If he had an organization in mind, he may have meant the Kingdom of God is among you, but if he was speaking of a condition, he probably meant the Kingdom of God is within you. In passing, it might be pointed out that that is also where the Kingdom of Hell is.

When there is faith, courage, righteousness, ability, spirituality, and understanding manifesting themselves in people, then the Kingdom of God is within us. Actually every individual always carries within himself the very things that he seeks. If one seeks faith, he needs only look within himself, as God has already planted within each of us the seeds of faith waiting only for us to make them grow. If one seeks courage he needs only to develop that which he already has. Success and life and love aren't in New York, or London, or Paris, or San Francisco — they are all in people. If we don't find peace and happiness within ourselves, we certainly won't find them in any other place.

A disturbed wife, in speaking about one of her husband's problems, said: "It's all in his mind." That is also where most of our problems and all of the answers are. That is also the place where our joys and sorrows are located. John Milton said: "The mind in its own place and of itself can make a heaven of hell or a hell of heaven." It is how we look at things that determines how much of heaven or hell we get into our hearts, our habits, our memories, and our futures. A squirrel stores up acorns in the fall to keep himself healthy, warm, and happy during the winter, and we can store up faith for our trials, abilities for our successes, and memories to keep us warm when life's winters arrive. Someone once wrote a poem about the ability that some people have for providing themselves with roses in December.

During the June periods of our lives when we are young, strong, well, and successful, we may lay away an extra supply of righteousness, love, and the memories of success so that when the season changes we may use this accumulated supply for our current motivation and strength. Then if the frost should wither our present sources of happiness, we may still be cheered by the beauty and fragrance of those preserved blossoms gathered during the friendly days of life's summertimes. The acorns of our previous successes will stand us in good stead as long as the winter lasts.

In his story "The Vision of Sir Launfal" James Russell Lowell tells of a gallant knight leaving behind him the comforts of his castle and the security of his wealth to spend his life searching for the holy grail. After many years of apparent failure, he returned poor and old to the area that had once been his home. Penniless and friendless he sat outside the castle that had once belonged to him. Although it was now bitterly cold, he warmed himself by letting his mind dwell on those wonderful happy days of his youth. Mr. Lowell said:

Sir Launfal's raiment thin and bare
Was idle mail against the barbed air,
For it was just at the Christmas time,
So he mused as he sat of a sunnier clime.
And sought for some shelter from cold and snow,
In the light and warmth of long ago.

Memories of warmth and comfort can be very satisfying, and those that had been stored in the mind of Sir Launfal were now being released to keep him warm and happy. Mark Twain had this idea in mind when he said that he could live for two weeks on a compliment. The memories of one's successes can be a kind of mental equivalent of the old yule log tradition. For a hundred years a tree might grow in the forest, storing up the warmth of the sun's summer rays within itself. Then the log is cut down to make the Christmas fire. As it is burned, the heat of a hundred past summers is released to warm those now surrounding the Christmas hearth.

When the winter of her life came upon Mary of Nazareth, she was warmed by the thoughts of the part she had played in the great drama of human salvation. The scripture says: "But Mary kept all these things, and pondered them in her heart." (Luke 2:19) Many times she must have relived these memorable experiences when the angel said: "I am Gabriel that stand in the presence of God." Frequently she must have pondered the angel's greeting when he said to her: "Hail, thou that art highly favoured, the Lord is with thee: blessed art thou among women." (Luke 1:28) He said: "The Holy Ghost shall come upon thee, and the power of the Highest shall overshadow thee: therefore also that holy thing which shall be born of thee shall be called the Son of God." (Luke 1:35) These flowers then bloomed in her heart and she said: "My soul doth magnify the Lord, and my spirit hath rejoiced in God my Saviour. For he hath regarded the low estate of his handmaiden: for, behold, from henceforth all generations shall call me blessed. For he that is mighty hath done to me great things; and holy is his name." (Luke 1:46-49)

What memories she must have stored away at the birth of her son when a multitude of angels from the presence of God sang heavenly anthems of joy when she brought him forth! The shepherds also paid their tributes to her son and the wisemen laid their treasures at his feet under her direction. It would be

interesting to feel as she felt, or we might try to imagine the
kind of person that she must have been to have been chosen by
God to be the mother of such a son, and during the years that
he was growing up there must have been many more wonderful
experiences that she had stored away. Then the climate changed
and we see her again, standing at the foot of the cross watching
them crucify the greatest son who had ever lived. But he was
still her son and from the cross Jesus said to John the Beloved,
"Behold thy mother." Then there followed what must have
been many long wintry years filled with severe loneliness. Difficult experiences are always much easier to be borne if we have
some offsetting memories of previous joys or hopes of future
triumphs. From both the past and the future we may draw
strength, love, joy, and courage.

While a young medical student is enduring the difficult
privations of his early years of study, he can draw strength from
his own future by preliving the successes that he knows must
eventually follow his toil. Frequently banks advance money to
a medical school student, based on his prospects of future earn-
ings. Through the right kind of spectacles we can see our own
eternal futures and we can be greatly strengthened by that por-
tion of our own success that we are able to draw on in advance.

I have a relative who, when she reads a novel, always reads
the last chapter first. She wants to know before she begins just
where she is going to be when she gets through. That has some
pretty good suggestions for us, as the anticipation is frequently
even more productive than the realization.

The apostle Paul was preliving the future when he said:
"For ye had compassion on me in my bonds, and took joyfully
the spoiling of your goods, knowing within yourselves that ye
have in heaven a better and an enduring substance." (Heb.
10:34) Paul was looking beyond the grave when he said, "For
I am now ready to be offered, and the time of my departure is
at hand. I have fought a good fight, I have finished my course,
I have kept the faith: Henceforth there is laid up for me a
crown of righteousness, which the Lord, the righteous judge, shall
give me at that day: and not to me only, but unto all them also
that love his appearing." (II Tim. 4:6-8)

A few years ago a workman told me about walking through
the cold and the snow toward his home at the end of a long,

hard day of labor. The weariness it caused was pleasant and to his tired muscles even the struggles and cold were stimulating and strengthening, because he had worked at his best and he knew that up ahead there was a hot supper awaiting him and that there would be dry clothing, a cheerful fire, and loving hearts to greet him upon his arrival. And so it can be with every accomplishment, including life itself. As we can look through the spectacles of our faith and our works and our love and our righteousness, we can see an eternal life and an eternal happiness.

It has been said that this picturing power of the mind is the greatest gift that God has ever given to man. It has the ability to construct images of success before the actual experiences are born. It can paint pictures that will fire our wills and exalt our spirits. This ability to travel ahead of our own success can also set up some giant, magnetic attractions at the very end of the trail that will draw us on with the greatest pleasure toward the most worthwhile objectives. When we buy an expensive picture we always hang it in the best possible light, and with the right kind of life's spectacles we can enjoy the finest satisfactions while progressing toward the most magnificent successes. May the Lord help us to make the most and the best of both the journey and the destination.

The Resurrection

AT EACH EASTER time we rethink those important thoughts having to do with our rescue from death and our resurrection from the grave. We remember the first glorious Easter sunrise that took place over nineteen hundred years ago when the universal resurrection was initiated upon this earth. Easter has been called the festival of the dawn for more than one reason. It took place at the beginning of a new day, but it also signifies some other new beginnings. It is a time when all nature is awakening in anticipation of the enjoyment of a new life. It also initiates the beginning of an eternal, everlasting existence for everyone who has ever lived or who ever will live upon this earth.

The greatest of all our human concepts concerns the immortality of the personality, the literal resurrection of the physical body, and the eternal glory of the human soul. God is the author of life and he is also the author of a divine program involving our eternal progression and everlasting happiness. We may not always understand the details of his plans and procedures, but then neither do we understand how the grass grows or what electricity or gravity is or how light and heat operate. All that we do understand teaches us to trust God in those things that may not be entirely clear to us. God has said: "For as the heavens are higher than the earth, so are my ways higher than your ways, and my thoughts than your thoughts." (Isa. 55:9) Of course, our faith should tell us that the God who created all life knows what he is doing and is able to fulfill his promise that "as in Adam all die, even so in Christ shall all be made alive." (1 Cor. 15:22) From the beginning he has promised that every human being who ever has or who ever will be born into the world will have a literal bodily resurrection. Some will come forth in the resurrection of the just and some in the resurrection of the unjust. (See Acts 24:15)

Because our resurrection is of such great importance we should always have the facts clearly in mind. Because our judgment is no better than our information, it naturally follows that when we underestimate God we shortchange ourselves. As our doubts and skepticisms increase, and as we half believe that God is dead or has lost his significance, to that extent we lose the power to uplift our own lives. It is likely that our most important possible idea for Easter time or for any other time is that God lives, that Jesus Christ was and is the literal Son of God, and that the gospel message as recorded in the holy scriptures is true.

God still has the same almighty power by which the universe was created and is operated. He has the same omniscience that ordained the laws of the universe. He has the same ability to reveal himself as when he talked with Moses face to face on the top of Mount Sinai. And yet in our day of intelligence and enlightenment there are some who insist on depriving God of his body, taking away his faculties and senses, and robbing him of his personality — yet this at the very time when he is preparing to come to the earth again with his holy angels in power and great glory to cleanse the earth of its sins and establish his own government upon it.

God has ordained our happiness to be the purpose of life. One of the primary conditions of happiness is to have a cleansed and purified spirit, inseparably joined together with a resurrected, glorified body. Next to the wonder of the human spirit the greatest of all of God's creations is the human body. However, there are some who profane God's masterpiece by looking upon the body as a disadvantage or as a harmful imprisonment of the spirit.

Occasionally we ought to go to the library and get some good books on physiology, psychology, personality, and religion and try to understand what a tremendous investment God has made in our hands, our eyes, our brains, and our immortal spirits. God never does anything that is superfluous or whimsical.

Harry Emerson Fosdick said: "A reasonable person doesn't build a violin with infinite care gathering the materials and shaping the body of it so that it can play the composition of the masters and then by some whim of chance caprice smash it to bits." Neither does God create in his own image this great masterpiece of flesh and bones, vision and personality, mind and spirit that we call a human being and then when it has just begun to live, throw it utterly away. If a human body were not necessary, it never would have been created in the first place. If it were not necessary for eternity, the resurrection would never have been instituted. If a body of flesh and bones were not necessary for God the Father, then God the Son would never have been resurrected.

The evidence of the resurrection is so overwhelming that it seems incredible that anyone should fail to believe it whole-heartedly. It is reasonable, advantageous, scriptural, and it is a proven historical fact. The promise of a resurrection has been continuously made to the prophets since time began. Job said: "For I know that my redeemer liveth, and that he shall stand at the latter day upon the earth: And though after my skin worms destroy this body, yet in my flesh shall I see God." (Job 19:25-27)

David said: "But God will redeem my soul from the power of the grave. . . ." (Ps. 49:15) Isaiah said: "Thy dead men shall live, together with my dead body shall they arise. Awake and sing, ye that dwell in dust. . . ." (Isa. 26:19) Daniel said: "And many of them that sleep in the dust of the earth shall awake, some to everlasting life, and some to shame and ever-lasting contempt." (Dan. 12:2)

Then this central fact of our world history was actually initiated on that first Easter morning in the garden tomb of Joseph of Arimathaea on the outskirts of Jerusalem over 1,900 years ago. Matthew records this thrilling event as follows: "In the end of the Sabbath, as it began to dawn toward the first day of the week, came Mary Magdalene and the other Mary to see the sepulchre. And, behold, there was a great earthquake: for the angel of the Lord descended from heaven, and came and rolled back the stone from the door, and sat upon it. His counte-nance was like lightning, and his raiment white as snow: And for fear of him the keepers did shake, and became as dead men. And the angel answered and said unto the women, Fear not ye: for I know that ye seek Jesus, which was crucified. He is not here: for he is risen, as he said: Come, see the place where the Lord lay. And go quickly, and tell his disciples that he is risen from the dead; and behold, he goeth before you into Galilee; there shall ye see him: lo, I have told you." (Matt. 28:1-7)

The scriptures are clear about the literalness of these facts. The *graves* were actually opened and real *bodies* came out of them. Following this event Christ personally ministered among the people as a resurrected being for forty days. He was seen and touched by many people on many occasions during this period. Once he was seen by over five hundred brethren at once. (See 1 Cor. 15:6) He was handled and felt. The scripture says: "Then the same day at evening, being the first day of the week, when the doors were shut where the disciples were assembled for fear of the Jews, came Jesus and stood in the midst, and saith unto them, Peace be unto you. And when he had so said, he shewed unto them his hands and his side. Then were the disciples glad, when they saw the Lord. . . . But Thomas, one of the twelve, called Didymus, was not with them when Jesus came. The other disciples therefore said unto him, We have seen the Lord. But he said unto them, Except I shall see in his hands the print of the nails and thrust my hand into his side, I will not believe. And after eight days again his disciples were within, and Thomas was with them: then came Jesus, the doors being shut, and stood in the midst, and said, Peace be unto you. Then saith he to Thomas, Reach hither thy finger, and behold my hands; and reach hither thy hand, and thrust it into my side: and be not faithless, but believing. And Thomas answered and said unto him, My Lord and my God. Jesus saith unto him, Thomas, because thou hast seen me, thou hast believed: blessed are they that have not seen, and yet have believed." Then the record says: "And many other signs truly did Jesus in the presence of his disciples, which are not written in this book: But these are written, that ye might believe that Jesus is the Christ, the Son of God; and that believing ye might have life through his name." (John 20:19-31)

The commemoration of this event is for this same purpose — that in believing we might have life through his name. After the miracle at the wedding feast at Cana where Jesus changed the water into wine the guests said: "You have saved the best till the last." God has also saved the best of life to the last. The faithful will find that the best and the most of life lies beyond the boundaries of mortality. It seems that it should not be difficult for anyone to believe in the resurrection who can believe in his own birth. That is, if you can believe that two microscopic bits of protoplasm can come together to create a life cell and then by a series of subdivisions create other cells completely unlike the original to form this great masterpiece of human life, it should be comparatively easy to believe

244 THE STRENGTH OF GREAT POSSESSIONS

that this great creation once established could continue upward and onward forever.

If a resurrected being had only been seen once, we should be convinced forever. We know the resurrection of Jesus was real. He was seen and handled many times by many people during this forty-day period. He cooked breakfast for his disciples on the shores of Tiberias. He walked and talked with them for forty days. As he ascended into heaven the angels who stood by him said: ". . . this same Jesus which is taken up from you into heaven shall so come in like manner as ye have seen him go into heaven." (Acts 1:11)

Some sixty years after the ascension he again appeared to John the Revelator as he served out his lonely exile on the Isle of Patmos. John says that he was in the spirit on the Lord's day when he heard a great voice behind him as of the voice of a trumpet. He turned to see who had spoken to him and he saw one like unto the Son of God clothed with a garment down to the foot and girt about with a gold girdle. Then John tried to describe the radiant glory of this great being. He said: ". . . his countenance was as the sun [when it] shineth in its strength. And when I saw him, I fell at his feet as dead. And he laid his right hand upon me, saying unto me, Fear not, I am the first and the last. I am he that liveth and was dead; and, behold, I am alive for evermore, and have the keys of death and hell." (Rev. 1:16-18)

But in addition to this, some new information about the resurrection has come into the world in these latter days. Since his visit to Patmos the resurrected Jesus has again been seen on several other occasions. Soon after his ascension into heaven he made a visit to the people of ancient America who were then living in an advanced state of civilization. He organized his Church among them and taught them the principles of the gospel, which we still find evidence of in the hieroglyphs and traditions of their American Indian descendants. As with Thomas he showed these ancient Americans the wounds that he had received on Calvary.

Centuries after the apostasy following his crucifixion, he came to the earth again in the early spring of 1820 to reestablish among men a belief in the God of Genesis, the God of Calvary, the God of John the Revelator, the God of the western continent, and the God of the latter days. While Joseph Smith was kneeling in the Sacred Grove, praying for wisdom to know which of the contending creeds was right, he had an experience which he partially describes as follows: ". . . I saw a pillar of light exactly over my head, above the brightness of the sun, which descended gradually until it fell upon me. When the light rested upon me, I saw two Personages whose brightness and glory defy all description, standing above me in the air. One of them spake unto me, calling me by name and said, pointing to the other — This is my Beloved Son, hear Him!" (Joseph Smith 2:16-17)

On another occasion the Prophet Joseph Smith and Oliver Cowdery were praying in the Kirtland Temple on April 3, 1836. The Prophet says, "The veil was taken from our minds, and the eyes of our understanding were opened. We saw the Lord standing upon the breastwork of the pulpit, before us; and under his feet was a paved work of pure gold, in color like amber. His eyes were as a flame of fire; the hair of his head was white like the pure snow; his countenance shone above the brightness of the sun; and his voice was as the sound of the rushing of great waters, even the voice of Jehovah. . . ." (D&C 110:1-3)

In our own day the Lord has officially opened the great and final dispensation of the gospel of Jesus Christ upon the earth to prepare the way for his glorious Second Coming. Other resurrected beings have visited the earth, restoring their various keys and authorities. Many wonderful Christian peoples of the world say that they *believe* in the resurrection, but this is supported and supplemented by many people presently living upon the earth bearing their solemn and reverent testimony that they *know* that this same resurrected Jesus is as much alive now as he was that day in Jerusalem when he showed himself to Thomas. I bear my own witness that again in our own day the divine assurance has been given that his promise of a glorious resurrection will be kept to all those who believe in him and obey his commandments. I humbly pray that God will bless our lives at this wonderful Easter season and help us to look forward to this promised event in our own lives.

The Shortcomings of Repentance

ONE OF THE GREATEST ideas in our world is repentance. It is also one of our most productive activities. The Savior of the world made it the second principle of the gospel. It was sponsored by him as the best means of bringing about the eternal exaltation of the earth's inhabitants. Closely connected with repentance is the vicarious atonement made by Jesus Christ when he took upon himself our transgressions and suffered for our sins on condition of our repentance. Repentance means a forsaking of evil and a turning of one's life upward to more worthwhile things. Try to imagine the amount of improvement that would be brought about in every department of human life if all criminals, all trouble-makers, all communists, all Americans, all sinners, and all Christians would wholeheartedly repent of their sins. Instead of being notorious as the originators of evil, we could then be famous as the producers of righteousness.

There are usually several steps to be followed in this important process of repentance: one is a recognition of guilt; two is a genuine sorrow for having done wrong; three is a firm determination to discontinue our sins; four, a wholehearted desire for reformation; five, an obligation to make restitution for the wrong we have done; and sixth, a firm resolve to adopt a new and better way of life. Some of the greatest men of the world have been reformed evil-doers.

For a long time Saul of Tarsus fought against the Church and was a persecutor of the saints. However, some new experiences caused him to change his ways, and he became one of the greatest Christian missionaries. Some men who have been held down by their own ignorance and inability have thrown off their evil and have developed great qualities of virtue and leadership within themselves. When this great power of repentance has been utilized, very frequently the pendulum has swung to the extreme in the opposite direction. Repentance is an effective procedure with more things than just our sins. We can also get rid of our weaknesses, and we can also exchange our poor judgment for a much better article.

The Bible probably makes more references to fools than to sinners. Everyone in the world wants to do well. Mostly we fall down because we don't know how, or we don't try hard enough, or we don't stick to our guns long enough to give our reformation a real chance to work. One of the interesting things about life is that it is much easier to fail than it is to succeed. We can fail merely by default, whereas we can only succeed by design. Failure is falling. Success is climbing. Wouldn't it be interesting if it were the other way around so that we always succeeded when we did nothing, or that we had to expend a lot of intelligence, industry, and thoughtfulness in order to fail?

Someone has said that success in life is like success in making a golf shot. There are 50 ways to hit a golf ball, but there is only one way to hit it right. There are innumerable ways to do things wrong, but not so many ways to do things right. A genuine repentance requires a firm desire and a whole-souled effort to turn our lives upward. We need to develop the power to effectively go from weakness to strength, from sin to righteousness, from mediocrity to excellence, from failure to success, and from misery to happiness. No matter how you look at it, this change in our lives — wherein we earnestly begin striving for better things — is one of the most productive ideas of our world. Sometimes we use this great power as a source of weakness by counting on it too much without doing anything about it.

Sometimes we tolerate evil because we think that repentance will always be so easily available. We are frequently more vigorous in sowing our wild oats when we believe that the whole crop that results will just disappear at a later date. We are also more prone to tolerate weaknesses and let them grow in us when we believe that they can be easily eliminated later on. One of the biggest problems of the murderer is to get rid of the dead body. That is also the biggest problem of the sinner.

Lillian Roth was a great movie actress. Then her fiance died suddenly, causing her great mental and emotional distress. For several weeks she was very nervous and upset. Finally, her nurse induced her to drink a glass of brandy before going to bed. Because this gave her such a wonderful night's rest, she repeated the treatment the next night and the next and the next. Finally, it was suggested that she may be going too far, but she felt sure that she could stop drinking at any time that she wanted to do so. When she got around to actually trying to let go of her alcoholic support, she found that it was not so easy.

She had now gone too far, and all the repentance that she could muster was not enough to save her. She lost all her money and suffered many disturbing experiences in trying to get rid of the bad habit that she had unintentionally acquired. What a great benefit it would have been to her if an easy repentance had still been available! This experience indicates that we should take advantage of this great gift of repentance while we have power over it.

Miss Roth later wrote a book entitled *I'll Cry Tomorrow*, illustrating that many of us think that we can do as we desire now and then take care of solving our problems when we feel like it. Sometimes our wild oats build up such an affinity for the soil in which they grow that they are almost impossible to eradicate. Sometimes we become so accustomed to a particular weakness or bad habit that we don't want to let it go; or we are so weakened by our sins that we lose our power to fight them.

The rules say that in playing baseball everyone is out if he can't hit the ball in three strikes; and if we can't make our football yards in four downs, we are asked to give up the ball to our opponents. Life is also like that. It also allows us only a limited time to get the job done. With each failure life becomes more difficult and finally we may lose the ball. However, life has given us this wonderful power of repentance, which has no equivalent in any other idea. In such activities as athletics or finances, no one is arbitrarily permitted to have his unprofitable plays wiped out and his losses excused and taken off the record merely by feeling sorry for having made them. The introduction of this principle of repentance into the game of life will enable all of us to be champions, if we merely learn how to use it effectively. If it is used early enough and frequently enough and with the right kind of understanding, it can even save our eternal souls.

However, sometimes we allow ourselves to get too far out before we call for help. Before we realize it, we may pass the point of no return so that we can't get back. Taken in the early stages, Lillian Roth would have had no problem at all with alcoholism, but when she tried to deal with it later, it cost her several million dollars and several disastrous marriages. It wrecked her career, her reputation, and her self-respect. There are likewise many dope addicts, atheists, lung cancer victims, and slaves of immorality, who in the same way die in their sins, being unable to redeem themselves from the habits that they had allowed to carry them too far out before applying the remedy.

Shakespeare's Claudius murdered his brother, married his queen, and ascended the throne of Denmark. With all these prizes in his possession, he sought forgiveness through repentance. After unsuccessfully attempting to pray, he said:

> My words fly up, my thoughts remain below.
> Words without thoughts never to heaven go.
>
>   Pray can I not,
> Though inclination be as sharp as will:
> My stronger guilt defeats my strong intent . . .
> What if this cursed hand
> Were thicker than itself with brother's blood,
> Is there not rain enough in the sweet heavens
> To wash it white as snow? . . .
>   Then I'll look up;
> My fault is past. But O, what form of prayer
> Can serve my turn? 'Forgive me my foul murder?'—
> That cannot be, since I am still possess'd
> Of those effects for which I did the murder.
> My crown, mine own ambition and my queen.
> May one be pardon'd and retain the offence?
>
>   (Hamlet)

Claudius had left the ingredient of restitution out of the formula, and that had made repentance impossible for him. Repentance also has a number of other shortcomings. Repentance cannot always heal the wounds that the sin has left. A murderer may feel sorry for what he has done, but even the most genuine repentance cannot bring the dead man back to life. Of course, whatever its limitations may be, it is always proper to repent. That is, no one ever steps into sin so deep but that repentance is a far better way than a continuance of the evil.

Even though one may truly repent of his immorality, he may leave ghastly wounds that will never completely heal. The story is told of a young man who adopted an interesting method of doing the bookkeeping while he was sowing his wild oats. For each evil thing he did, he drove a nail into the wood paneling of his room. Then he tired of his sins and wanted to repent. As he conquered a bad habit or eliminated a vice, he drew out the particular nail that had represented that sin. Finally, all his evils had been discontinued and all the nails had been withdrawn, but what he had left was what had been beautiful paneling — now marred with a lot of ugly nail holes. It is sometimes very difficult to erase the ugly marks of sin. So frequently past ugliness remains with us and destroys the joys of our future successes.

I know of no particular advantage in falling into a mud hole, merely because someone will arrive on the job in time to pull us out. Even if one does get out of the mud holes, he is always dirty as a consequence, and the cleaning-up process is expensive, depressing, and usually time-consuming. In his capacity as the Savior of the world and the Redeemer of men, the Son of God has promised us that he will take upon himself our sins and suffer for our evil deeds if we will repent of them.

About this situation Isaiah said: "Surely he hath borne our griefs, and carried our sorrows . . . he was wounded for our transgressions, he was bruised for our iniquities: the chastisement of our peace was upon him; and with his stripes we are healed." (Isa. 53:4-5)

In this spirit, we sometimes sing a song in which we say with some enthusiasm: "Cast your burdens on the Lord and trust his constant care." The more we sin the greater his suffering. It should not be particularly pleasing to us to know that we have caused the wrong man to be whipped. The shortest verse there is in the Bible is composed of just two words: "Jesus wept." Our present generation is probably causing more tears than those of any other day, and we ought to be responsible enough to carry our own burdens. We always cause pain for others when we are sinful. We can save a lot of suffering if we eliminate our sins, instead of casting their burdens of suffering upon an innocent person.

Jesus set us the proper example when he avoided all sin. Because he didn't fall into any mudholes, he didn't cause anyone any of those problems involved in getting out and getting cleaned up. In this way we can also avoid suffering for ourselves and others. We can avoid the unhealable wounds and the perversions that they cause in our lives by staying away from mud holes. We can also eliminate the intense regret, the wasted opportunities, the broken plans, the ruined hopes, and the loss of time by following the Master.

The story is told of a horse that once ran away from its master. After a time, the horse repented and returned to his master and said: "I have come back." The master said: "Yes, you have come back, but the field is unplowed." How does one go about repenting of unplowed ground, or good deeds not done, or lessons not learned, or blessings not attained?

In football we only have four tries before we lose the ball. The ancient prophet Jeremiah seemed to have about the same thing in mind when he tried to caution us by saying: "The harvest is past, the summer is ended, and we are not saved." (Jer. 8:20)

We have been allotted just enough time for our lives if we don't make too many detours or get on too many dead-end streets. We can't afford to waste too many years while we are sowing our wild oats and then using the balance of our strength to try to stamp them out. The losses are always greater for the sinner than the non-sinner. When we sow the wind, we should always expect to reap the whirlwind. Many of our lives are shortchanged because of the time wasted cleaning ourselves up after our mud-hole experiences. The poet said:

> Do right, though anguish be thy lot,
> Thy heart will cheer thee when thy pains forgot.
>
> Do wrong for pleasure's sake, then count thy gain—
> The pleasure's soon forgot, the sins remain.

Repentance is one of the greatest ideas in our world. It is one of our most productive activities, but it is only the second principle of the gospel, not the first. It will always rank second to faith, righteousness, and obedience to God.

The Short Course

A<small>N</small> INTERESTING STORY is told of the experiences of a young man enrolling in college. He had some ideas about what he would like to become, and in trying to help him orient himself in his new undertaking a school counselor was going over the curriculum step by step. He was explaining to this young man the various classes that would be required for graduation and the order in which they should be taken. The prospective student was a little impatient with the amount of work that was involved, and the time that would be required in order to reach his objective. He said to his adviser, "Don't you have a short course?" The professor said, "Oh yes, we have a lot of short courses. It all depends on just what you want to make of yourself."

Then he tried to explain to this young man some of the basic requirements in his preparation either for a professional career or for life itself. In trying to help him get a better perspective, the professor said to the young man: "When the Lord starts out to make an oak tree, he takes a hundred years to do it in, but he can make a pumpkin in ninety days." More or less, education as well as life itself is like that. And as individuals, we ourselves must choose whether we desire to become an oak tree or a pumpkin.

One of the very serious problems in our world and in our lives generally is that so frequently we are unwilling to pay the price demanded by success. The proper preparation often seems like a waste of time, and so we become dropouts from education. It is often true that in our minds we want to be oak trees or even giant redwoods, but if one's determination is weak, he may end up by becoming just a pumpkin.

Because we don't understand this law of preparation, many people frequently sacrifice their great goals, their possible capability and their ultimate success in order to travel with the crowd along the easy path of least resistance. Benjamin Franklin once told an interesting story about a man who had a rusty ax that was so corroded by disuse that it had a dull-brown appearance. The axman wanted to have a bright, shiny ax like the other workmen. Accordingly, he took his ax to a grinder. The grinder agreed to make the workman's ax sparkle like new by holding it aginst the grindstone which was to be turned by the owner of the ax. The axman was very pleased and both went to work accordingly. But putting a polish on an ax, like putting a polish on a human being, can't always be done in a minute. And after a period of long, hard turning the axman began to tire. Finally he told the grinder that he thought the ax had been ground enough. The grinder pointed out that the job was only partly done. He said to the axman, "Your ax is now only a speckled ax." And he said, "Turn on, turn on, and it will be bright and shiny soon." But as weariness had set in, the axman had had a change of heart about shiny axes, and he now said, "I think I like a speckled ax best."

It is a common phenomenon to have our viewpoints change as our muscles tire or as our patience begins to wear out. A shiny ax seems much less important when it requires the "long course" of grinding. And sometimes for success in life our minds or our spirits need to be held against the grindstone for some long hard grinding. Sometimes we become dropouts while we are still speckled with ignorance or atheism or irresponsibility, whereas with a little more grinding and some extra polishing, our abilities, our faith and our self-discipline would sparkle with a satisfying radiance.

A woodsman once said that he didn't understand how his fellow workers cut down so many trees when they wasted so much time sharpening their axes. And in about the same way we all tend to be more or less like the old country deacon. Someone once asked him whether or not he was a Christian. He said he was in spots. So frequently we stop turning the grindstone while we are still marred by the rust spots of our irresponsibilities, our immaturities, our insecurities, and our inferiorities. I suppose that it may be better to be a spotted Christian than to be rusty all over. But life is much more profitable and pleasant if we are sharp and shiny. When we have too many rough spots interspersed with our shiny places, conflicts develop. A little longer course devoted to grinding out the rusty spots and getting rid of the corrosion can be very profitable to us.

It can be very helpful to remember that most of life is preparation. We prepare for school. We prepare for marriage. We prepare for our life's work. We prepare for death. In our antemortal existence we prepared for this life. In this life we prepare for the next life. And an eternal life and an eternal progression involves an adequate preparation. No one is ever happy while he is standing still or going backward. Here and hereafter we bring many problems upon ourselves when we stop turning the grindstone of preparation. Each month I listen to a recital of many marital problems, and most of them are caused because those involved took some variety of the short course. For example, many of the people who begin their marriages as teenagers have a pretty rough time in making a go of it because they are not prepared. They just haven't lived long enough. It takes time to learn to build those strong foundations of basic fundamental character. And the short course does not give enough time for our personalities to mature or to adequately build up our judgment. Frequently, the short course leaves some rough spots of selfishness, laziness, irresponsibility, and lack of self-discipline.

Actually most education is about ourselves. We study medicine to learn how to keep ourselves well physically. Psychology, psychiatry, and the other mental studies will teach us how to keep ourselves well mentally. Agriculture is how to feed ourselves. Business is how to deal with each other. The law teaches us how to be orderly. Sociology is how we live together agreeably. And then we have that great study of religion which shows us how to keep ourselves well spiritually.

Those people who have held their axes against the grindstone until they are no longer speckled have a great advantage in marriage or in business or in life. When we still have some rusty moral spots, or some brown spots of atheism, or some corroded spots of selfishness, or some rough spots of ignorance, or some bothersome spots of immaturity, we are found to have an increase of troubles. Life can also be pretty difficult when we have some spots of sloth or lethargy or indifference that haven't been ground off. Someone has said:

> The man who wants a garden fair,
> Or small or very big,
> With flowers growing here and there,
> Must bend his back and dig.

The things are mighty few on earth
That wishes can attain,
Whatever we want of any worth
We've got to work to gain.

It matters not what goal you seek,
Its secret here reposes.
You've got to dig from week to week
To get results or roses.

To take the short course in planning or industry is the way we shortchange ourselves and bypass our blessings. The best course always includes the philosophy of the second mile. We need to do more than we get paid for. Someone once pointed out that "the shortest distance between two points is a straight line." Then his friend said, "Ah, but I know a short cut." Those who tamper with premarital sex are looking for a short cut. Those who practice dishonesty in their businesses are trying to find a short cut. They hope to get some of life's experiences and benefits by taking a shorter route than the one provided by a straight line. All of those who take short cuts on the straight and narrow way are headed for an unhappy ending. The hippies and dope addicts are all enrolled in one of life's short courses. They don't plan on paying the price that all real success inevitably demands. They want to eat their bread before they earn it.

In fact, many don't want to earn their own bread at all. And many people want to eat the bread that others have produced. Some entire groups specialize in idleness. They don't want to work or to wait to be deserving of retirement from their jobs. They want to retire before they have worked. Many want to graduate before they have studied. By the self-delusion of dope they want to take trips into make-believe lands that do not exist. They don't want to merit the attention of their fellowmen by service and character. And they think they have found a short cut when they quit shaving, dress in ludicrous dirty clothing, and stop combing their hair or taking a bath. It is easy for some people to persuade themselves that God was wrong when in his command he said, "Six days shalt thou labor." And his old law of morality is now out of date, in their opinions. They have found a number of short cuts that apparently God didn't think about when he was planning our lives in our interests.

To some, God uttered an unintelligible concept when he said, "Be ye clean that bear the vessels of the Lord." And many people have rejected the philosophy of "Peace on earth, good will toward men." They think that peace and righteousness are not as profitable as troublemaking, subversion, disloyalty, and deception. But we are on much safer ground when we understand that God did not make any mistakes when he enacted his laws, nor did he overlook anything that would be in our interests. And we had better be very careful when we try to shortcut the straight lines that he has drawn, for when we bypass the law, we are certain to miss the blessings.

We live in a great free land founded by God upon Christian principles. Freedom, righteousness, order, and human dignity were designed to be the order of our lives. And when we attempt short cuts to greater freedom in bypassing legislatures and legally constituted bodies, we are only laying a snare for our own feet. Many are taking the law into their own hands and are making their appeal for success to race riots, fear, force, clamorous demonstrations, and distorted propaganda to accomplish their purposes. Although we are supposed to live in a stable, civilized, orderly society, instead of fully supporting the orderly processes of a trial by jury we have substituted such disorderly procedures as trials by marches and trials by threats or trials by race riots and troublemaking. In all of these new short cuts in government, many Americans are changing to the short course in living and in many cases they are ignoring God and leaving all thought of eternal life out of the picture.

In one of the greatest of all commands, the God of creation came down onto the top of Mount Sinai and to the accompaniment of lightning and thunder set aside one-seventh of all of the days of our lives as days to worship God, to study the scriptures, and to improve our own quality of living. One of our greatest errors is that we don't want to obey this law, don't want to spend enough time in spiritual preparation, so we have drastically shortened our all-important long course in religion. As an inevitable consequence, many of us place a handicap upon ourselves comparable to the prospective doctor who severely limits his medical school experience. Abraham Lincoln once said that a man is only about as happy as he makes up his mind to be. Likewise we are only about as capable and as successful as our preparation entitles us to become.

I once heard of a hive of bees that took a short course in honey-making. They gave up flowers as the source of their raw material and transferred their patronage to some discarded syrup barrels at a Coca Cola plant. It seems that an English investigator made a survey about the effort required by a bee to carry on his life's work of honey-gathering. One pound of honey contains 7,000 grains of sugar which presents the concentrated sweetness of 62,000 clover blossoms, each of which is made up of 60 florets. To obtain one pound of honey, therefore, the bee is obligated to make two million, seven hundred thousand trips to and from the flowers, covering a distance of approximately five million miles.

In the process of extracting the honey, he inserts his tiny proboscis into each separate floret, which means that he performs the operation 60 times 62,000, or three million, seven hundred and twenty thousand times, to get nectar enough to make a pound of honey. But then, with a kind of "new morality" glee, the bees discovered an abundant supply of Coca Cola syrup in the barrels. So they shifted their loyalty and effort as they transferred to the short course in honey-making. Their only problem was that thereafter their honey was no good and the bees themselves soon died.

A group of seagulls had a similar experience. Instead of catching their own fish, they settled down at a fish cannery, where each day they stuffed themselves with the scraps and waste discarded from the cannery. Soon they were like stuffed ducks. They forgot how to fish and they forgot how to fly, and large numbers of them died from the occupational disease connected with their short courses in fishing.

When the Lord said "Go to the ant thou sluggard, consider her ways and be wise," he was not talking about life's short courses.

Life is the greatest commodity ever known in the universe, and making the most of it is our greatest opportunity.

Sightseeing

IT IS PROBABLE that the most popular entertainment in the world is sightseeing. Human beings have a strong inclination to travel. We like to go places and do things. We enjoy making new friends and talking to new people.

The Greek poet Homer illustrated this human characteristic some nine centuries, B.C., when he wrote the story of Ulysses, King of the little Greek state of Ithaca. Ulysses and his men had spent ten years fighting in the Trojan War, but when the war was over they spent another ten years getting back to their homes, which were only three hundred miles away across an island-dotted sea. On their way home they stopped at the happy isles and listened to the enchanting songs of the sirens. They had some exciting experiences with man-eating giants, terrible monsters, roaring whirlpools, and romantic interludes. Only a few of Ulysses' soldiers were killed in the Trojan War, but he was the only one who survived the sightseeing of their return trip.

Recently I read about a young woman who was paralyzed in the lower half of her body. She was a natural lover of history and geography, and even though the paralysis confined her body to the wheel chair at home, she devised a procedure by which her mind and heart visited every part of the earth.

She selected one country at a time and then fully devoted herself to visiting it. She wrote to steamship companies and airlines for travel information. She got many beautiful pictures of people and places. She studied the history books and the great literature. She read interesting stories about the people that she would soon be visiting. She studied each country in the greatest depth. Before she visited Greece she learned all about the interesting myths and legends of the people. She put herself on a kind of first-name basis with the greatest of the heroes, heroines, philosophers, and military leaders. She dressed herself in Grecian costume and took part with them in their golden age. She stood on the top of famous Mount Olympus and loved this wonderful little country lying at her feet. She discussed philosophy with Socrates and watched the heroic deeds of Hercules. With her wonderful Grecian friends, she ate and laughed and loved and lived to her heart's content. After this most delightful journey that had been made strictly on her own terms, she would return home to prepare for her next adventure.

Someone has said that this picturing power of the mind is one of the greatest gifts that God has ever given to man. In one paragraph of President David O. McKay's great book, *Gospel Ideals*, he says: "Last night I dreamed about my mother." Then he said: "I would like to dream about my mother more often." In his dream he went back into his childhood and relived those important experiences at his mother's knee that had brought him to his high place in the world. He didn't learn to be President of the Church when he was eighty or seventy or sixty; he learned that in his mother's presence when he was five and ten and fifteen. Then in his maturity he went back and relived those important periods while he re-absorbed the strength of his mother's love and inspiration.

In some ways the benefits of our dreams exceed those of our realities. One doesn't necessarily have to be asleep in order to dream, nor is a dreamer limited to reliving the past. We can also prelive the future. This picturing power of the imagination builds the roadway on which all future success will someday travel.

In the year 1265 there was born an Italian poet by the name of Dante Alighieri, who also had some rather unusual sightseeing experiences. He read a lot of the Bible and other travel literature, and then in his imagination he made a journey through hell and talked with some of its inmates. He recorded his experiences in a book called *The Divine Comedy*. In those days a comedy was not something that was funny; a comedy was something that had a happy ending. Therefore, a more understandable title for our day would have been *The Divine Experience*, or Homer might have called it *The Divine Odyssey*.

Dante's book is divided into three parts. He called the first "The Inferno," and in it he describes his trip through the lowest regions of the world of spirits. Before he began, Dante had made himself thoroughly familiar with the Bible accounts of hell, to which he added generously from his own reason and imagination. To Dante, hell was a place inhabited by those

spirits who were forever lost. These despairing souls lived forever without hope. Then Dante made his way upward through
purgatory. Purgatory differed from hell because it had an exit
as well as an entrance, and its punishments were less severe
because the inmates still had a chance to be delivered. Purgatory was the place where human souls were purged of their
evils, with the hope that through their suffering, repentance,
and education, they might be prepared for entrance into one
of God's kingdoms of glory. This was the place where the dross
was burned out of their lives. About this place, Jesus said: ". . .
Thou shalt by no means come out thence, till thou hast paid
the uttermost farthing." (Matt. 5:26)

Dante pictures hell and purgatory as a series of circles or
elevations. The top levels are inhabited by the spirits who have
sinned least, and then as one descends from one layer to another
into the depths of hell, the corruption and consequent suffering
increase. Dante tries to picture the worst conceivable suffering
of which his mind was capable. But human imagination — even
at its best —is very limited in its power and often is not capable
of giving more than a faint suggestion of the real experience.

For example, no one ever suffers as much from a toothache
in his imagination as he does from one in his tooth. It is probable that no matter how vivid a verbal description of hell might
be, it would still fall far short of an actual experience in its
ability to convey understanding to us. No one has ever yet
discovered the limits of human suffering. We do know that
it can be so intense as to unhinge our minds and produce insanity.
The scriptures tell us that while the body of Jesus lay in the
tomb, his spirit went and preached to the spirits in prison who
were disobedient in the days of Noah. (See I Pet. 3:18-20) The
purpose of his visit was to arrange for the release of those who
were worthy. Jesus went into the eternal prison house in person,
whereas Dante did the next best thing by going there in his
imagination. Certainly his mental pictures have been very
thought-provoking for millions of people since that time.

As Dante made his way through hell, he tried to describe
the depression, pain, and hopelessness of those he interviewed.
Speaking of hell, he said: "Now I perceived its flames and heard
the cries that set me trembling, as I crouched in dread." He
tries to describe the misery in the distorted ill-formed minds
of hell's inhabitants as they sadly contemplated their bygone

folly and suffered with no hope of deliverance. One of hell's inmates said to Dante: "There is no greater grief than to recall a bygone happiness." Trying to help us, another of hell's spirits said to Dante: "We beg if ever you escape from these dark places to look again upon the stars of heaven, see that ye speak of us to other men." Then Dante adds his own comments and says: "Reader, as God may grant you reason, gather fruit from reading this and then take council with yourself."

Then Dante visited in purgatory where human souls were being cleansed of sin and made worthy to ascend to heaven. Here, some of the inmates told Dante how they had arrived in this dreadful place. One said: "As our eyes intent on earthly things were never lifted up to heaven so now hath justice fixed them here upon the ground. And even as greed destroyed our love for good whereby the labors of our lives were lost, so now doth justice hold us captive here fettered in close restraint." Another of these imprisoned spirits said: "Not what I did but what I failed to do lost me the right to live with God on high." One confessed that he had been a *secret* Christian and had kept putting off his repentance until it was too late. One woman told about the nettles of remorse that were constantly torturing her soul. She described herself as "an ailing crone who finds no rest upon her bed of down, but tosses to and fro to ease her pain. The allurements of the moment turned my steps astray and every evil that I entertained is now my fierce oppressor."

Then Dante said: "Reader, sharpen well your eyes to truth," but he pointed out that even a blind man would not go astray if he walked faithful behind his guide. Finally Dante came to the wall of fire that marked the boundaries of the kingdom of purgatory. He fought his way through the flames and described its fire by saying, "I would gladly have jumped in molten glass to cool me from that heat which was beyond all measure." And here again an exaggeration may be an impossibility.

In a modern-day revelation the Lord himself has mentioned the extremes of punishment suffered by those who bring eternal death upon themselves. He has said: ". . . they shall go away into everlasting punishment, which is endless punishment, which is eternal punishment, to reign with the devil and his angels in eternity, where their worm dieth not: and the fire is not quenched, which is their torment — And the end thereof, neither the place thereof, nor their torment, no man knows; neither was it revealed, neither is, neither will be revealed unto man, except to them who are made partakers thereof. Nevertheless, I, the Lord, show it by vision unto many, but straightway shut it up again; Wherefore the end, the width, the height, the depth, and the misery thereof, they understand not, neither any man except those who are ordained unto this condemnation." (D&C 76:44-48)

It seems that we have three alternatives for solving our hell problems: one is to find out about it by a personal experience; the second is to so live the gospel that this suffering and attending reformation are made unnecessary; and the third might be to follow the example of Dante, and with the scriptures, our reason, and our imagination as travel guides, we might do a little spiritual sightseeing in this eternal reformatory on our own initiative. Incidentally, this is a pretty good idea.

Thomas Carlyle once said that in his opinion *The Divine Comedy* was the most remarkable of all books. Dante himself believed that he was divinely inspired and commissioned. He believed that it was his mission in life to show men hell. Of course, we are all aware that hell is a divine institution. It was established by God as a place of purification where men and women can be prepared for better things. Jesus probably talked of hell about as much as he did of heaven. One of the tremendous advantages of some effective sightseeing in this area is that we may save ourselves an actual experience, which may be far more unpleasant.

It is not very wise to try to dispose of hell merely by saying that we don't believe in it and therefore, that it doesn't exist. This is frequently what we do, as there are many surveys indicating that far more people believe in heaven than in hell. Even if we believe, it is pretty difficult to get ourselves to do any detailed meditation about situations that we think of as unpleasant, but unpleasant or not, there is a hell. Even our earthly society would have difficulties in trying to operate without some penitentiaries, hospitals, and reform schools. There is an unseen avenger that constantly stands guard in the universe to make sure that no sin goes unpunished. There is an unchangeable, inexorable, immutable, irrevocable law that says: "Whatsoever a man soweth that shall he also reap."

Nothing is more clearly stated in the scriptures than that everlasting eternal law that everyone will be rewarded or punished according to his works. The Lord said: "And the righteous shall be gathered on my right hand unto eternal life; and the wicked on my left hand will I be ashamed to own before the Father; wherefore I will say unto them — Depart from me, ye cursed, into everlasting fire, prepared for the devil and his angels." (D&C 29:27-28)

For Dante, the happy ending came when he finished his journey in paradise. That was the place where the righteous lived forever with God. And, of course, this is where all of us would like to finish. We might profitably advance our own interests by doing homework on hell's travel literature before we find ourselves booked for a personal visit. Like Dante, we should also arrange for a visit to paradise. The Prophet Joseph Smith once said that if you could look into heaven for five minutes, you would learn more than by reading all of the books that had ever been written on that subject. What could be more profitable to us than to do a little spiritual sightseeing among the glories and pleasures of celestial conditions?

Someone has said that "the best argument for an eternal life is the existence of someone who deserves one." Nothing in life would make sense without a heaven. The existence of Satan, our crime waves, our atheism, and our sins make it abundantly clear that there has got to be a hell, for as Jesus has said: "My blood will not heal them if they hear me not."

A great Sunday School teacher was once asked: "Is there a hell?" He replied: "Yes, there is a hell all right, but we won't go into that now." It is thought, however, that maybe we should go in occasionally. We should also make some visits to heaven, and we probably have some friends in both places who could furnish us with some very interesting information and suggestions. Inasmuch as sightseeing is our most popular entertainment we ought to do it in a place where it will also be the most productive.

A Somebody

As NANCY HANKS LINCOLN lay on her deathbed, she said to her nine-year-old son: "Abe, go out there and amount to something." Lincoln loved his mother and was devoted to her ideals, and he spent the rest of his life doing those things he knew would please her. In honoring her, it was easy for him to be strictly honest and completely fair, because he knew that was what she wanted him to be. Later in his life Lincoln said: "All that I am or ever hope to be, I owe to my angel mother."

When from the top of Mount Sinai God said: "Honor thy father and thy mother," he was actually saying to all of his children: "Go out there and amount to something." This has probably been his most urgent cry all down through the ages since that time.

One great father said: "If I had only five minutes of life left to spend with my son, I would try to set him on fire with a love of truth and give him a passion to make his own life meaningful." The purpose of life is growth. It was intended that every life should have meaning and significance. It is one of the most serious tragedies of our world when this great aim sometimes miscarries and potentially great human beings formed in God's image make themselves into something less than creation intended.

Norman Vincent Peale tells about a young woman with whom he visited after one of his lectures. She greeted him with a weak, limp handshake and said in a timid, apologetic voice: "I wanted to shake hands with you, but I really shouldn't be bothering you. There are so many important people waiting to speak to you and I am just a nobody. Forgive me for taking your time." Dr. Peale asked her if she would remain until he had shaken hands with the others, as he wanted to talk to her.

When the others had gone he said: "Now, Miss Nobody, let's sit down and have a little visit." In surprise she said: "What did you call me?" He said: "I called you by the only name you gave me. Didn't you tell me that you were a nobody? Do you have another name?" She replied: "Of course I do." He said: "I thought you must have."

Then Dr. Peale said to this fine young woman: "One of the reasons I wanted to talk to you was to find out how anybody could get the idea that she was a nobody. I also wanted to tell you that by such a belittling reference to yourself, you are probably making a serious affront to God." She exclaimed: "Dr. Peale, you can't be serious!" Then Dr. Peale said in substance: "Young lady, you are a child of God; you have been created in his image and you have been endowed with a set of his attributes and potentialities. In view of the great possibilities that God has given you, it must greatly disturb him to hear you so profane his work as to refer to yourself as a nobody."

Then in an encouraging conversation Dr. Peale tried to assist this fine young woman to see herself in a little better perspective by pointing out her great potential as a child of God. Every human being has an incalculable importance to himself, but everyone is also important to God and to the world in which he lives. God did not create anybody to be a nobody, and yet consciously or unconsciously so many people are willfully making those degrading decisions to be nobodies.

A prominent doctor said that man does not die; he kills himself. All of our spiritual, moral, social, and intellectual deaths are usually brought about by our own hands. God has decreed that in the eternal scheme of things everybody can be somebody. And we ourselves must do something about it. It seems that everyone needs a discoverer as well as a developer. All parents should be talent scouts for their children to help them discover themselves on an eternal-life basis.

When Lincoln's mother died that did not end her interest in her son, and wherever she was during his famous mortal career, think how proud Nancy Hanks Lincoln must have been of him as he overcame his difficulties and gave his own life its great significance! On Father's Day, we might well think of the greatest of all "parent and child" combinations and how on four different occasions God the Father introduced his Only Begotten by saying: "This is my beloved Son in whom I am well pleased." What would have pleased God or Lincoln's mother more, either on earth or in heaven, than the success and welfare of their children? Probably our greatest Father's Day prayer is that one saying, "Go out there and amount to something."

In the world of spirits, it must have been even a greater thrill than we can now understand for Mrs. Lincoln to have known that her young son was always scrupulously honest and absolutely fair. He always devoted himself to the better things in life and was finally given the greatest honor that his countrymen could bestow upon him, but it would probably be an even greater thrill for God to look down upon an earth filled with his children who are bringing themselves up in his image to become what he is. Because God wants our lives to have significance and happiness, he has gone to great pains in giving us detailed directions as to exactly how we can make them the most worthwhile. Many years ago, one seeker after the most worthwhile things said to Jesus: ". . . Good master, what shall I do that I may inherit eternal life?" Jesus answered: "Thou knowest the commandments, Do not commit adultery, Do not kill, Do not steal, Do not bear false witness, Defraud not, Honour thy father and thy mother." (Mark 10:17, 19) We must also understand that every time we violate one of these great eternal laws, we subtract from our own significance and tend to make ourselves into nobodies.

The most severe shock that any mortal is ever asked to endure in this life is to have an acute awareness of his own uselessness. To begin with, Lincoln didn't have many advantages in the usual sense. He was motherless at age nine; his early life was spent in abject poverty; he was almost entirely deprived of the usual privileges of education. More or less, he was all alone in the world. He was awkward and ungainly in physical appearance. He was heartbroken at the death of his sweetheart and later married a woman who was a serious burden to him all his life. He was unsuccessful in many ways. A great majority of his political contests went against him, but because he didn't give up and because he kept this mother's goal firmly in mind, he eventually became one of the finest human beings who has ever lived upon this earth. A hundred years after his death, he is still being quoted and loved throughout the entire world, and many people are trying to pattern their lives after him. His mother might well have said of him: "This is my beloved son in whom I am well pleased."

By comparison, how different it must be for mothers and

fathers who have gone back to that great world of spirits and have found out that their children are dope addicts, idlers, atheists, and advocates of weakness and immorality.

Some time ago a book was written entitled *How to Be Somebody*. What a great title that would be for a book that we might write with ourselves in mind! God has also written some books on this subject — we call them the Holy Scriptures. Their purpose is that we might become even as God is. That would mean that we should really become somebody. Because the teacher usually learns faster than the student, and the writer learns faster than the reader, we should write our own book entitled *How to Be a Somebody*.

Usually we know enough to fill up our own book on this subject, but writing it down may help us to make some additional determinations about it. A salesman once complained to his sales manager that he was failing in his business, and he solicited the aid of the sales manager to help him be more successful in providing for his family. The salesman knew that the sales manager was very capable, and the salesman was delighted when the sales manager agreed to help him.

The sales manager said: "There are two general rules that, if you will agree to follow them, we can quadruple your income in a very short time." The salesman was delighted with the prospect and agreed to do as he was directed. The sales manager said: "Rule number one is that you are to immediately stop doing all those things that you are now doing that you know you should not do. Rule number two is that you are to begin immediately to do all those things that you are sure you should do that presently you are not doing." The salesman was disappointed and discouraged, as he had not expected to receive any instructions that were so difficult to follow. More or less, we all tend to make ourselves into nobodies because we want some glamorous thing to do, but won't do those things that we already know to be right.

Just think what tremendous people we would all become, if we merely followed the simple rules of success. For example, a lot of people are having trouble with overweight who are praying for an easy way to reduce, but they will not practice the simple rules of self-control. One man once said that he had a diet in every pocket of every suit, but he didn't follow any of them. Another man asked for someone who could help him stop the disgusting habit of swearing. There are many people who have serious troubles with profanity, dishonesty, immorality, ignorance, and laziness that greatly reduce their success. A little self-discipline could solve almost all our problems, and any one of us could easily write the formula that would result in the finest accomplishment if we were only willing to follow what we already know. In carrying out his mother's wish, Lincoln merely did those things that any nine-year-old boy would know that he should do.

Lincoln didn't have many books in his early years, but he read and followed the ones he did have, and that was one of his greatest success secrets, which anyone of us may practice. One of Lincoln's books was *The Life of Washington* written by W. R. Weems. Another of Lincoln's books was the Bible. The Bible doesn't do much good for those who don't know what it says. I have always felt a great admiration for this young, unschooled Abraham Lincoln, lying before the open fire in that backwoods cabin reading the Bible. To begin with, the Bible is not easy to read, even for people with much better educations. It was written a long time ago, and many of the things discussed are not easily understood, but Lincoln kept reading until he did understand.

Lincoln's success comes partly because of his natural interest in the kinds of things that the Bible discusses. It might be said that Lincoln not only obeyed God, but he also agreed with him. Someone once suggested that he thought the Lord was on Lincoln's side. Lincoln said he was not concerned about whether or not the Lord was on his side, but he knew that everything would be all right if Lincoln was just always on the Lord's side. We might try to imagine what our own lives would be if we were always on the Lord's side in every situation.

As the communists go about their business of enslaving people and causing trouble, they are disobeying God's proclamation of peace on earth, good will to men. The communists have also banished God from their countries. We may also banish him from our personal lives when we disregard his laws and break his commandments. When we lie, steal, cheat, kill, become drunkards, and act like criminals, we are making ourselves into eternal nobodies. Nations disappear and individuals fail when they disobey God and do the wrong things. We also tend to lose our own significance when we identify with inferior causes and take part in projects that are not worthwhile.

Presently many people are actually killing themselves by their abnormal depressions, their guilt complexes, and their deserved feelings of inferiority. It is said that before an alcoholic can be given any help, he must understand that he has a problem, and he must admit to himself and those who are to assist him that he needs help.

There is a lot of evidence pointing to the fact that all of us presently need help. Things are not necessarily right, merely because we think that way. A great scripture says: "Let no man think he is a ruler; but let God rule him. . . ." (D&C 58:20)

The greatest joys come to most parents when they see their children making something worthwhile out of their lives. With this in mind the Lord said to us: "Be ye therefore perfect." (Matt. 5:48) He indicated our potentials when he said: "Ye are gods; and all of you are children of the most High." Ps. 82:6) We should cling to our inheritance and constantly reaffirm it in our lives. God our Eternal Father is far more anxious about us than Lincoln's mother was about him. Speaking of his own life's mission, God has said: "This is my work and my glory — to bring to pass the immortality and eternal life of man." (Moses 1:39) It is his mission to help us amount to something and we will be able to succeed if we have our own full and complete cooperation.

Son, Behold Thy Mother!

ONE OF THE MOST impressive scenes from sacred literature took place at the foot of the cross during the crucifixion. Most of the friends of Jesus had deserted him and many of his disciples had run away, but his mother stayed close by and waited out with him those long, lonely hours of his death struggle. In recalling that agonizing period the scripture says that Jesus looked down upon his mother and his beloved apostle John. The record says:

"When Jesus therefore saw his mother, and the disciple standing by, whom he loved, he saith unto his mother, Woman, behold thy son!

"Then saith he to the disciple, Behold thy mother! And from that hour that disciple took her unto his own home.

"After this, Jesus knowing that all things were now accomplished, that the scripture might be fulfilled, saith, I thirst. . . .

"When Jesus therefore had received the vinegar [which was offered] he said, It is finished: And he bowed his head, and gave up the Ghost. (John 19:26-30)

This scene has also been presented to our minds in poetic form as follows:

> When Jesus hung upon the tree,
> He looked to John entreatingly
> And said, "Son, behold your mother."
> John hearkened to his Lord's request
> And to his home and to his breast
> He took his Other Mother.
>
> And Other Mothers since that day
> Whose blessed sons have gone away,
> Concern our Elder Brother;
> And on this holy Mother's Day,
> To you, to me, does He not say,
> "Son, behold your mother"?

This ancient scene between a son and his mother indicates one of the greatest of all our human relationships. The son owes almost everything to the mother, and the mother's greatest duty is to her children. It seems appropriate to use this challenging line as a fitting title for our own observance of this important day as we say, "Son, behold thy mother." We mean that we should honor her, love her, serve her, and make her life happy.

This important parent-child relationship is two-directional. Again, God is saying, "Woman, behold thy son." What he will become is in her hands. There is an old Chinese custom to the effect that if you were to save someone's life, you become responsible for him as long as the life that you have saved continues. A friend told me about making it possible for a cousin living in a foreign land to come to America. The immigration authorities required him to sign some guarantees that he would be responsible for his cousin, and when a mother helps to bring a human soul from the world of spirits to live on this earth of sin and trouble, she too signs up to be responsible for him. She not only bestows upon her child life, which is the greatest of all gifts, but she also incurs an obligation as to how that life will be lived. A mother becomes a partner with God and accepts some responsibility for the strength and perpetuity of the race. On this important Mother's Day, we honor that very special person who stands next to God in our lives. She was the one who provided the mold in which our bodies were formed, but she also carries the chief responsibility for nourishing our minds and inspiring our spirits.

There are some teachers who claim that the greatest thing in the world is education. There are doctors who think that the most noble calling centers in the practice of medicine. There are many other wonderful professions which make important claims. Great artists put new visions on the canvas for our inspiration. Poets express great thoughts in the most uplifting language; engineers transform deserts into bounteous fields and fill the waste places with prosperous towns and thriving cities. Scientists discover new elements and better ways of doing things, but a mother functions on a far higher plane. In compliance with God's eternal laws, she becomes a co-partner with him. She not only brings immortal souls into the world, but she also feeds our faith, molds our ideals, and leads us along that path of righteousness to our own eternal destiny.

A great man once said: "If we work upon marble it will perish; if we work upon brass, time will efface it. If we rear temples, they will crumble into dust. But if we work upon immortal minds, imbue them with just principles and a righteous fear of God, if we write in human hearts a love of one's fellowmen, then we do that which time cannot efface but which may endure untarnished through all eternity."

Each year the President of the United States gives all Americans a great message called his State of the Union Address. He reports on his stewardship to the people over whom he presides and for whose welfare he carries the primary responsibility.

The mothers of the world have a continuing responsibility, and they are not free to lay down their office at the end of four years. Throughout her life she must report her own stewardship in her "state of the family message" and her "state of the home message." She must also be aware of the conditions prevailing in our individual lives. God is continually saying to her: "Woman, behold thy son." What a tremendous reward comes to her if her sweat, toil, and tears have been expertly expended! That mother who instills into the souls of her children a proper respect for each other, a love of parenthood, a love of righteousness, a love of industry, and a love of law and order is rendering the greatest possible service to the church, the community, and humanity in general. Any mother lives at less than her best if she allows the impurities of sin, weakness, or atheism to make her son less than was intended when he was created in the image of God. And so we might say, "Woman, behold thy son."

The offices of both the mother and the father are important, but women have been so designed by the Creator that frequently they are just better human beings than men. But recently Satan seems to have greatly increased the vigor of his attack against women. Many men have been drunkards since time began, whereas in the main, women have kept themselves aloof from this debauching sin. Women have usually maintained a higher moral level than men, but in the face of the increase of this current Satanic thrust, more women are getting their tissues saturated with booze and their blood streams filled with nicotine. We are now teaching female children about the advantage of the new morality with the greater sex freedoms that are spoiling so many lives. Some women are being enticed by Satan to abandon their cleanliness and their sense of beauty. Some are becoming hippies, and with uncombed hair and dirty clothing they are living in sin. As given in the parable of Jesus, the enemy is coming by night and is sowing some deadly tares among the wheat.

A man once got into a building elevator with two women. Because of his instinctive respect he immediately removed his hat, but after listening to these women talk for a few minutes, he put his hat back on. As a safeguard against too many tares, we might occasionally look into the mirror of truth and say: "Men and women, behold thyselves."

Even before our births our mothers are sowing those seeds that will determine what our harvest will be, both in this life and in the life beyond. The scripture says that we reap as we sow, but that is only a part of the fact. Mostly, we reap as somebody else sows for us. Largely, we reap as our mothers have sown. And those godly thoughts that she plants in our hearts when we are young will largely determine what the harvest of our lives will be. Jesus gave a great parable, indicating that all the seeds that are sown are not equally productive. We can help to prepare the seedbed into which our mothers' love may take root. Our pre-existence was the childhood of our immortality and now is the period when we grow up. Sowing and reaping are so much parts of life that we might make a kind of Mother's Day philosophy out of this idea. A great author says:

We are sowing, daily sowing countless seeds of good and ill,
Scattered on the level lowland, cast upon the windy hill;
Seeds that sink in rich, brown furrows, soft with heaven's gracious
  rain;
Seeds that rest upon the surface of the dry, unyielding plain.

Seeds that fall amid the stillness of the lonely mountain glen;
Seeds cast out in crowded places, trodden under foot of men;
Seeds, by idle hearts forgotten, flung at random on the air;
Seeds, by faithful souls remembered, sown in tears and love and
  prayer.

Seeds that lie unchanged, unquickened, lifeless on the teeming mold;
Seeds that live and grow and flourish when the sower's hand is cold.
By a whisper sow we blessings; by a breath we scatter strife;
In our words and looks and actions lie the seeds of death and life.

Thou who knowest all our weakness, leave us not to sow alone!
Bid thine angels guard the furrows where the precious grain is sown,
Till the fields are crowned with glory, filled with mellow, ripened ears,
Filled with fruit of life eternal from the seed we sowed in tears.

One of the great precautions of life should be to make sure that the enemy is not permitted to come by night and sow tares among the wheat that our mothers have planted. Sometimes the tares even get into the lives of the mothers themselves. I rode in an airplane across the aisle from a mother and her little three-year-old son. The mother was a nervous chain-smoking woman in improper clothing. She was also getting far more than her share of the airline's supply of free liquor. I shuddered a little bit as I thought what this little boy was likely to reap.

In the early life of Jesus, Joseph and Mary, conforming to the ancient law of Israel, took the infant child to the temple to be blessed. Simeon, the temple priest, had been told that he should not die until he had seen the promised Messiah. When Jesus was brought into the temple by Joseph and Mary, Simeon took the child in his arms and blessed God and said: "Lord, now lettest thy servant depart in peace, according to thy word: For mine eyes have seen thy salvation. Which thou hast prepared before the face of all people; a light to lighten the Gentiles, and the glory of thy people Israel. And Joseph and his mother marvelled at those things which were spoken of him. And Simeon blessed them, and said unto Mary his mother . . . [in foreshadowing the manner of his death], Yea, a sword shall pierce thine own soul also." (Luke 2:29-35)

A renowned artist has painted an impressive picture based on this prophecy. It shows Mary kneeling by the side of the cradle as she lovingly caresses her sleeping child. Tears are in her eyes as she peers into the future for some glimpse of those great responsibilities that he must assume. Though he were the Son of God, yet many sacrifices would be required of him before he would be able to say: "It is finished." Now, as Mary stands before the cross, watching her great son die, she feels the sword twisting in her heart as she suffers with him for the sins of other sons as well as those of other mothers.

True motherhood is the mightiest force in the world, and Mother's Day is the time for a return of our love in a fostering of her interests. The older I grow, the more deeply grateful I become for the life and influence of my own mother. Among my most precious soul treasures is the memory of my mother's bedside prayers and her daily loving care and sacrifice. I specifically remember some personal talks with her about some of life's most important issues, which are now yielding their own abundant harvest. Because I loved my mother and wholeheartedly believed in her, I made up my mind at a very early age on some of life's most important questions, which have guided me as nothing else could have done. Thrice fortunate is that boy whose mother's companionship is his daily guide and inspiration; and that girl is also thrice blessed whose personal life constantly radiates the pure and self-sacrificing influence of a loving mother. We should never, even for a day, lose sight of her benefactions, but we should constantly say, "Son, behold thy mother."

God has made the benefits of the pure air we breathe and the glorious sunshine in which we live automatic, whereas we must make effective utilization of those benefits that are available to us from God and from our parents. Therefore, we have the Sabbath Day, Memorial Day, Christmas, Easter, the Fourth of July, Thanksgiving Day, Father's Day, and Mother's Day to remind us of our duties. We must never lose sight of God, and we should always keep the ideals of our mothers in view.

It has been said that the time to prepare a ship for the storm is not when it is in the middle of the ocean, being mauled by the waves. The time to prepare a ship for the storm is when it is still in the dockyard, while the planks are being picked and the rivets are being driven. As each new child is born and the mother lovingly holds his hand, she might well let her mind go forward a few years when the storms of life will be beating upon him. How she does her work will determine her satisfactions when she says to herself, "Woman, behold thy son." May there be no sword to pierce her soul because the tares have smothered out the wheat!

And so on this sacred Mother's Day, we might remind ourselves of our double duty and say to each other, "Woman, behold thy son," and "Son, behold thy mother." And may God help us to make this great cooperative effort successful!

Statues

THE ANCIENT ROMANS used to have an interesting custom of making statues of their greatest men and setting them up in their homes. Then each day each family member could lift himself upward by absorbing the good traits of those who had thus become a part of the family circle. In a little different way we do about the same thing when we set aside as national holidays the birthdays of some of our greatest men. As we think about their virtues and pattern our lives after their admirable qualities, we also draw ourselves upward. Two of these great days come in February.

George Washington was the man chosen to become the father of a very special country that was destined to become the greatest nation ever known upon the earth. We have the direct word of the Lord that God raised up special men to write the American Constitution and to give the United States its start toward a glorious destiny. How grateful we ought to be that men like Napoleon, Lenin, Stalin, Hitler, or Castro were not chosen to stand in the forefront of our country's history. Another great American named Abraham Lincoln appeared upon the scene to keep America solid and united in a time of great danger and trouble.

Washington and Lincoln, among others, were divine instruments in helping us get started in the right direction. Washington and Lincoln died an average of 137 years ago and yet each of them is still a living presence throughout America, and particularly on government hill in our nation's capital. The capital city of America has been given the name of our first president, and a beautiful 555-foot monument pierces the sky in his honor. A memorial has also been erected to Lincoln wherein he everlastingly watches over the welfare of his country. We have pictures of these men on our calendars and elsewhere in our homes. We write their speeches in our books and quote them in our daily conversation. As their birthdays come around on this particular year we find ourselves with a serious need for their help. What a great benefit our country would receive if lawmakers, businessmen, teachers, students, dropouts, hippies, criminals, and all other Americans would set up in their homes and in their hearts a living statue of Washington and Lincoln, in such a way that their patriotism, their honesty, their fairness, their reverence for God, and their love of truth would become important parts of us.

Both Washington and Lincoln spent a great deal of time on their knees and a lot more doing whatever was necessary to bring about the welfare and happiness of all people. Someone has said that the wealth of a nation can be counted in the number of its great men. Even their common, everyday experiences are helpful, and there are many ordinary men and women in America today who have in their hearts the important traits that have made America great. A man recently tried to reenlist in the army at age 42. Someone said to him: "Don't you think you have done enough for your country?" He said: "Can anyone ever do enough for his country?" All great Americans who serve their country are not presidents.

There are many unknown soldiers and unsung heroes who are entitled to our praise and appreciation. I have never worn the uniform of my country but I wish I had, and I greatly envy those who have. Many years ago Mr. R. D. Robbins wrote a great Lincoln Day story entitled "The Soldier's Reprieve." I would like to share this with you now as we pay our own tribute to the life of this great man, a great American soldier, and his great little sister who were a part of this experience. This account is appropriate for several reasons — one is because we are again involved in the terrible activity of war, and serving our nation in many ways are some other great Bennies and Blossoms.

THE SOLDIER'S REPRIEVE

"I thought, Mr. Allen, when I gave my Bennie to his country, that not a father in all this broad land made so precious a gift — no, not one. The dear boy only slept a minute, just one little minute, at his post. I know that was all, for Bennie never dozed over a duty. How prompt and reliable he was! I know he only slept one little second: and he was so young, and not strong, that boy of mine! But, he was as tall as I, and only eighteen! And now they shoot him — because he was found asleep when doing sentinel duty. 'Twenty-four hours,' the telegram said, only twenty-four hours! Where is Bennie now?"

"We will hope with his Heavenly Father," said Mr. Allen, soothingly.

"Yes, yes: let us hope. God is very merciful! 'I should be ashamed, father' Bennie said, 'when I am a man to think I never used this great right arm' (and he held it out so proudly before me) 'for my country, when it needed it. Palsy it rather than keep it at the plow.' 'Good, then — go my boy,' I said, 'and God keep you!' God has kept him, I think, Mr. Allen!" And the farmer repeated these last words slowly as if in spite of his reason his heart doubted them.

"Like the apple of his eye, Mr. Owen: doubt it not!"

Little Blossom sat near them, listening, with blanched cheek. She had not shed a tear. Her anxiety had been so concealed that no one had noticed it. She had occupied herself mechanically in the household cares. Now, she answered a gentle tap at the kitchen door, opening it to receive a letter from a neighbor's hand. "It is from him," was all she said.

It was like a message from the dead! Mr. Owen took the letter, but could not break the envelope on account of his trembling fingers, and held it toward Mr. Allen, with the helplessness of a child. The minister opened it and read as follows:

"Dear Father: When this reaches you I shall be in eternity. At first it seemed awful to me, but I have thought about it so much that now it has no terror. They say they will not bind me nor blind me, but that I may meet my death like a man. I thought, father, it might have been on the battlefield for my country, and that, when I fell, it would be fighting gloriously: but to be shot down like a dog for nearly betraying it — to die for neglect of duty! — O, father, I wonder the very thought does not kill me! But I shall not disgrace you. I am going to write you all about it: and when I am gone, you may tell my comrades. I cannot now.

"You know that I promised Jimmie Carr's mother I would look after her boy; and, when he fell sick, I did all I could for him. He was not strong when ordered back into the ranks, and the day before that night I carried all his luggage, besides my own, on our march. Toward night we went in on double-quick, and though the luggage began to feel very heavy, everybody else was tired too. And as for Jimmie, if I had not lent him an arm now and then, he would have dropped by the way. I was all tired out when we went into camp, and then it was Jimmie's turn to be sentry, and I would take his place: but I was too tired, father. I could not have kept awake if a gun had been pointed at my head: but I did not know it until — well — until it was too late."

"God be thanked!" interrupted Mr. Owen. "I knew Bennie was not the boy to sleep carelessly at his post."

"They tell me, today, that I have a short reprieve — 'time to write to you,' our good Colonel says. Forgive him, father; he only does his duty: He would gladly save me if he could. And I do not lay my death against Jimmie. The poor boy is heartbroken, and does nothing but beg and entreat them to let him die in my place.

"I can't bear to think of mother and Blossom. Comfort them, father! Tell them I die as a brave boy should, and that, when the war is over, they will not be ashamed of me, as they must be now. God help me; it is very hard to bear! Good-by, father. God seems near and dear to me, not at all as if he wished me to perish forever, but as if he felt sorry for his poor, sinful, broken-hearted child, and would take me to be with him and my Savior in a better life."

A deep sigh burst from Mr. Owen's heart. "Amen," he said solemnly, "amen."

"Tonight, in the early twilight, I shall see the cows all coming home from the pasture, and precious little Blossom standing on the back stoop, waiting for me; but I shall never, never come! God bless you all! Forgive your poor Bennie!"

Late that night the door of the "back stoop" opened softly and a little figure glided out and down the footpath that led to the road by the mill. She seemed rather flying than walking, turning her head neither to the right nor the left, looking only now and then to heaven, and folding her hands as if in prayer. Two hours later the same young girl stood at the mill depot, watching the coming of the night train; and the conductor, as he reached down to lift her into the car, wondered at the tear-stained face that was upturned toward the dim lantern he held in his hand. A few questions and ready answers told him all;

and no father could have cared more tenderly for his only child, than he for our little Blossom.

She was on her way to Washington to ask President Lincoln for her brother's life. She had stolen away, leaving only a note to tell them where and why she had gone. She had brought Bennie's letter with her. No good, kind heart, like the President's, could refuse to be melted by it. The next morning, they reached New York, and the conductor hurried her on to Washington. Every minute, now, might be the means of saving her brother's life. And so, in an incredibly short time Blossom reached the Capital and hastened to the White House. The President had just seated himself to his morning task of overlooking and signing important papers, when without one word of announcement the door softly opened, and Blossom, with down-cast eyes and folded hands, stood before him.

"Well, my child," he said, in his pleasant, cheerful tones, "what do you want so bright and early this morning?"

"Bennie's life, please sir," faltered Blossom.

"Bennie! Who is Bennie?"

"My brother, sir. They are going to shoot him for sleeping at his post."

"O, yes," and Mr. Lincoln ran his eye over the papers before him. "I remember. It was a fatal sleep. You see, my child, it was a time of special danger. Thousands of lives might have been lost by his culpable negligence."

"So my father said," replied Blossom, gravely. "But poor Bennie was so tired, sir, and Jimmie was so weak. He did the work of two, sir, and it was Jimmie's night to watch, not his; but Jimmie was too tired, and Bennie never thought about himself, that he was tired, too."

"What is this you say, child? Come here: I do not understand." And the kind man caught eagerly at what seemed to be a justification of the offense.

Blossom went to him. He put his hand tenderly on her shoulder and turned up the pale face toward him. How tall he seemed! And he was the President of the United States, too! A dim thought of this kind passed for a minute through Blossom's mind, but she told her simple, straight-forward story, and handed Mr. Lincoln Bennie's letter to read.

He read it carefully; then, taking up his pen, wrote a few hasty lines and rang his bell.

Blossom heard his order given: "Send this dispatch at once."

The President then turned to the girl, and said: "Go home, my child, and tell that father of yours, who could approve his country's sentence even when it took the life of a son like that, that Abraham Lincoln thinks that life far too precious to be lost. Go back, or — wait until tomorrow: Bennie will need a change after he has so bravely faced death; he shall go with you."

"God bless you, sir!" said Blossom.

Two days after this interview, the young soldier came to the White House with his little sister. He was called into the President's private room, and a strap fastened upon his shoulder. Mr. Lincoln then said: "The soldier that could carry a sick comrade's baggage, and died for the act so uncomplainingly, deserves well of his country." Then Bennie and Blossom took their way to their Green Mountain home. A crowd gathered at the mill depot to welcome them back, and, as Farmer Owen's hand grasped that of his boy, tears flowed down his cheeks, and he was heard to say fervently:

"Just and true are thy ways, Thou king of saints."

And so it is and may God bless our present America and help us to help it faithfully fulfill its great mission in the world. May we properly adjust our lives to the service of God and our country.

The Strait Gate

THE GREATEST AUTHORITY on success who ever lived upon this earth was Jesus of Nazareth. He was the Son of God and came here in his official capacity as the Savior of the world and the Redeemer of men. He was a great teacher and the world's greatest authority on religion. In addition to being a great moralist, he was also an outstanding efficiency expert. He gave expression to one of our most important success laws when he said: "Enter ye in at the strait gate: for wide is the gate, and broad is the way, that leadeth to destruction, and many there be that go in thereat: Because strait is the gate, and narrow is the way, which leadeth unto life, and few there be that find it." (Matt. 7:13-14)

Everyone wants to be successful and happy, and yet many fall down. The primary reason for our failure is our natural tendency to require a broader road than real success will permit. The broad road leading to destruction maintains its popularity because it is easier to follow. It makes fewer demands upon its travelers, and it allows much more room for sidestepping, meandering, and turning around. It is significant that most people want more latitude than the narrow road can give. Almost all failure begins merely by broadening the way. Too frequently we yield to our natural enticings to explore the side roads and travel the dead-end streets. Because the road leading to death is broad enough to permit many forbidden activities, many travelers never arrive at their desired destinations. No one ever leaves the success highway at right angles, and instead of an acknowledgement that we are stepping out of bounds, we try to keep ourselves in good standing with ourselves and make things appear legal to others by merely broadening the way.

A worthy objective is important to success; a fine ambition is wonderful; enthusiasm gives us power, but we should also make certain that the road itself leads to the right destination. Success has much in common with itself wherever we find it. Whether our efforts are spent in intellectual, social, physical, spiritual, or financial pursuits, the highest objectives are always reached by this narrow-road concept in the exact meaning that Jesus attached to it. Not only is the road to every success and every happiness narrow, but we must keep ourselves within its bounds.

When Gladstone was asked the secret of his brilliant career, he answered with one word: "Concentration." Concentration is achieved by limiting the scope. Emerson said: "The one good is concentration, the one evil is dissipation." Jesus was limiting the scope when he cautioned us to keep our eye single. A single vision should also have a narrow focus. Jesus was proclaiming this same philosophy when he said: "No man can serve two masters."

James points out that "A double-minded man is unstable in all his ways." We also have some triple-minded men and some quadruple-minded men. These are men who have not tuned out enough of their distractions. The secret of success is to limit the scope, narrow the vision, and concentrate the effort with a finer focus on a single objective.

Decision is one of the very important ingredients of success, and decision is also narrow. We must definitely make up our minds on specific points. Holding a narrow focus on our attention, we should drive with full power down the middle of the straight and narrow way. It is only when we become specific and exact that we eliminate the success deterrents of confusions, conflicts, whims, guesses, speculations, and rationalizings. Success demands that we give up our vagueness and generalities by setting up mental and moral limits of latitude beyond which we must never go. Success demands that our meanderings must be restricted and all inharmonious things ruled out of bounds. The song that says "Don't fence me in" does not describe the conditions along the straight and narrow way. Not only should we have a fence, but it should be a very strong one. Those people who are trying to reduce their weight have discovered that *this* success also requires a straight and narrow discipline. When our dietary way is made broad enough to include three pieces of pie, the cause is placed in jeopardy. If obesity is to be controlled, certain food items must be placed out of bounds. Limitations must be placed on intake, and a tighter rein should be held on the appetite. The greater the desired weight reduction, the narrower the road must be made.

In the Word of Wisdom the Lord so narrowed down the width of the road leading to health that he placed alcohol, nicotine, and caffeine out of bounds. None of our several million American alcoholics or our other millions of lung cancer victims ever deliberately headed for the dreadful places at which they finally arrived. They made their mistakes merely by making the road broad enough for some extra indulgences in the wrong things.

We like to think of ourselves as broadminded, but sometimes our thinking span gets so broad that many undesirable elements get into it. We sometimes describe an interesting human trait called tolerance, which usually implies a yielding up of territory. We practice a peaceful co-existence with too many evils. As a nation we have given up too much ground to the communists; and as individuals we are giving up too much ground in morality and those other Christian ideals and principles on which our country was founded.

Many years ago when violations of the prohibition law became too great, we merely widened the way by making liquor legal. As we have become more immoral, we have appeased our minds with the doctrines of the new morality. We have diluted the American spirit of success with some un-American attitudes. By our many compromises with evil, we have so widened our national way and are now going where we don't want to go. With too much tolerance for evil, we are losing our convictions and our self-respect.

We can easily expand the road to such width that nothing is excluded. We can get ourselves into a situation where everything goes. Crime waves, race riots, and dope addiction now seem to some not to be very far out of line. We have developed a great tolerance for atheism, sin, and too many side-road interests that are antagonistic to our eternal salvation. In spite of the fact that Jesus asked us to shun the broad road leading to death, the traffic thereon continues to get more and more crowded. Some of our broadmindedness has been compared to the Powder River, which is very broad and very shallow. We never get much power from a river that is a mile wide and an inch deep; rather, it is the narrow torrent that tears away the mountainside.

Isn't it interesting how narrow the laws of nature are? Water boils at 212 degrees, not at 210. It freezes at 32 degrees above zero, not at 34. Water that contains 20% salt will not freeze until 2.4 degrees above zero. Alcohol will not freeze until the temperature gets down to 30 degrees below zero. I don't understand how the water knows when it is time to freeze, but it never makes a mistake. It never forgets, and it is never influenced by anyone's opinion. Like all other natural laws, it performs right on the nose every time. The sciences are narrow and they are never repealed. They are never suspended. The verdict has been handed out even before the act is committed. The smartest lawyers, the most sympathetic witnesses, or the most powerful judges cannot change the verdict in the slightest degree. The sentence is not softened because of mental or physical incompetence, and there is no time off for good behavior.

Each year our planet makes a 595-million-mile orbit around the sun. It always travels at the rate of 66,600 miles per hour, and it completes its journey in exactly 365 days, 6 hours, 9 minutes, and 9 and 54/100 seconds. The time of the completion of this 595-million-mile journey can be more accurately foretold than your trip from the living room into the dining room. No planet is ever given any latitude or any time for meandering or for making any stoppings or startings.

Electricity is also a little bit on the narrow-minded side. A compass always points to the magnetic north — never to the east, the west, or the south. Mathematics is narrow. Two times two is always four — never three and seven-eighths. If you have ever had an airplane ride through a violent storm that required an instrument landing, you will remember how you prayed for a narrow-minded pilot who would never get even a little way off the beam. One flash of broadmindedness from a meandering pilot might have brought about your sudden death.

In piloting our own flight through life we also need to stay right on the beam. Just as science is narrow and nature and happiness are narrow, so success in life is narrow. If we do certain things, we succeed; if we do certain other things, we fail, and it is as simple as that. We start to fail as soon as we begin getting a little bit broadminded with evil. The main direction for achieving excellence in any field is to carefully follow the narrow road. That is the way to happiness; it is the way to leadership; it is the way to effective weight control. It is the opposite of that road that is broad enough for vague decisions, unbridled thoughts, loose morals, and unrestricted activities. The Ten Commandments follow the straight and narrow way and so does the Sermon on the Mount. The broad, easy, meandering, gypsy trail always leads to that place where destruction and failure lurk.

Think how narrow the road to loyalty is! It binds us to definite devotions. Harry Emerson Fosdick has written convincingly about the narrow way in an article entitled "On Catching the Wrong Bus." He said: "The man who swears allegiance to a cause places upon himself limitations that are stronger than any slave's because he has given his heart."

Success and happiness in marriage always go along a straight road and over a narrow way. When two people, by their own choice give themselves to each other and to no one else, they are no longer loosely or irresponsibly free to wander wherever passing fancy may attract them. Marriage is not a broad, double street with double standards of morality; neither is patriotism; neither is life. Any person's greatest glory always lies in the straightness of his gate and the narrowness of his way. The unfaithful, the disloyal, and the disobedient are all traveling the broad road. They may have a variety of attachments, or they may have no attachments at all. They may be devoted to many or to none. They may live without restraint under the philosophy of "don't fence me in." That particular road is labeled "The Broad Way," and everyone can tell in advance where it leads. Mostly we miss the way because we take down the fences, erase the yellow lines, remove the guard rails, and change the laws. We do away with the out-of-bounds signs and feel no compunction about getting off the track occasionally.

Whoever conceives the pathway of life as a big, broad, double highway with plenty of room for hypocrisy, sidestepping, and confusion gets into trouble very quickly. Too many double standards are responsible for the discords between deed and creed that lie at the root of the innumerable wrongs vexing our civilization.

Double standards give institutions and men split personalities. It is one thing to talk about high goals; it is another to stick rigidly to those conditions that will make sure that we reach them.

We frequently hold in our minds great objectives and high ideals at the very moment when our hands reach for forbidden things. Our minds may be on the narrow way that leads to life, while our feet are taking us down that broad road that leads to destruction. Everyone desires to do right, but we must also keep our feet on that narrow road leading to our planned objective. Despite the boasted reason and scientific attitudes of our day, consciously or unconsciously, we still more or less believe in a sort of black magic in religion. It is a common philosophy that regardless of which road we take, somehow we will all come out all right in the end. By this philosophy we not only class ourselves as failures but as fools as well, for nothing that travels the wrong road can ever come out at the right destination. The foundation law of the universe is that fundamental, unchangeable, irrevocable, immutable, inexorable law of the harvest that says: ". . . whatsoever a man soweth, that shall he also reap." (Gal. 6:7) We are all going to be judged by our works. As the resurrected Jesus was about to leave this earth and ascend to his Father from the Mount of Olives, he said to his disciples: "Go ye into all the world and preach the gospel to every creature. He that believeth and is baptized shall be saved; and he that believeth not shall be damned." (Mark 16:15-16) To some, that may sound like a very narrow way, but it is the law, and we should not forget it; nor should we count too heavily on the possibility of God changing his mind.

And so we come back again to the statement of the Master, saying, "Enter ye in at the strait gate: for wide is the gate, and broad is the way, that leadeth to destruction, and many there be that go in thereat: Because strait is the gate, and narrow is the way, which leadeth unto life, and few there be that find it." (Matt. 7:13-14) And that's how it must always be!

Testimony

ONE OF THE serious problems of our present world is the lack of faith in God of those who live in it. So many people are seriously bothered by disabling doubts and disturbing fears. Some are half afraid that God is dead and others are half afraid that he is not. We may not know what his promises are and consequently are not greatly motivated by the thought that they will be kept. Someone said that he would give anything to know that the gospel of Jesus Christ was true, but this man was making no attempt to live those principles that he desired to believe. So frequently we depend on a miracle for our convictions, and we pray for some kind of a ready-made conduct to go with them. Throughout the history of our civilization many people have depended on omens and waited for signs to determine what their faith and their works would be. However, the Lord has instituted a kind of do-it-yourself program where we can earn a testimony of every necessary truth for ourselves.

Faith is a gift from God, and it is given as a reward for our obedience to his commandments. We have been created in God's image and we have been endowed with a set of his attributes. We have had planted within us some of the greatest powers. The scriptures indicate that we "are fearfully and wonderfully made." (See Ps. 139:14) We are equipped with a miraculous brain and a personality with stupendous possibilities. We have a divine gadget inside of us that will tell us when we need food and rest. We have an equally wonderful conscience that tells us what is right and wrong. We also have some godly powers of reason. Emerson said: "We live in the lap of an immense intelligence." God has made it possible for us to channel this intelligence into our own minds for our own benefit. Jesus said: "If any man will do his will, he shall know of the doctrine. . . ." (John 7:17) He also said: "And ye shall know the truth, and the truth shall make you free." (John 8:32) God makes his will known to those who keep his commandments. He has promised us that we may have every blessing where we are willing to obey the law upon which that blessing is predicated. (D&C 130:20) If we wallow in wickedness while waiting for signs of righteousness, we will probably be disappointed. We must first live the blessing that we desire to have.

An ancient American prophet has said: ". . . dispute not because ye see not, for ye receive no witness until after the trial of your faith." (Ether 12:6) He further said: "For if there be no faith among the children of men God can do no miracle among them; wherefore, he showed not himself until after their faith." (Ether 12:12) Why should we expect further blessings when we fail to practice the virtues that we already have? Think of the things that we already know that we don't do much about.

When Moses was standing in the immediate presence of God, he didn't know a bit more surely than I know or than you know that it is right to be honest and that it is right to be fair, kind, considerate, and helpful to other people. If we would only practice these things that we know for sure, then our knowledge would be greatly increased. On that exciting day when God stood on top of Mount Sinai in fire and gave us the Ten Commandments to the accompaniment of lightnings and thunderings, at that moment the people who heard him didn't know then, any better than we know now, that every one of the Ten Commandments is good and should be obeyed. Even if there were no God, I am still absolutely certain that it would be fundamentally wrong to kill, steal, lie, covet, worship false gods, violate the Sabbath day, commit adultery, use profanity, bear false witness against our neighbors, or dishonor our parents. These laws are right not only because God gave them, but he gave them because they were right. They will always be right — regardless of our preferences or appetites or what we do about them. And it was probably just as difficult for an adulterer or an alcoholic to behave himself then as it is now.

Over nineteen hundred years ago Jesus gave a great discourse that we call the Sermon on the Mount. We were not there and yet those who heard him did not understand these truths any better then than we can understand them now, nor did the ancients believe them any more wholeheartedly than we believe them now. Jesus selected twelve men to carry on his work. But there are a great many people in our day who have had far more experience with life and with people than these young fishermen and tax collectors had. We can understand the Golden Rule now as well as they understood it then, and we can also understand right and wrong as well as they did. If we do not live our convictions as faithfully as they did, that is our fault and we should not be disturbed because we lose the blessings.

Someone complained to his friend that the reason he lacked spirituality was that he was not sure that the gospel was true. His friend said to him: "Bill, I *know* that the gospel is true. While you are getting a testimony for yourself, why don't you lean on mine."

When a doctor recommends that a patient undergo surgery the patient must either lean on the knowledge of the doctor or put off having his operation until he can get a medical education for himself. We can best serve our own interests by leaning on the testimony of scientists, businessmen, geologists, and historians in those fields where they have knowledge. One of the greatest privileges of our lives is that we can get an inspired testimony of the truth of the gospel for ourselves if we live the law on which that blessing is predicated. In the meantime we can use the testimony and draw on strength that others have already developed.

Jesus said to his disciples: "But the Comforter, which is the Holy Ghost, whom the Father will send in my name, he shall teach you all things, and bring all things to your remembrance, whatsoever I have said unto you." (John 14:26)

While the apostles were waiting for this promise to be fulfilled they studied and prayed and prepared themselves for the promised blessing. That law has not been changed, but there are better things to do while we are waiting for these blessings than to merely twiddle our thumbs or get drunk: While we are gaining a certain knowledge for ourselves suppose that we lean on the testimony of Moses. Some 3,460 years ago while the children of Israel were encamped at the foot of Mt. Sinai, Moses and some of his people were invited onto Mt. Sinai for a conference with God. The record says: "Then went up Moses and Aaron, Nadab, and Abihu, and seventy of the elders of Israel: And they saw the God of Israel. . . ." (Exo. 24:9-10) "And the Lord spake unto Moses face to face, as a man speaketh unto his friend. . . ." (Exo. 33:11)

The scriptures are full of accounts where men have seen and conversed with God and other heavenly beings face to face.

If God had only been seen once, that is good proof that he exists, but he has been seen many times. For the 40 days of his post-mortal ministry the resurrected Jesus showed himself to many people. There are always those who won't believe. When all ten of the apostles told Thomas that they had seen the Lord, he said: "Except I shall see in his hands the prints of the nails, and thrust my hand into his side, I will not believe." Eight days later Jesus personally confronted Thomas and said: "Reach hither thy finger, and behold my hands; and reach hither thy hand, and thrust it into my side, and be not faithless, but believing." Then Jesus said: "Thomas, because thou hast seen me, thou hast believed: blessed are they that have *not* seen, and *yet* have believed." (John 20:25-29) Thomas may not be entitled to much credit for this experience because under the circumstances it would have been almost impossible for him not to have believed. Jesus indicated that greater credit belongs to those who don't have to have every detail proven to them.

If God had intended for us to live in a world where everything was cut and dried with nothing left for us to do he would have made it that way. God wants us to learn to walk a little way by faith because no one knows all the answers. God wants us to solve some of our own problems, and to be able to resolve some doubts on our own power makes us stronger. Some people can only be faithful when there is no chance to be anything else. On the other hand some people would do right even if they had never heard of God's laws, and some would be better followers of Christ by faith than others would be if they had a dozen angels constantly reminding them to do their duty.

Our world now has a modern and more powerful testimony to lean upon. In the early spring of 1820 in upper New York state, God the Father and his Son, Jesus Christ, appeared to a young prophet, Joseph Smith, to re-establish in the world our faith in God and to re-establish his church and his authority upon the earth. The Prophet partially describes this tremendous event as follows: ". . . I saw a pillar of light exactly over my head, above the brightness of the sun, which descended gradually until it fell upon me. . . . When the light rested upon me I saw two Personages, whose brightness and glory defy all description, standing above me in the air. One of them spake unto me, calling me by name and said, pointing to the other, This is My Beloved Son. Hear Him!"

The Prophet said: "My object in going to inquire of the Lord was to know which of all the sects was right, that I might know which to join. . . .

"I was answered that I must join none of them, for they were all wrong; and the Personage who addressed me said that all their creeds were an abomination in his sight, that those professors were all corrupt, that: 'they draw near to me with their lips, but their hearts are far from me, they teach for doctrines the commandments of men, having a form of godliness, but they deny the power thereof.' " (Joseph Smith 2:16-19)

Then in discussing the persecution that followed, the Prophet said: "However, it was nevertheless a fact that I had beheld a vision. I have thought since, that I felt much like Paul, when he made his defense before King Agrippa, and related the account of the vision he had when he saw a light, and heard a voice; but still there were but few who believed him; some said he was dishonest, others said he was mad; and he was ridiculed and reviled. But all this did not destroy the reality of his vision. He had seen a vision, he knew he had, and all the persecution under heaven could not make it otherwise; and though they should persecute him unto death, yet he knew, and would know to his latest breath, that he had both seen a light and heard a voice speaking unto him, and all the world could not make him think or believe otherwise.

"So it was with me," said the Prophet. "I had actually seen a light, and in the midst of that light I saw two Personages, and they did in reality speak to me; and though I was hated and persecuted for saying that I had seen a vision, yet it was true; and while they were persecuting me, reviling me, and speaking all manner of evil against me falsely for so saying, I was led to say in my heart: Why persecute me for telling the truth? I have actually seen a vision; and who am I that I can withstand God? . . . For I had seen a vision; I knew it, and I knew that God knew it, and I could not deny it, neither dared I do it; at least I knew that by so doing I would offend God, and come under condemnation." (Joseph Smith 2:24-25)

Disbelief does not solve many of our group or individual problems. Disbelief and disobedience usually go together, and they did not solve the problems of those who crucified Christ or those who have slain the apostles and rejected the prophets since the beginning of time. Disbelief and disobedience are not solving our problems now, and only faith in God and obedience to his laws can save our world. If we still can't develop a testimony of our own, we can lean on that of Moses, Jesus, Peter, Thomas, the apostle Paul, and Joseph Smith until we do.

In helping us to prepare we might remember that none of these knew a bit more surely than we can know that it is wrong to be immoral, drunken, ignorant, and addicted to dope and profanity. The ancient and modern prophets may have known some things better than I know them, but they didn't know any better than I know that it is right to study and work and be kind and helpful to people. There are two ancient laws that will guarantee any desired success: the first is never do anything that you know to be wrong, and second, always do everything that you know to be right. If we obeyed these two laws this earth would be God's paradise, and we would have powerful testimonies of God, truth, and our own destinies.

Jesus has said: "For everyone that asketh receiveth; and he that seeketh findeth; and to him that knocketh it shall be opened." (Matt. 7:8) In this asking, seeking, and knocking Jesus was not speaking about mere lip service. He was talking about the kind of investigation where we study and think and believe, and then we roll up our sleeves and do something about it. When we do our parts then only those who fail to seek fail to find, and only those who fail to ask fail to receive. May we do those things that will enable us to deserve and to receive a strong testimony of God and his truth.

The Therapy of Words

ONE OF THE MOST important ambitions of our lives is to build up a strong, vigorous, good health within ourselves. John Locke once said: "A healthy mind in a strong body is a short but full description of a happy state in this life." In order to develop strong bodies, we pay special attention to our diet and take regular exercise, but we also want to have clear minds, happy spirits, friendly hearts, and constructive personalities.

When at our best, we live the oath of the Boy Scouts and make our own pledge to keep ourselves physically strong, mentally awake, and morally straight. A good way to reach all of these objectives is to make a wise use of language. The other day I learned a big, helpful word called *bibliotherapy*. It was compounded from some Greek words meaning books and treatment. It has to do with a very valuable kind of self-improvement. It is a literary remedy for our problems, and it describes a cure that can be brought about by the effective use of the good ideas that may be extracted from books. Many years ago John Milton approved of this therapy when he said: "Books are not dead things, but contain a certain potency of life in them as active as the soul whose progeny they are. They preserve as in a vial the purest efficacy of the living intellect that bred them." There are other helpful kinds of language treatments that can come direct from people or that we may produce for ourselves. From various experiences I know that a stimulating idea in one's mind, a great love in his heart, or a holy ambition in his soul can increase his temperature, quicken his heartbeat, step up the happiness content of his life, and actually raise the level of his general health and performance.

Jesus quoted an old proverb, saying, "Physician, heal thyself." Most of the means for bringing about our welfare have been placed in our own hands. The apostle Paul gave us one technique for promoting our own interests when he said: ". . . be ye transformed by the renewing of your mind. . . ." (Rom. 12:2) There are many things that can be done to lift our spirits, fill our minds with light, and give our bodies life and power.

The great word "holy" comes from words meaning whole and wholesome. To be holy means to be complete, to be perfect with none of the good things left out. The opposites of holy would be described by such words as incomplete, unrighteous, diseased, distorted, weak, and imperfect. In addition to practicing the proper diet to maintain good physical health, we also need to take in a lot of good mental and spiritual food. We can help ourselves become vigorous, whole, wholesome, happy, and holy by hearing, thinking, and saying a lot of the right kind of words. These words that inspire hope, build morale, arouse ambition, and increase know-how can actually destroy disease. We can get these words out of books, from other people, or we ourselves may create them.

The night before General Robert E. Lee surrendered his arms to end the Civil War, Ulysses S. Grant had been sitting up all night, trying to cure a terrible cold. He had his chest packed with mustard plasters and his feet soaking in a tub of hot water. In the early morning hours an officer rode up to General Grant's tent and told him that General Lee was waiting to surrender his sword. Upon hearing this good news, all General Grant's aches and pains immediately left him. He hurriedly dressed, mounted his horse, and was a perfectly well man as he went to preside over the closing scenes of this destructive Civil War. General Grant had been cured of his infirmities by the great words that a fellow officer had put into his ears. More than anything else, this particular medicine was exactly what he needed.

We are not always aware that the mainsprings of one's emotional health can be most quickly reached through his ears. Many of our bodily ills are caused by our mental and emotional problems, both large and small. A few words of sincere commendation and a little genuine praise can make anyone a better person. Kindness and love have actually prolonged the lives of many people, whereas a discouraged man is always a weak man and a sick man. A sinful man is also a sick man. People become both weak and ill when they have conflicting ideologies and antagonist interests. Almost all of these complaints can be cured and the individuals concerned can be made whole, wholesome, and holy by a proper use of word therapy.

Even a discouraged, mistreated dog can usually be revived

by some kind words and a few love pats. A dog's eyes can be made brighter, his coat glossier, and his tail will wag more quickly when a few kind words are translated into the friendly pats and strokes that he understands. On the other side of the picture, a recital of some bad news or hearing tidings of some serious evil can actually make a person deathly ill. There is an old jingle that I remember from my childhood that says: "Sticks and stones may break my bones, but words can never hurt me." Of course, nothing could be farther from the truth. Many people have actually died of the heartbreak, loneliness, boredom, and discouragement caused by the wrong kind of communications. One's blood pressure can be increased, his heart can be made to pound, and his breath can actually be knocked out of him by a few angry, evil, hateful words. Many people have felt their blood run cold while listening to a profane oath or some other form of foul, hateful, depressing language. Many employees have had their interest in their work destroyed, and their jobs have become dull and depressing because of having many derogatory or belittling words piled upon their hearts.

Hundreds of wives live lives of boredom, loneliness, and despair because of unfair criticisms, hateful abuse, or words representing other forms of ugliness. We talk a great deal about the healing power of modern wonder drugs and how effective they can be in wiping out disease and helping heal our crippled bodies, but a few words of encouragement, a warm expression of confidence, or some words of deserved appreciation can accomplish even greater miracles. A few words of love can often heal the scars on one's soul. There are words of faith, words of good will, and words of righteousness, which, if properly used, can lift us up to God.

Twenty centuries ago Jesus went around healing sick bodies, causing blind eyes to see, and bringing the dead back to life by using the right words backed up by the great powers within himself. On a lesser scale we can perform similar miracles of wonder healing. Everyone ought to see to it that he experiences some feelings of real happiness every day. In addition, everyone ought to get some fun and satisfaction out of all the good that can be said and done. Edward Everett Hale once said that the best education is to be perpetually thrilled by life. One of the best ways to keep ourselves healthy, wealthy, happy, holy, and successful is to use on ourselves the magic therapy that is found in words and meanings.

We might try the challenging ideas of keeping our minds, spirits, and personalities in a condition comparable to that exemplified by the expert skier as he flashes down the hillside and flies across the landscape with tingling blood and taut muscles. Of course, every feeling of physical, mental, or spiritual well-being puts a new joy into our hearts. It puts happiness into our minds and success into our spirits.

Someone has designated the skylark as the symbol of high purpose and happiness. It has been thought that no bird equals the skylark, either in heart or in voice. The skylark's mission is music and happiness. In a still hour you can hear its thrilling notes at nearly a mile's distance. Long after the skylark's form is lost to our sight in the upper air, it still floods a thousand acres of sky with its song that is made available to our ears. The movement of the skylark is swift and sure. In almost perpendicular flight it rises quickly toward the upper areas of the sky. It seems to be lifted up by the ecstasy of its own happy heart. On the earth the skylark seems timid, silent, and unsure of itself. Actually, it has little by way of color, features, or form to recommend it. Its inspiration comes from the fact that it is always soaring and that it is always pouring out its rapturous song in a flood of exciting musical delight. Although the skylark flies high, it always builds its nest on the ground.

Dr. Henry Jowett once said that the apostle Paul had a mind like a skylark. He was always soaring. He flew high enough to catch the vision of life at its best. He attained the mental heights of a searching education. The songs of his heart always radiated his devotion. He rose quickly from his challenging experiences on the Damascus road and thereafter believed in his new mission without reservation. Never did he do things poorly or by halves. Although he flew high, he always kept the common touch. He taught the divine philosophy of exaltation, but he never got his feet off the ground or lost the balance of his down-to-earth common sense. Untiringly, with his voice and with his life, he served the God of heaven, but he kept his base of operations among humble men.

All of us need a little more of this skylark spirit. An increased elevation in our point of view can give us a clearer look at life. A happier song leads to a greater accomplishment. A good dose of inspiration now and then enlarges our vision and increases our pulse rate. The spirit of the skylark is a strong antidote for boredom; it is a deterrent to sin and a preventive of negative living.

The spirit of the skylark in the heart of Isaiah made him say: "Sing, O heavens; and be joyful, O earth; and break forth into singing, O mountains; for the Lord hath comforted his people, and will have mercy upon his afflicted." (Isa. 49:13) He also said: "How beautiful upon the mountains are the feet of him that bringeth good tidings, that publisheth peace; that bringeth good tidings of good, that publisheth salvation; that saith unto Zion, Thy God reigneth!" (Isa. 52:7)

An interesting story is told of a lady who once bought the wrong typewriter. As she was exchanging it, she pointed out that this particular typewriter didn't have an exclamation point. She said: "My letters are just full of exclamations." To her, a typewriter without an exclamation point would be worse than useless. What a serious handicap we have when our minds and hearts are without some exclamations of love, praise, and worship! Even the greatest words lose much of their meaning when they have no exclamation points.

How drab a skylark's life would be without her song, her love of the upper air, her thrilling speed of flight! Suppose some tragedy required the skylark to lower her altitude. The perspective of all life is less interesting when one flies at the level of the tree tops. Most of the darkest moods of life are born when one is flying on the lower levels of living and going at a snail's pace. Only when one flies high can he see the beauties of creation, and only when he is going at top speed can he feel the sheer joy of being alive. A high accomplishment doeth good like a medicine. With a skylark's love of life, one is likely to have better health, clearer thoughts, and greater purpose in his living. Anyone can live on less when a faithful expression of love gives him more to live for. Think what wonders lovers can perform in the hearts and ambitions of each other with a few wonderful words.

Most of the controversy about sex education revolves around the question of what kinds of ideas should be put into youthful minds through youthful ears. The present shocking increases in immorality, disloyalty, and atheism can also be traced through the ears. The problems of our present day are that we are using our verbal destructive powers too much and our verbal healing powers not enough.

One woman spent many years trying to get her husband to tell her that he loved her. He would always beat around the bush, and she could never get him to use the actual words. Then she tried to get him to merely say the word "love" in a sentence with some other meaning, but he just couldn't bring himself to say what apparently seemed to him to be a forbidden word. This is just one manifestation of what is actually a very common kind of speech impediment among us. Sometimes we just can't bring ourselves to say those words that are involved in prayer, worship, and expressions of appreciation to our Heavenly Father. Many people can only use sacred words when they are dressed in the foul sacrilege of some profane oath. Many people don't hesitate to use obscene, ugly, hateful words that tear themselves and others down, but they are strangers to those great words that heal and bless and enlighten.

Many people are actually starving to death for a few words of appreciation. They would be wonderfully strengthened if someone would ask them for their opinion or how they felt on some important or even unimportant subject. Sometimes we can't bring ourselves to say words of praise, even though our lives depend upon it, as indeed they often do. Without some exclamation points and an ability to use those words that go with worship, healing, love, sympathy, encouragement, and under-standing, we become like the mudlark, who, instead of getting his life from the upper air, gets his sustenance from the slime of the low tide. When we get our support by wallowing in the mud, we are likely to become downcast, depressed, sinful, and unsuccessful. One of the greatest opportunities of our lives is to fill our spiritual medicine cabinets with a lot of great words. We need some words of encouragement, some words of faith, some words of worship, some words of strength, and some words of love. We need some tranquilizing words, some skylark words, and some success words. We need words that can spiritualize us and warm us up on the inside. We need a lot of words that have been fashioned into great philosophies, powerful scriptures, inspiring poems, and motivating ambitions. When these are run through our minds, they can clear out our depressions, destroy our sins, cure our moral aches and pains, and put the spirit of the skylark into our blood streams.

"This Day We Sailed On"

THOMAS CARLYLE ONCE said that no one could look upon a great man without gaining something from him. It is probable that the greatest power in the world is the power of example. The way we learned to walk, the way we learned to talk, and the reason we speak with the particular accent we do is because we saw or heard someone else doing it that way. Example is also the way we get our manners, our morals, our ambitions, and our leadership. Man does not live by bread alone. We need a good dose of inspiration occasionally. We need a model to look at, an ideal to think about, and an example to go by. With a good example we can wind up our faith and recharge our enthusiasm with power. It is a well-known law that we become like those with whom we habitually identify. That nation is the most fortunate that claims the largest number of good men. How grateful we should be that we had such God-fearing men as our Founding Fathers to stand in the forefront of our civilization to give our nation its course and direction.

In our nation's capital we have erected a statue of Abraham Lincoln and set it apart as a national memorial. And Lincoln's spirit still lives on Capitol Hill. Another of the great men to whom we might well erect a memorial in our hearts is Christopher Columbus. It is to him that we give credit for discovering our land in the first place. On more than one occasion Columbus wrote in his diary that he believed himself commissioned by heaven to accomplish some grand design for God. He had no money, no ships, and no men, but he did have an idea and some faith, and after being turned down by several nations he finally persuaded Queen Isabella of Spain to outfit him with three little ships.

When once in charge he pointed their noses westward out into the vast, unexplored regions of the north Atlantic. His sailors were apprehensive and as they proceeded, their fears climbed daily. They said to Columbus: "Are there no graves in Spain that you should bring us here to perish?" Terrified by the variations shown in the compass, these homesick and discouraged sailors were always in a state of near mutiny, and frequently they threatened to throw their leaders overboard. But Columbus held firmly to his purpose, declaring that he had to get to the Indies and with the help of the Lord he would go until he found them.

The great faith and dauntless courage of this one man kept his men going ever deeper and deeper into the unknown. Day after day Columbus wrote down in the private log of this famous voyage: "This day we sailed on, course west by southwest." Conditions were about as adverse as they could possibly be. Storms had damaged their ships; the *Pinta* had lost its rudder. And the crews of all three vessels were constantly threatening to turn back. In his day most people believed his cause to be an insane enterprise. And yet we have no indication that his own confidence ever wavered. This unusual man set his course by his own intuition and logical intelligence. His spirit told him that he was right and his dogged courage and determination kept him always going forward.

Finally on that dark night of October 12, 1492, a spark of light from an Indian campfire told him that his ships were approaching land. Columbus landed on the low, sandy shore of a small island, which he named San Salvador or the Holy Redeemer in appreciation for his preservation from harm. Joaquin Miller has put into verse the seeming hopelessness of this voyage from the point of view of the men as contrasted with the unmovable determination and singleness of purpose possessed by its leader. As a spokesman the mate represents the utter dejection, discouragement, and lack of hope of the crew. But always the admiral remained confident. Mr. Miller wrote:

> Behind him lay the gray Azores,
>   Behind the Gates of Hercules;
> Before him not the ghosts of shores;
>   Before him only shoreless seas.
> The good mate said: "Now must we pray,
>   For lo! the very stars are gone.
> Brave Adm'r'l speak! What shall I say?"
>   "Why say: 'Sail on! sail on! and on!' "
>
> "My men grow mutinous day by day;
>   My men grow ghastly, wan and weak."

The stout mate thought of home; a spray
    Of salt wave washed his swarthy cheek.
"What shall I say, brave Adm'r'l, say,
    If we sight naught but seas at dawn?"
"Why, you shall say at break of day:
    'Sail on! sail on! sail on! and on!' "

They sailed and sailed, as winds might blow,
    Until at last the blanched mate said:
"Why, now not even God would know
    Should I and all my men fall dead.
These very winds forget their way,
    For God from these dread seas is gone.
Now speak, brave Adm'r'l, speak and say—"
    He said: "Sail on! sail on! and on!"

They sailed. They sailed. Then spake the mate:
    "This mad sea shows his teeth tonight.
He curls his lip, he lies in wait,
    He lifts his teeth as if to bite!
Brave Adm'r'l, say but one good word:
    What shall we do when hope is gone?"
The words leapt like a leaping sword:
    "Sail on! sail on! sail on! and on!"

Then pale and worn, he kept his deck,
    And peered through darkness. Ah, that night
Of all dark nights! And then a speck—
    A light! A light! At last a light!
It grew, a starlit flag unfurled!
    It grew to be Time's burst of dawn.
He gained a world; he gave that world
    Its grandest lesson: "On! sail on!"

Because of the sturdy faith and relentless persistence of this great discoverer whose life was shaped by God's call to service, we might well erect a great statue in our hearts to help us remember our grandest lesson. To go forward is an idea that we should never forget.

Fifty-three years after the United States was officially established, a book of ancient scripture was revealed from its burial place in western New York state, which had been written by the prophets who lived during the civilization that had flourished in America in pre-Columbus days. In this book the Prophet Nephi records a vision shown to him by an angel in which he was permitted to see the future coming of Columbus to reopen this land to the world. This record says: "And it came to pass that the angel said unto me: Behold the wrath of God is upon the seed of thy brethren. And I looked and beheld a man among the Gentiles, who was separated from the seed of my brethren by the many waters; and I beheld the spirit of God, that it came down and wrought upon the man [Columbus]; and he went forth upon the many waters, even unto the seed of my brethren, who were in the promised land." (1 Nephi 13:11-12) And the angel said: ". . . the Lord God will raise up a mighty nation among the Gentiles, yea, even upon the face of this land. . . ." (1 Nephi 22:7)

Modern scripture tells us that the United States Constitution was written by inspired men whom God had prepared for this very purpose. Wise old Benjamin Franklin pointed out that if a sparrow cannot fall to the ground without God's notice, then certainly this great American nation could never rise without his aid.

The prophets of this earlier American civilization also knew of the divine decrees that God had dedicated this land to liberty and had given it his choicest blessings. God also gave it the divine mission to keep freedom, righteousness, and human dignity alive in the world. Pre-Columbus American prophets foresaw the problems of sin and trouble that would envelop this great American nation in our own time. It is an interesting fact that almost all of the prophets on both continents saw our day, and some of them almost lived in our time.

Near the end of his life, as the Master sat on the Mount of Olives, his disciples came unto him privately and said, "Tell us, when shall these things be? and what shall be the sign of thy coming, and of the end of the world?" (Matt. 24:3) Jesus seemed to be fully informed about world conditions in our time and told them of the wars and rumors of wars that should fill our earth with strife. He said: "For nation shall rise against nation, and kingdom against kingdom: and there shall be famines, and pestilences, and earthquakes, in divers places. All of these are the beginning of sorrows. . . . And then shall many be offended, and shall betray one another, and shall hate one another . . . and because iniquity shall abound, the love of many shall wax cold." (Matt. 24:7-12)

He made an interesting comparison for our times when he said: "But as the days of Noah were, so shall also the coming of the Son of man be." (Matt. 24:37) Then he brightened the picture somewhat by saying: "And this gospel of the kingdom shall be preached in all the world for a witness unto all nations; and then shall the end come." (Matt. 24:14)

Every American should know that it was God's will that America should be made available as a home for freedom-loving people and that God inspired the organization of our democratic form of government. It is his present desire that each one of us should have his own part in carrying forward the American mission. We need to adopt the great faith and develop the never-ending courage of Columbus, the great discoverer. We need to get some directions clearly in mind for ourselves and then according to God's will we should so conduct ourselves that we might also be able to write in the log of our own lives: "This day we sailed on."

We know with great certainty what God wants us to do. We know that he abhors all kinds of vice, sin, unfairness, and uncleanness. We know that he wants us to be free and to accept the full responsibility for our deeds. We know that he wants us to go forward, to grow bigger, to be happier, and to spread peace, good will, and righteousness throughout the world. It is very displeasing to him when we lose any of those high ideals and Christian standards on which this nation was originally established.

The knowledge explosion, which began in America, and the speeding up in the tempo of human life were foretold thousands of years ago, and we are now headed toward the grand winding-up scene. America will play an important part in the world's future. The spirit of America has always been one of freedom, progress, and comparative righteousness, and Jesus Christ is the God of this land. In the journey we are making toward our objectives we should not camp too long in the same place.

The spirit of America is forward, and we must not get away from that course that God has charted for us. The ships of Columbus were damaged by the storm, and we are also having a lot more trouble than is good for our journey. God's purposes are being damaged by the mutiny of atheism and the rebellion against morality and religion that is taking place. Our strikes, our race riots, our marchers, scoffers, disbelievers, and false teachers are holding up our progress. The Russian communist leaders have banished God and outlawed religion to make their own course seem more consistent. However, we sometimes do about the same thing as individuals, when, by our disobedience, we make law and order of little effect and we substitute a mediocre accomplishment for what should be lives of excellence. We should have a lot more days when we write in our log book: "This day we sailed forward."

We are sailing backward when we glamorize sin and use liquor, tobacco, immorality, dishonesty, and disobedience for our own destruction. It is ridiculous to entice ourselves with all kinds of those evils that God has forbidden to us in this promised land. In becoming dropouts from education, dropouts from religion, and dropouts from righteousness, we are riding those winds that are tending toward failure. One of the most appalling comments on our present-day life is that in spite of our intelligence and education one-half of our hospital beds are filled with patients suffering from nervous diseases and mental illnesses. We are being battered into ruin by those self-induced conflicts with our own evil.

Too many people bring about their own collapse by taking on the crushing burdens of the accumulated errors of our sinful yesterdays and the worries and dreads of our fearful tomorrows. This is not proper for the people who live in the land of Columbus. It is our sailing backward that has made the inferiority complex the most widespread disease in our land. We do ourselves a great injustice when we load up our lives with the conflicts of evil, while our guilt complexes make us physically, mentally, and morally ill.

Every one of us was created in God's image and we were designed to go forward. As one of the very important events that should precede his Second Coming, Jesus said: "And this gospel of the kingdom shall be preached in all the world for a witness unto all nations; and then shall the end come." (Matt. 24:14) John the Revelator saw this event in process of fulfillment when, from his lonely vigil of Patmos, he looked down to our time and said: "And I saw another angel fly in the midst of heaven, having the everlasting gospel to preach unto them that dwell on the earth, and to every nation, and kindred, and tongue, and people, saying with a loud voice, Fear God, and give glory to him; for the hour of his judgment is come. . . ." (Rev. 14:6-7)

We bear a solemn and humble witness that the angel has flown, and like Columbus, under divine command, he came to

America. The Lord has again established his Church upon the earth, and men have again been commissioned by heaven to carry out God's grand design. His Church is a world church. When it was originally established by Jesus its headquarters were upon the eastern continent, but the people there not only rejected him but also those who later represented him as well. In this last dispensation the headquarters of his Church have been established in America. Some thirteen thousand messengers are now going throughout the world, two by two, without pay. They are bearing the important message of the angel and teaching the doctrines taught in the original Church. We need to repent of our sins, recharge our faith, and then in God's name we should sail on with all our hearts.

Every person in this land should share in the responsibility for carrying out the divine mission of his church. May God help us to write in the largest letters in the daily log of our lives: "This day we sailed on."

The Trail

S OME TIME AGO, I heard a man give an account of a hiking expedition, which he had taken with his family.

The family had been spending a few days on a camping trip in the mountains. They had already done the usual things, such as enjoying the scenery, doing some fishing, riding horses, and playing games, but something was lacking. The children decided that in order to make the trip complete, they should climb the mountain. When this ambition was expressed and the matter discussed by the family, the mother expressed a grave concern about the dangers that might be involved. She mentioned such possible problems as falling rocks, poison ivy, rattlesnakes, and other dangers that might be encountered along the way, but every department of life involves risk, and it was finally agreed that the climb should be made. The mother compromised by exacting a promise from each that they would be careful.

Climbing is always one of the most exciting of life's experiences, and this particular adventure was above the ordinary. They found some beautiful patches of wild flowers growing along the trail, and they came upon some refreshing snowbanks and a beautiful waterfall. As they rose from one mountain level to another, they marveled at how much their point of view was changing. The valley below seemed much more interesting when viewed from a great height, but the experiences on this dizzy level also frightened them a little. Frequently they held their breath as they crossed over narrow ledges, where they knew that one misstep could mean a fall of hundreds of feet, or one loosened boulder tumbling down from above could send them all crashing to their deaths. In spite of all the dangers and the hard climbing, they were all greatly enjoying the experience.

To the youngest daughter, the adventure was particularly exciting. With unusual energy, she was running back and forth, making the most of every situation. She said to her father: "I am not afraid of anything, as long as you are with me."

During her few years of life, this little girl had developed a happy, safe confidence in her father's ability to handle difficult situations. To her, he was very wise, and she knew that he was more than ordinarily interested in her safety. She felt that he would be able to spot any danger in advance and that he could effectively handle any difficulty that might threaten them along the way.

One of the interesting facts about life is its similarity to an interesting adventure in the mountains.

As if it were yesterday, I remember my own first mountain hike. Almost every day for all of my previous short life, I had looked up to the mountain tops from the valley below, but when I was actually upon the mountain slopes they seemed very different. They seemed much bigger and more exciting. When, in beginning the trip, we had stood at the foot of the mountain, it seemed to me that the top of the first steep ascent was the top of the mountain itself. But after a lot of hard climbing, we came near the top of the first section, and I was very surprised to discover that another long, steep ascent reached far up beyond the first. This experience was repeated several times before the top of the mountain finally came into view.

Alexander Pope compares this to the learning processes of life. In his poem he says:

> Fir'd at first sight with what the Muse imparts,
> In fearless youth we tempt the heights of Arts,
> While from the bounded level of our mind,
> Short views we take, nor see the lengths behind;
> But more advanc'd, behold with strange surprise
> New distant scenes of endless science rise!
> So pleas'd at first the tow'ring Alps we try,
> Mount o'er the vales, and seem to tread the sky,
> Th' eternal snows appear already past
> And the first clouds and mountains seem the last:
> But, those attain'd, we tremble to survey
> The growing labours of the lengthen'd way,
> Th' increasing prospect tires our wand'ring eyes.
> Hills peep o'er hills, and Alps on Alps arise!

(A Little Learning)

Climbing mountains, like living successfully, always involves many challenges. There is a lot of hard work and many great adventures, and in each we always have some new experiences that we have never had before. Like the mountain trails, the trails of life are also beset with dangers and there are various kinds of casualties in both instances.

The Bureau of Vital Statistics makes it clear that not all the people born in any given year will even survive the year of their birth. Each subsequent year will take an increasing toll of life. There will also be many kinds of disabilities and disappointments. Some of these will come from carelessness, some from accidents, and some from disease.

One of the most disturbing things on either trail is that we seldom know from what source the danger may be expected.

The newspaper told of a little boy riding his brand new tricycle. At the very height of his joy with his new possession he was run over by an automobile, backing out of a driveway. Another small boy fell into a canal, and another was stricken down with polio and condemned to a lifetime of inactivity. Each of these young men had in one moment given a wonderful promise of life, but an hour later only blight and hopelessness remained.

So many of life's most serious dangers are not physical at all. Because a promising young businessman became so involved with a conflict of opposing philosophies that in his confusion and bewilderment, he committed suicide.

A great many people nourish within themselves the very germs that will destroy them. Sometimes even our misstep will send our lives crashing in failure.

In following this urge to climb upward, we may often feel that the fears of those who stay in camp are groundless, but each year many people have some serious troubles along the trail of life that they didn't expect.

A rattlesnake has the noble habit of always sounding a warning before he strikes, but along the trail of life one may come in contact with other rattlesnakes that are not so generous. It was *men* that Jesus had in mind when he spoke of wolves in sheep's clothing. This single disguise does not exhaust the possibilities of this metaphor. Sometimes rattlesnakes also dress as men and carry a charge of poison much more deadly than any of their crawling brethren that may coil up along a mountain trail.

The scriptures mention the many who lie in wait to deceive. The little girl felt perfectly safe as long as she stayed close to her father. He could spot the danger in advance and help protect her against it.

Neither this little girl nor any of the rest of us will always have our fathers closeby, but God is our Heavenly Father and if we always keep close to him, we will always be safe. He has written some safety rules to help us climb life's mountains. To be successful, we should love God and goodness and industry. God has anticipated all the dangers of the trail and has vigorously warned against those missteps that would make our journey unhappy or unsuccessful. Satan is both miserable and unsuccessful in real accomplishment — only because he has done the wrong things. There can never be any happiness for him or for us in evil, or in idleness, or in discouragement, or in wickedness. The scripture says: "Wickedness never was happiness."

I once saw a person who had gotten involved with some poison ivy. Sores had broken out all over his body. They itched and hurt and were unsightly. They made him useless, miserable, and unhappy. He reminded me of the beggar mentioned in the parable, who laid by the rich man's gate full of sores, hoping to be fed the scraps that the rich man threw away. The beggar's only companions were the dogs that came to lick his sores. Sores are not a very pleasant kind of companionship. Some of our worst sores are those that form in our minds and hearts because of our own evil.

Recently I talked with a young woman who had developed some pretty bad moral sores. She hadn't actually intended to do anything that was wrong. Like the parable of the lost sheep, she had just nibbled her way out of bounds. She had gone from one bunch of grass to another until she had passed the point of no return and was unable to find her way back. Then some feelings of rejection and unworthiness had developed as a consequence of her troubled conscience. Like itching and smarting sores, these were making her life miserable — almost to the point of being unbearable. Like so many, her problems had started small but they had gained enough ground to start an avalanche. She is being destroyed because she didn't stay close enough to God, and she now seems unable to stop this landslide of trouble.

Some time ago I saw a man who had once been a great salesman. He was a real leader, but he got off that straight and narrow trail and did things that were disapproved by his company and his own conscience. When he was questioned, he became offended. Because he was unable to take criticism, his offense grew quickly into antagonism. The more anyone tried to correct and help him, the farther the pendulum of his opposition swung in the other direction. We frequently talk about the many martyrs who have given up their lives for some righteous cause, but what a tragedy when one gives up his life for some worthless evil!

This man's great ability only made his misdirected zeal more serious. He was trying to prove to people that he could do as he pleased. In attempting to prove this unprofitable point, he lost his employment and became involved in several serious lawsuits. The other day when I saw him again, after a number of years, he was a broken, bankrupt, disagreeable old man, still spending his years in getting his own way and causing everyone unpleasantness, including himself. He has lost the respect of his former friends and no one dares to befriend him, because they know that sooner or later anyone whose life touches his can only reap trouble as their reward. He is quarrelsome and unhappy in his church, and his personality sores are exuding a foul odor that makes him offensive, even to those who would like to help him.

When this man started to climb the mountain of his life, one might have predicted for him the greatest possible success. His problems came because he didn't stay close enough to righteousness; he got off the trail of fairness and had too many contacts with the poison ivy of egotism and self-interest, which have now largely destroyed him. Instead of accepting any correction, he just moved the yellow line far enough to the left to make everything seem to him to be within bounds. As a usual thing, he recognizes no fixed line running between right and wrong. He has set himself up as his own judge as to where that line ought to be. After so many bad habits have now been developed and so many sores are hurting him, it is pretty difficult for him to change his ways.

Recently I read an article written by a man whose occupation is that of finding missing persons. He says that anyone can be located if you know enough about him. He points out that it is very easy for one to disguise his appearance. He can color his hair, grow a mustache, and even make his face over with plastic surgery. But this finder of lost persons says that it is not so easy for one to change his habits. When one becomes critical, unrighteous, selfish, or loaded with complexes, these habits that he cannot change always make him a marked man.

It is interesting to look back to one's school days and think about the early lives of our friends. We remember the good and poor students. Some were stars in athletics, some in debating, and some in drama. Some were prominent in social affairs and were fine friends and good conversationalists. There was another group of students who seemed not to excel in anything. After many years have passed, it is interesting to think about what has happened to each of them. Some have died physically; others have died mentally and spiritually. In some cases, the promising and the unpromising have changed places. Some without any obvious advantages have gone to the top; some with great financial prospects have lost their money because of missteps or miscalculations. Some have become the victims of poison ivy, and some have died of rattlesnake poison. Some have started political, economic, and personality avalanches that have done great damage. Some have rejected their Heavenly Father as their guide and companion along the way of life. Among the casualties, by far the greatest number are those who have committed some kind or some degree of personal suicide.

Jesus talked about the most desirable trail when he described the straight and narrow path leading to eternal life. Then, after he had marked out the way, he said: "Follow me." And every human soul will finally be judged by how well he carries out that single direction. Mostly our problem is that we can't follow. Judas couldn't follow. Most of our present world problems are because we are not following. Too often, we get off the trail and strike out on our own without realizing where we are going. Then so many of us fail; we fail in our reason, we fail in our objectives, and we generate complexes and unhealthy attitudes.

We lose out along life's way because we don't stay close enough to our Heavenly Father. If we only learn to understand his point of view and live by his principles, we are safe.

If we always follow divine instructions, we will be able to

say to our Heavenly Father: "I am not afraid of anything as long as you are with me."

One of our greatest abilities is to learn to effectively climb our own mountains of life, and may God help us to get great joy in the process.

The Ugly Duckling

OVER A HUNDRED years ago Hans Christian Anderson wrote an interesting fairy tale called "The Ugly Duckling." It seems that by some mischance a swan's egg had gotten into the nest of a mother duck and had been hatched out as her own. From the beginning this one member of her brood seemed to be more than ordinarily awkward and ungainly, and it soon acquired the title of "the ugly duckling." For this peculiar little duck to be so singled out for her ugliness caused her a great many unpleasant problems. As the time passed, however, things became a little better. Some changes began to take place in the little duck itself until one day, in the reflection of the water, the ugly duckling discovered that she was not a duck at all but a graceful, beautiful swan. It is interesting that Mr. Anderson did not write this story for the benefit of ducks or swans. Actually, this story was a disguised biography of Mr. Anderson's own life.

Probably there are few people who go through life without experiencing some of those devastating human emotions wherein one feels that he is ugly, inferior, and unwanted In writing this story with the spotlight on an awkward, misplaced, ugly duckling, Mr. Anderson was merely reviewing and reliving some of the sufferings connected with his own early growing-up years. The recital of some of the experiences of this lonely, guilty, grief-stricken little duck strikes a familiar chord in the lives of many human beings. It seems to be a part of the program of life for people to start at the bottom, and many are required to make their own transformations from failure to success, from misery to happiness, from weakness to strength, and from ugliness to beauty. Life itself, both here and hereafter, was planned to be a matter of constant growth and improvement. There are some big dictionary words that are called by such impressive names as metamorphosis and evolution. Then there are the more common names for growth such as self-development, or just plain progress. Metamorphosis implies a change in form. The dictionary gives the examples of a caterpillar becoming a butterfly and a tadpole turning into a frog. To these Mr. Anderson adds his own story of an ugly duckling becoming a graceful swan. There are also some other kinds of progress. Our living standards are going up. Our scientific accomplishments are becoming greater. The old oxcart with which our pioneer forefathers crossed the plains was changed into a powerful steam locomotive, and now jet propelled planes carry us through the air faster than sound.

The dictionary speaks of evolution as an unfolding or an unrolling. There are some people who believe that the highest types of life have evolved from some very simple forms. They believe that lowly prehistoric, unintelligent creations are the ancestors of that complex organization that we know as man. Anyone who believes that George Washington and Thomas A. Edison evolved from a caterpillar or a tadpole can have great expectations for the future of our race, if the upward progress is continued in the same way at the same rate. On the other hand we might accept the scriptural declaration that God created man in his own image, endowed him with a set of his own attributes, and made him heir to his own glorious destiny. This also might give us some very high hopes for our own futures. Either way we look at it, we might expect a lot of excitement ahead as we climb the heights and change our present ugly duckling status into that of a beautiful swan.

We have one problem connected with this idea and that is that recently something seems to have gone wrong, as in some cases our evolutionary machinery seems to have slipped into reverse. There are numerous evidences pointing to the idea that instead of going from caterpillar to butterfly and from animal to man, some of us are presently heading in the other direction. The crime reports and the divorce proceedings indicate that in some ways the current order is from man to animal. What a sorry state it would be if all the beautiful, graceful swans had to spend the rest of their days as ugly ducklings. Suppose the Washingtons and the Edisons had to spend their eternities in some ignorant sub-human forms of life; or suppose that some of the children of God were required to live forever among the unbearable miseries of hell; or suppose that instead of being servants of God we were required to serve as servants of an evil, offensive, sinful, ugly devil.

The dictionary defines "ugly" as something that is extremely unattractive. Ugliness is something that is unpleasant to look at, or to think about, or to associate with. Ugliness not only offends our sense of beauty, but it also disturbs our feelings of tranquility and peace. Ugliness is disagreeable in form and displeasing in appearance. It may be morally revolting and cause unpleasant discords with righteousness. Ugliness may show itself in disfigured bodies, sick minds, or depraved spirits, and ugly moods and ugly ambitions always leave their disfiguring marks upon the soul.

A disturbing trend has recently arisen in some segments of our society where some people seem to take a strange, unnatural pride in their own ugliness. They seem to delight in wearing soiled, untidy, peculiar - looking clothing. They have dirty, uncombed, unclean hair with smelly bodies, smelly morals, and smelly habits. Unfortunately this violent downturn in personal appearance and in the personal pride of people is having far more than mere physical significance. Ugliness, like cancer, is hard to stop when once it gets going. Actually it is not very many steps from an ugly personal appearance to an ugly personal attitude and an ugly personal performance. With an ugly set of situations we can only expect to have an ugly set of consequences.

One member of an idle, rebellious, retrogressing group recently said that their aim was "to kick the establishment." He meant that it was their purpose to pull down and destroy those things that had already been built up by others. He said: "Look at the mess we are in. What has anybody ever done for us?" It therefore seemed logical to him to make things as much worse as he could. His father was a doctor, devoting his life to helping people. Both of his parents had worked hard for him, but he was against his parents. He was against education. He criticized those who invested their time in learning to carry forward the necessary work of the world. He made fun of those who live orderly lives with rules and schedules to go by.

Comparing him to his father and mother it appeared to me that surely his evolution must have changed its direction. It seemed that we were witnessing a beautiful swan hatching out an ugly duckling and where he will go from there is something else. It is a law of God that sooner or later rewards must always follow merit. However, the young man wanted the rewards without the merit. He talks a great deal about freedom and love without understanding either one. He wants his freedom without its accompanying responsibility. He wants to be free to loaf, free to be immoral, free to be a dope addict, free to be lazy, and free to live without being accountable to anyone. He wants to be free to be ugly, free to be sinful, free to disobey God. He is working vigorously on his freedom to go to hell. He wants love without the need for honor, respect, or responsibility. Actually there is no excellence without labor, and there are no causes without consequences. When we undertake to bring about such a reversal in the law, we also bring about a reversal in our own progress.

Washington Irving said: "It is the divinity within us that makes the divinity without." It is also the ugliness within us that makes the ugliness without Ugliness on the outside also tends to make ugliness on the inside. Because the great God who created us has divinity within, it is manifest in the glory and radiance that shines in his person. When Jesus was transfigured on the high mountain the scripture says that "his raiment was white as the light." Luke describes the angels that appeared on the hills of Judea on that first Christmas by saying, "And the glory of the Lord shone round about them."

We make a beginning approach to this situation in ourselves when on the Lord's day we prepare ourselves for his spirit. Then we pay particular attention to the washing of our bodies; we put on fresh, clean clothing and dress ourselves in smiling faces and our most pleasant attitudes. We are more able to acceptably perform our devotions to God. The proper observance of any divine law helps us climb upward in spirit, success, and beauty. There are some who use the Sabbath as a time for lowering themselves. They let their whiskers grow, allow their bodies to remain uncleaned, and permit their minds to go undisciplined. Sunday is a day when they wear their dirtiest clothes and do their dirtiest jobs and therefore make the Sabbath day their dirtiest day. By this desecration we not only foster physical ugliness; we also build up within ourselves ugly attitudes and an ugly spirit. In down-grading ourselves we also reverse the Cinderella fairy tale where a fairy godmother transformed a poor little cinder girl into a princess. She lifted her above the ashes and dirt by dressing her at her best to attend a wonderful ball.

Often the mere memory of some pleasant, beautiful occasion

can permanently change our attitudes and transform us into something that is better than we were. When we send ourselves to the ball of life dressed as hippies, ne'er-do-wells, cowards, atheists, and sinners, that is what we are likely to become.

Some business establishments post notices requesting improperly dressed people to stay off their premises. God does something similar when he excludes those from his presence who don't measure up. A good fisherman throws back the fish that have little value, and so does life. We always hang a picture in the best possible light, but unfortunately many of us are not that considerate of ourselves. We habitually put ourselves in the worst light by putting on our most unsightly clothing and by engaging in sinful conduct. How sad it is when we defend all manner of human perversions, fill our own minds with violence, participate in many crimes and evils and put a grim mask of ugliness upon ourselves!

The usual plot for a movie used to be to follow the pattern of the ugly ducklings and the caterpillar and climb out of our lowest situation reaching for something better. Formerly the hero always started out in a hole and then worked himself upward to live happily ever after. Now we seem to start out on top of the world and descend until we end up as hippies, dope addicts, and sinners. Nowadays when the movie ends, the villain is frequently on the throne, the mortgage has been foreclosed, and the hero is on a dope binge on the very outskirts of hell. Of course, when we devour the ugliness from our screens and out of our books and practice it in our dress and our thoughts, how can we help getting it into our souls? Whenever we glamorize sin, take pride in ugliness, and worship Satan, we are evolving backward. We are climbing downhill. We are advancing toward failure. And we need to re-stablish the better order.

Schlegel said: "There is no more potent antidote to a low sensuality than the adoration of beauty." Aristotle said: "Beauty purifies the thoughts and passions." Socrates, who was a very homely man, prayed to God and said: "Make me beautiful within." We can all make ourselves beautiful by holding in our minds and hearts beautifying thoughts. Everyone has seen plain people who have become beautiful by the working of a radiant spirituality. A godly spirit will make the plainest body beautiful. Great mental and spiritual qualities transform our bodies into their likeness. A dirty mind and dirty clothing contaminate each other. Among the greatest energy builders and the most important health tonics are a clean shave, a good hair cut, a hot soapy bath, and modest, appropriate, clean clothing, and a vigorous repentance. "God's house is a house of order." "Cleanliness is next to Godliness." "Beauty is the mark that God sets on virtue." God made the earth beautiful. He covered it with beautiful grass, flowers, and trees. He used some of his most brilliant colors to beautify the sunset, the ocean, and the sky. He gave a friendly twinkle to the stars. He made the moon shine with a beautiful light and luster. He put energy and vitamins into the sun's rays that are able to kill germs. Then, as the crowning scene in the great drama of creation, God created man in his own image and gave him God's own plan for eternal progression, that man might be glorious also.

Those who earn the right to live with God will be glorified celestial beings. Their lives will have a heavenly beauty from which all evil and ugliness will have been removed. Then filth, ugliness, death, and disease will be the lot only of those who have insisted upon living it. In referring to this situation John the Revelator said: "Then he that is filthy shall be filthy still." How horrible it would be if we were unable to take an occasional bath in the cleansing waters of righteousness! God has given us a conscience, an ambition, and a faith to help us keep our lives clean and beautiful. He has said that only those who have clean hands and a pure heart will ascend the hill of the Lord and stand in his holy place. One of the greatest of all our opportunities is to outgrow our "ugly duckling" status and put on the beauty that God intended for us to have.

Winning Arguments

A GREAT SALES supervisor once said that the best way to lose sales was to go around among one's prospects winning arguments. This sales supervisor spent a lot of time trying to eliminate from his salesmen that serious human weakness of always wanting to have one's own way. Whether our objective is to be effective in the business of selling, in the business of marriage, or in the business of living, we should be careful about winning too many arguments, unless we want to lose the larger prize of making sales. We should not join the old Sophists in their boast that they could make the worse appear to be the better cause.

So frequently we lose our prospects and even our friends because we hold them on too tight a rein. We should keep in mind that other people also like to win occasionally. Often the best way to gain an advantage for ourselves is by giving up ground. Frequently the best way to win is by yielding. Someone once wrote a tombstone epitaph, saying:

> Here lies the body of William Jay,
> He died defending his right-of-way,
> He was right — dead right — as he sped along,
> But he's just as dead as if he'd been wrong.

Sometimes we can save ourselves by giving up some of the highway. Often we can advance fastest by retreating. One of the most common methods of closing sales comes in making concessions. Jesus gave this law its finest statement when he said: ". . . he that loseth his life for my sake shall find it." (Matt. 10:39) Losing ourselves in what we are doing is a great idea. This process demands that we dim our own lights occasionally. It is the soft answer that turneth away wrath. It may not be a good idea to always play at the organ of life with all our stops pulled out. The shortest distance between two points is *not* always a straight line. Sometimes we can reach our destination more quickly by circling the field a few times and then coming in from the other side. Someone once wrote an interesting story about this philosophy entitled "She Stoops to Conquer."

A salesman once called on a farmer. The farmer suggested that three months in the future would be a more appropriate time to complete the sale. The salesman came back as requested and walked down into the field where the farmer was working. As he came within earshot the farmer greeted him by saying, "Here comes this blankety-blank sales pest again."

While the remark was largely made in jest, the salesman was seriously offended. The salesman's first impulse was to put the farmer in his place with a good punch on the nose. At least the farmer should be made to apologize for his discourtesy. The salesman was about to make the prospect eat his words; however, he caught himself in time by realizing that he hadn't come to win any arguments. Try as he would he couldn't remember of ever making a sale by punching people on their noses, either physically or verbally. Neither could he think of anyone who had ever failed in sales work because he had too many people who liked him. Therefore, he quickly changed his attitude and put on his most friendly geniality.

To remember that genuine good will is the doorway leading to every success usually makes losing arguments a real pleasure. Accordingly, this salesman shook his prospect's hand, told him how well he looked, and patted him on the back. He lost himself in his prospect and got the order. He had advanced his own cause by yielding the right-of-way. He had dimmed his own lights in order to give the prospect the full benefit of the spotlight. By abandoning his natural urge to attack he also kept the prospect's good will. This idea of losing oneself in righteousness has a great many applications. It has built excellence into many personal relations and has promoted a lot of marital success.

A woman recently took her husband through the divorce court because he felt that as the "head of the house" he was obligated to win all the family arguments. Therefore, whenever *she* sent up an idea *he* always shot it down. He jumped on her logic with his many reasons why her ideas wouldn't work. She soon became afraid to express herself to him. Gradually she almost completely abandoned the field of marital communication and left her husband alone to do all the family thinking and managing of their joint affairs by himself.

In filling her with fear and inferiority he soon drained from her the initiative and satisfaction that made her a person. His unwise domination had transformed her into a "thing," for all practical purposes. What a boost it would have given her ailing ego if her opinion had been a little more sought after! What if she did make a mistake occasionally — that is the way we learn. And to have been permitted to win just one little argument may have been a lifesaver to her. However, all hope of any victory for her was abandoned wherever he was concerned. In the interests of her own self-preservation she decided that she must divorce her husband, if she was to salvage any of herself.

Many of the most serious sins in the world are those committed against the human personality. Even without meaning to do so, some people frequently dominate, inhibit, or distort the personalities and the wills of others because of their stronger and more aggressive arguing ability. Almost invariably these people lose by winning. In fear and trembling some wives must prostrate themselves before a supposedly superior partner to induce him to supply the financial small change required for her personal or household needs. Some men pressure their wives into becoming naggers and beggars, rather than building them up into responsible, happy partners.

Child growth is also frequently retarded by an unjust domination and false rule that should not be confused with discipline, principle, or righteousness. Even older people are sometimes treated like children and kept in unjust subjugation by magnifying their weaknesses and by rehearsing, coloring, and enlarging their mistakes. By this process self-confidence is often destroyed and personality strength diminished. The void is filled by some disabling inferiority and guilt complexes. Sometimes this damaging oppression is heaped upon people because of either a conscious or unconscious selfishness or thoughtlessness. Sometimes by our own sins we bring these problems upon ourselves, but whoever is responsible, it is unlikely that this unpleasant, unprofitable oppression of the human spirit is ever justified.

Of course, this excessive winning of arguments is not entirely a male sin. I know a wife who rates above her husband in debating ability, who carries on an aggressive and continual war against him. There is no question about whether or not he has some faults, but with a kind of master oratory, his wife inflates his faults and uses them as her weapons to beat him into nothingness. She invokes against him all the emotional sanctions that are available to her and she tells him off in no uncertain terms. With the self-assurance of ignorance she casts herself in the role of one who can do no wrong, and by her assumed authority she thoroughly unsells him upon himself.

His unrealized love of peace combines with his feelings of guilt, rejection, and inferiority to push him further and further down into the mire. He is now like a man struggling in the quicksand, and he sinks a little deeper each time he struggles and loses. The fact that she is so convincing in her speech and so forceful in her delivery is causing far more trouble than it is curing. To let her husband win one argument, even on a minor point, might be like throwing him one end of a rope on which he could save himself. There is no question that the wife is winning the arguments, but as a consequence her own happiness is being destroyed and her marriage is tottering on the brink of divorce. In finding her dominion she is losing her life.

Winning arguments is sometimes like one burning a house down to roast the egg, or destroying some other worthwhile program to correct one of its faults. There are better ways to cure a man of his dandruff than by cutting off his head. One woman said that if her husband would only be reasonable everything between them would be all right. But everyone would get along fine if we were always reasonable. Our problem is that there are so few people who are completely reasonable beings. None of us always do exactly as we should and frequently we can much better advance our own interests by making a few allowances for others. The Lord has said that the basis we use in forgiving others will be used by him to judge us. No one ever travels straight along his own mountain top of life without making an occasional dip in altitude.

There is a natural ebb and flow in human affairs that we should take into consideration in our relations with other people. Someone has said that marriage is a fifty-fifty proposition, but it should be much more than that. When one insists on a fifty-fifty marriage, with no allowances made for an occasional shortage, there is bound to be trouble. Frequently there isn't enough length in a fifty-fifty marriage to cover all the needs. That is, if one party to a fifty-fifty marriage drops back to forty in his performance, there isn't enough marriage to reach. A sixty-

sixty marriage would provide some margins and would be more likely to hold itself together. An eighty-eighty marriage would be even better. Jesus probably had a hundred-hundred situation in mind when he advised people to go the second mile. That is twice as far as was expected. Any citizen was required to carry the burdens of a Roman soldier for one mile but Jesus recommended that, if necessary, they go another mile of their own choice. Marriage is one of those places where we should go farther than we are required to go and do more than is expected of us. We are practicing a kind of stupid aspect of this fifty-fifty law when we demand "an eye for an eye" and a "tooth for a tooth." This procedure, if followed to its ultimate, would eventually end in making everybody blind. It is as true in marital relations as in our military affairs that no one wins in a war. In addition we frequently unsell ourselves on ourselves and load each other down with inferiority and guilt complexes.

In trying to help an argument-winning wife keep her family together, it was suggested that she get a better understanding of her possible alternatives. She had been trying to bring about their marital compatibility by shaming her husband and putting various pressures upon him. She embarrassed him before his friends. She was also using threats, but he just couldn't bring himself to do what she wanted him to do. By divorce she could take away his home, deprive him of his family, and force him into a great deal of extra expense. It is not denied that sometimes a good shock treatment might be very helpful. On the other hand it can be the straw that breaks the camel's back. In World War I many soldiers had their nervous systems permanently ruined by shell shock. Even in a little cold war, shame, threats, or force are likely to increase in tempo and drive us farther and farther from our objectives without our being able to do much about it. Sometimes a hard bump on the head may actually restore one's senses, but one can also lose his mind that way.

However, there is still another available weapon that might be used in making one's marriage a success, and that is the mysterious power of love. This wife said: "How can I love him when he does wrong?" She was a wonderful woman and probably was far above her husband in her moral, mental, and spiritual stature. But as soon as his problems began to develop she began turning off her love in favor of the weaker instruments of shame, fear, force, and frigidity. She was trying to whip him into line with condemnation. She was winning all the arguments. She didn't leave him a leg to stand on, but she was losing the sale and so was he.

Jesus commented on this situation when he said, "For if ye love them which love you, what reward have ye? do not even the publicans the same?" (Matt. 5:46) Almost anyone can get along with those who are always kind, reasonable, obedient, and successful. If every woman could always depend upon her husband doing and saying those things that would always keep her love and happiness turned on, we would have a lot fewer problems. But even the Publicans could get along under those circumstances. Another way to solve our problems is to develop this technique of a hundred-hundred marriage. There are some people who when necessary can go all the way. They can turn on their own love if their partner doesn't do it for them. That is, there are some people who have enough love, fairness, forgiveness, and charity to get both partners through the rainy season of their problems. They can maintain the marriage single-handed until the necessary qualities can be generated in the one who is running the deficits. No matter what the field may be this idea of going the second mile or of returning good for evil is the greatest success strategy of our time. The surest way to get the best of someone is to be kind to him. No one ever argues very long or very hard with one he loves. The hottest coals of fire ever heaped upon the head of an enemy are the coals of human kindness.

The story is told of a colored girl on the auction block during American slave days. A prospective buyer approached and said: "If I buy you and give you a good home and feed you well and treat you kindly, will you promise to be honest?" This wonderful little slave girl said: "I will promise to be honest whether you buy me and give me a good home and treat me kindly or not." That is the spirit of real success; that is the spirit of the Master; that is the spirit of the second mile; and that is the spirit of a hundred-hundred marriage.

The power of love is much stronger than the power of hate, shame, fear, force, or frigidity. It is also more profitable and more pleasant. The "eye for an eye" philosophy not only makes people blind but it also causes bitterness, fosters resentment, and breeds a counterforce of evil and wrong. May we develop this godly ability to lose our lives in order to find them and lose a few of the arguments in order to win the sales.

Index

Couple, young, with marital problems, 82
Courage, already within ourselves, 163
 of Columbus, 300-302
Course, short, 252-257
Covenant, new, with Israel, 63
Covenants, of faith, 141
Coveting, weakens abilities, 10
Creation, 94
Creator, 58, 71 ,78, 86, 94, 113 164, 181 272
 serious concerns of, 183
Criminal, tied by his crime, 19
Criticism, magnifying glasses of, 235
Crucifixion, 270
Cruelty, enjoyment in, 76
Curie, Pierre and Marie, 222
Custom, old Chinese, 271

— D —

Dangers, in mountain-climbing and in life, 307-311
Daniel, 61, 92, 140, 242
Dante, 259
Dates, important, in one's life, 37-38
Daughter, unafraid while father present, 307-308
David, 100, 242
da Vinci, Leonardo, 2, 13
Day, that shall burn as an oven, 158
Death, ix, 60
 abolished during millennium, 113
 hour of, 70
 wide road to, 88
 task of recognizing, 185
Deaths, brought about by ourselves, 265
Decision, important ingredient of success, 283
Decisions, effective, review of, 66
 importance of firm, 9
Deeds, and consquences, relationship between, 74
Deficits, moral and spiritual, 135
Degrees of glory, 101
Demonsthenes, 3, 80, 83, 177
Dependence, upon fellow beings, 38
 upon God, 35, 38
Destiny, 117
 divine, 105, 107
 missed through distractions, 11
 of becoming like God, 87
Determination, 252
de Tocqueville, Alexis, viii
Detours, to be avoided, 251
Development, beings in different stages of, 164

Devotion, to God, 81
Dickens, Charles, 206
 Great Expectations, 103
Dictators, God tired of, 54-55
Dictionary, 49
Dignity, human, 256
Disability, measured in percentages, 185-186
Disbelief, solves few problems, 292
Discipline, rebellion aaginst, 60
Discouragement, 22, 162
 brings weakness, 61
 to be eliminated, 64
Discoveries, mostly made recently, 221
Disguise, 161, 162, 164, 165
Dishonesty, in business, 255
Disloyalty, 20, 170
 to God, greatest sin, 229
 to be shunned, 169
Disobedience, 27, 170, 292-293
 children of, 186
Dispensation, final, 245
Distance, shortest, between two points, 320
Distractions, impair success, 10-12
Divine Comedy, The, by Dante Alighieri, 259-263
Divorce, 79, 232, 321
Doctrine, of Jesus Christ, 84
Doctrines, of the Church changed, 32
 teaching of false religious, 136
Doubts, caused by neglect, 10
Dropouts, 305
 from eternal glory, 193
Drummond, Henry, 1

— E —

Earth, celestialized, 91, 182
 created for man's benefit, 42
 destiny of, 114
 honored by birth of Son of God, 181
 in the beginning, 94
Easter, 240
Economy, national, 133
Edison, Thomas A., 66, 117, 118, 315
Education, most, is about ourselves, 254
 the best, 178
Egypt, Israelites in, 59, 78
Elect, of God, 42
Elegance, of poetry, 197
Elias, 95
Eliot, T. S., 139, 142
Emerson, x, 35, 84, 192, 224, 288
Emotions, devastating, 39, 314
Emphasis, destructive, 234
Empathy, definition of, 46
Emptiness, spiritual, 139, 141

Ills, can be abolished by obedience, 35
Imagination, eclipsed by real
    experience, 260
Immorality, 20, 27
Imprisonment, worst kind of, 207
Inclinations, immoral, developed as
    rebellion, 233
Inflation, 133
Influences, personal, betray us, 224
Inheritance, as children of God, 269
Inspiration, 81
    from poetry, 198
    people receive and give, 226
Institutions, divinely established, 170
Intelligence, 102
    God the source of all, 38
Interests, 145
Inventor, resourceful, 194
Irresponsibility, awful sin of, 233
Irving, Washington, 317
Isaiah, 61, 89, 92, 144, 181, 205, 242,
    250, 298
    sees airplane, 92
Israel, 32
    children of, ix
Israelites, 34, 60, 61, 66, 116

— J —

James, 283
James, William, Harvard psychologist,
    22, 111
Japan, war with, 41
Japanese, victories in World War II,
    154-155
Jealousy, 22
Jefferson, Thomas, 56
Jeremiah, 166
    feelings of inferiority, 79
Jerusalem, Christ's triumphal entry
    into, 74
Jesus Christ, appears to Joseph Smith,
    244-245
    ascension of, 244
    assumes sins of men, 250
    birth of, 95, 237
    chosen before earth was organized,
        178
    contemporaries of, x
    creator, 94
    foreordained as the Redeemer, 181
    head of the family, 125
    in temple with Simeon, 274
    ministry as resurrected being, 243
    ministry to Nephites, 95, 244
    miracles, 179, 296
    mission of, 157
    modern sufferings of, 72
    resurrection of, 242

rule of, 111
    second coming, 91, 92, 111, 135, 157-
        160, 195, 305
    takes on our sins, 72
    with Samaritan woman 173
Job, 94, 177, 209-215, 242
Joel, 158-159
John the Baptist, the Lord's
    forerunner, 180
John the Revelator, 89-90, 112, 132,
    187, 244, 319
Jowett, Dr. Henry, 297
Joy, 27
    fulness of, 189
    through good literature, 200
Joys, individual, 252
Judas Iscariot, 229-230, 312
    betrayal of Jesus, 170
Judgment, God's, based on our
    forgiving others, 323
    no better than one's information,
        240
    snap, 69
    understanding dimensions of, 67

— K —

Keats, 199
Kennedy, John F., grave of, 57
Kettering, Charles F., 86
Kindness, can prolong lives, 295
    loss of, 124
    to an enemy, 23
Kingdom of God, revelation on, 32
    within us, 235
Knowledge, makes man godlike, 110
    of self, 163

— L —

Labor, 2
Language, instrument of persuasion,
    200
    pure, during millennium, 112
    several forms of, 197
Laodiceans, 7
    the Lord scolds, 4
Last days, compared with Noah's day,
    159
    Jesus' prophecy on, 303-304
    prophecy, 75
Law, eternal, of rewards and
    punishments, 263
    God's, in the heart, 63
    natural and eternal, 12
    obedience to, 33
    rebellion against, 228

Shortsightedness, spiritual, 196
Sickness, caused by seeking attention, 25
  spiritual, 131
  from unhealthy ideas, 131
Sightseeing, 258-263
  danger of being distracted by, 11
Significance, loss of, 269
Sin, abolished during millennium, 112
  concentration camps of, 157
  deterrent to, 298
  does not go unpunished, 19, 262
  God's view of, 206
  must be paid for, 72
  never permanently profitable, 137
  offence to order of heaven, 205
  sickness of, 295
Sins, evil consequences of, 60
  man chained to his, 19
  men punished for own, 29
  repentance effective with more things than, 246
Skylark, symbol of happiness, 297-299
Slave, colored girl, being sold, 325
Slaves, of habits and attitudes, 203
Smith, Joseph, 98, 166
  first vision, 291-292
  writes Articles of Faith, 28
Smuts, Jan, South African prime minister, 120
Snow, Eliza R., 149
Society, protection of, 204
  serious problems confronting, 128
Socrates, 121, 144, 163, 259, 318
Sodom and Gomorrah, viii, 76
Soldier's Reprieve, The, by R. D. Robbins, 277-281
Solomon, 66, 109, 117, 119, 127, 177, 191
Song, of the heart, a prayer, 83
Sons of Perdition, 102
Sophists, boast of, 320
Sores, of immorality, 310
Sorrow, abolished during millennium, 113
Soul, eternal glory of, 240
  eyes, are windows of, 82
  prison of, 208
  radioactive, 168
  value of one, 138
Souls, enriched by miracle foods, 174
  eternal, saved through repentance, 248
  hymns are food for, 146
  wastelands in, 142
Sowing, good or bad seeds, 273-274
Spectacles, using right kind of, 234-239

Spirit, empty, 51
  enlightens everyone born, 225
  productive area for expectations, 106
Spirits in prison, 135, 204, 260
Spiritual death, 143
  comes gradually, 141
Spiritual gifts, 32
Spirituality, 139
Stalin, 44, 156
Standards, double, produce split personalities, 286
Stanton, Edmund, 57
Statues, 276-281
  building one's own, 58
Stimulants, spiritual, 145
Strangers, entertaining, 164, 165
Strength, drawn from past and future, 238
Storage, of good qualities for future, 236
Story, of three medical students, 140
Success, 168, 236
  attitudes of, 103
  depends on preparation, 256
  Edison formula for, 118
  god of, 13
  great secret of, 119
  images of, constructed before experiences, 239
  importance of enthusiasm to, 216
  influenced by loyalty, 167
  Jesus' formula for, 22-23
  law of, 117
  law of love, 23
  laws governing parental, 124
  path to, is straight and narrow, 12
  plan for, ix
  price demanded by, 12, 252
  no limitations upon, 106
  requires good principles, 97
  shortest route to, 23
  simple rules of, 267
  source of, 174
  the big three of, 8-13
Successes, and failures, understanding of, 115
Suffering, of Jesus Christ, 250
  pictured by Dante, 260
Sufferings, people softened by, 218
Sun, storehouse of universe, 223
Sunflower, symbol of loyalty, 167-168

— T —

Tagore, Sir Rabindranath, Hindu poet, 203
Tale of Two Cities, A, by Charles Dickens, vii

Talents, 13
 pigmy, 194
 unused, repossessed by nature, 66
Taylor, John, 148
Team, spirit of, 175
Teen-agers, 24
Temper, loss of, 124
Temples, millennial work in, 112
Ten Commandments, ix, 45, 71, 77, 99, 101, 131, 190, 286, 289
Ten Tribes, 32
Tensions, self-induced, 220
Tennyson, 224
Testimony, 288-293
Testing, program of, 212
Thinking, clean, 67
 distorted, 75-76
Thomas the Apostle, 291
Thoreau, Henry, 37, 109
Thoughts, uplifting, most important possession, 58
Times, best and worst, vii
Title, to life, 7
Tongue, Moses' slowness of, 78-79
 slow, 78, 83
Tournier, Dr. Paul, European psychiatrist, 129
Tradition, Chinese, 103
Traits, come from seeds, 49
 godly, 233
Transfiguration, of Jesus Christ, 5
 of the earth, 113
Transformation, through regenerated mind, 116
Treason, Benedict Arnold's, 168
Treasures, earthly and heavenly, 2, 4, 7
Trees, degrees of death among, 186
Treptow, Martin, 174-175
Trojan War, 358
Truman, President Harry S., 40, 43, 155
Trust, 168, 169
 in oneself (poem), 85-86
 proper source of, 76-77
Twain, Mark, 237
Typewriter, without exclamation point, 298

— U —

Ugliness, 315-317
 destroys future joys, 250
 endured by wives, 296
"Ugly Duckling, The," by Hans Christian Anderson, 314
Ulysses, and men, returning from Trojan War, 258
United Nations, 45

United States, Christian standards of, 304
 great because good, viii
Universe, foundation law of, 287
Unkindness, forbidden by eleventh commandment, 72
 to God, 72-73
Unorthodoxy, rebels proud of, 230
Uselessness, shock of awareness of one's, 266

— V —

Vacuum, boy defines, 78
Values, 193, 196
 of God's gifts, 7
 poetry enhances awareness of, 197
Van Dyke, Henry, 166
Vengence, natural, 15
Virtue, assuming a, 49
"Vision of Sir Launfal, The," by James Russell Lowell, 236-237
Vision, people perish without, 191
 unclear, 193
Vital Statistics, Bureau of, 309

— W —

Wadsworth Henry, 18-19
Wainwright, General Jonathan, 155
Wake Up and Live, by Dorothea Brande, 188
War, greatest, 207
Washington, D. C., 53, 55
Washington, George, 53, 91, 104, 119, 169, 174, 225, 276, 315
 considered for king, 54
 prayers of, 277
"Wastelands, The," by T. S. Eliot, 142
Weakness, disabling human 40
Wealth, 2
Webster, Daniel, story of taking second look, 67-68
Weems, W. R., 268
Wentworth, John, 28
Whitman, Walt, 198
Wicked, destruction of, 111
Wickedness, never was happiness, 310
Wife, argument-winning, 324
 who castigates husband into nothingness, 322-323
Wilson, Woodrow, 65-66
Wisdom, 127, 144
 God's compared with man's, 214
Woman, twice-married, 88-89
 who conducts camaign against God, 231
 who had tried to commit suicide, 186